Chicken Soup for the Soul

Hope, Faith & Miracles

Chicken Soup for the Soul: Hope, Faith & Miracles
101 Awe-Inspiring Stories
Amy Newmark

Published by Chicken Soup for the Soul, LLC www.chickensoup.com
Copyright ©2025 by Chicken Soup for the Soul, LLC. All Rights Reserved.

No part of this publication may be reproduced, stored in a retrieval system or transmitted in any form or by any means, electronic, mechanical, photocopying, recording or otherwise, without the written permission of the publisher.

CSS, Chicken Soup for the Soul, and its Logo and Marks are trademarks of Chicken Soup for the Soul, LLC.

The publisher gratefully acknowledges the many individuals who granted Chicken Soup for the Soul permission to reprint the cited material.

Front cover image created by Daniel Zaccari using Adobe Firefly from the prompt "In the style of mosaic art, create an oil painting depicting dove flying over a mountainous background"
Back cover and interior photo courtesy of iStockphoto.com/AnnaNahabed (©AnnaNahabed)

Photo of Amy Newmark courtesy of Susan Morrow at SwickPix

Cover and Interior by Daniel Zaccari

Publisher's Cataloging-in-Publication Data

Names: Newmark, Amy, editor.
Title: Chicken soup for the soul : hope , faith & miracles , 101 awe-inspiring stories / Amy Newmark.
Description: Cos Cob, CT: Chicken Soup for the Soul, LLC, 2025.
Identifiers: LCCN: 2025937283 | ISBN: 978-1-61159-125-5 (paperback) | 978-1-61159-358-7 (ebook)
Subjects: LCSH Faith--Literary collections. | Faith--Anecdotes. | Miracles--Literary collections. | Miracles--Anecdotes. | Spiritual life--Literary collections. | Spiritual life--Anecdotes. | BISAC SELF-HELP / Motivational & Inspirational | SELF-HELP / Personal Growth / Happiness | SELF-HELP / Spiritual
Classification: LCC BL624 .C45 2025 | DDC 158/.12--dc23

Library of Congress Control Number: 2025937283

PRINTED IN THE UNITED STATES OF AMERICA
on acid∞free paper

30 29 28 27 26 25   01 02 03 04 05 06 07 08 09 10 11

Chicken Soup for the Soul.

Hope, Faith & Miracles

101 Awe-Inspiring Stories

Amy Newmark

Chicken Soup for the Soul, LLC
Cos Cob, CT

Changing your life one story at a time®
www.chickensoup.com

Table of Contents

❶ Miracles Happen

1. The Christmas Diamond, *Candy Allen Smith* 1
2. The Interview, *Cj Cole* 5
3. Knock, Knock, *Carole Harris Barton* 8
4. A Miraculous Departure, *J. Ross Archer* 11
5. The 115-Pound Miracle, *Tammy Ruggles* 13
6. Miracle in the Desert, *Geno Lawrenzi, Jr.* 16
7. The Voice, *Kristine Benevento* 18
8. The Palm Tree, *John Elliott* 21
9. The Day Nanny Died, *Karen Ekstrom* 24

❷ Divine Intervention

10. Miracle on Lake Travis, *Michael Evans* 29
11. A Voice in the Desert, *L. Thorburn* 33
12. My Interstate Navigator, *Nancy Emmick Panko* 36
13. Lifted, *MaryAnn Diorio* 38
14. Tsunami Survivor, *Sheoli V. Gunaratne* 41
15. Miracle on Mott Street, *Lynn Maddalena Menna* 44
16. September 15, 1998, *Kim Garback Diaz* 47
17. Frozen, *Melissa Bender* 50

❸
Angels Among Us

18. Last Words, *Bill Hess* 53
19. Mechanic Angel, *Mary Beth Magee* 56
20. The Garden Visitor, *Sheryl K. (James) Winbolt* 60
21. Leave Now, *Christine Trollinger* 63
22. Maybe, Under Some Circumstances, *Robyn Gerland* 65
23. The Doctor, *Catherine Kopp* 68
24. Bandit's Run, *David Magill* 70
25. Father, Son, and Brother, *Gary R. Hoffman* 73

❹
Random Acts of Kindness

26. Feeding a Family on a Prayer, *Hosanna Barton* 77
27. Giving Life to a Stranger, *Jen Eve Taylor* 80
28. Secret Santa, *Suzanne Lindsay* 82
29. Faith in Humanity, *Linda L. Koch* 86
30. A Mysterious Angel, *Mary M. Alward* 89
31. Fifteen Dollars, *Rachel Schmoyer* 91
32. Angels' Food, *Delores E. Topliff* 94
33. The Day I Met an Angel, *Jackie Eller* 97

❺
Comfort While Grieving

34. Miracle of the Green Tide, *Barbara A. Poremba* 100
35. The Messenger Daughter, *Lainie Belcastro* 104
36. Dragonflies, *Carmen Myrtis-Garcia* 107
37. Listening to The Boss, *Joshua J. Mark* 110
38. The Gift at the Grave, *Amanda Mattox* 113
39. A Message Delivered at the Museum, *Patricia Ann Rossi* 115
40. She Found Me, *Carolyn C. O'Brien* 119
41. A Golden Gift, *BJ Jensen* 122

Table of Contents

❻
Amazing Coincidences

42. The Boomerang Bible, *Judy Fleming* 126
43. At Last Sight, *Christina Metcalf* 128
44. Face-to-Face with a Miracle, *Denise Wasko* 131
45. The Night Santa Claus Cried, *Elizabeth Atwater* 134
46. The Painting, *Lisa McCaskill* 138
47. The Gold Ring, *Andrea Lebedovych Bilaniuk* 140
48. Love You Forever, *Amy B. Chesler* 143
49. Miracle Cat, *Angela Marchi* 146
50. Cold Goldie, *Daniel James* 148

❼
Messages from Heaven

51. Not Forsaken, *Kathryn Y. Pollard* 152
52. Feathers from Heaven, *Susan A. Karas* 156
53. One Last Visit Before the Light, *Lisa Wojcik* 159
54. The Beauty of Rubber Bands, *Julie Rine Holderbaum* 163
55. Snow Angels, *Wendy Portfors* 166
56. Walk Me Home, *Dan Boyle* 169
57. My Miracles and Me, *Richard Bennett* 172
58. A Stop on His Journey, *Michele Ivy Davis* 175

❽
Let Hope In

59. Turned Messenger, *Rebecca Radicchi* 179
60. Balloons of Hope, *Donna Teti* 182
61. Blessed Bloom, *Becky S. Tompkins* 186
62. Dinner with My Dad, *Jane R. Snyder* 190
63. My Mother the Bag Lady, *Sharilynn Hunt* 192
64. The Boxes in the Basement, *Skip Myers* 195

Table of Contents

| 65. | Surprise! You're Getting Married, *Rebecca Gurnsey* | 198 |
| 66. | A Matter of Hours, *Tamara Bell* | 202 |

❾ Faith in Action

67.	Escape from Hell, *Herchel E. Newman*	206
68.	A Miracle in Greece, *Mary Treacy O'Keefe*	210
69.	The Check, *Lettie Kirkpatrick Burress*	213
70.	Love's Farewell, *Linda Kinnamon*	216
71.	Covered, *Patti Wade*	220
72.	The Christmas Coat, *Donna Anderson*	223
73.	A Pink Dress and a Promise, *Gail MacMillan*	226
74.	The Voice, *Patrick P. Stafford*	229

❿ Miraculous Timing

75.	Thank You, Mr. Truck Driver, *Kayleen Kitty Holder*	233
76.	The Dog Days of Winter, *Laura Savino*	236
77.	The 430 Miracle, *Sandy Martin*	239
78.	The Perfect Wait, *Hannah Edmonds*	241
79.	Serendipity, *M.J. Shea*	244
80.	The Call, *C. Solomon*	248
81.	Fleas and Thank You, *David L. Bishop*	251
82.	Finding My Truth, *Sheila Quarles*	254
83.	One Rainy Morning, *Jennie Ivey*	257

⓫ Answered Prayers

84.	Prayers of Thanksgiving, *Jane McBride*	261
85.	Answered Prayer, *Annie Riess*	263
86.	Reflections of Hope in the Snowstorm, *Valaree Terribilini Brough*	266

87.	Miracle on the Hudson, *Warren F. Holland*	269
88.	Ask and You Shall Receive, *Gene F. Giggleman*	273
89.	The Healing Hand of God, *Donna Fawcett*	275
90.	Faith and Warmth, *Brenda M. Lane*	279
91.	Off the Hook, *Tina Wagner Mattern*	281
92.	A Patchwork of Hope, *Donna Volkenannt*	284

⑫
Dreams and Premonitions

93.	Not My Child! *Sara Nolt*	289
94.	Banking on My Inner Voice, *Gail Small*	292
95.	Her Final Lesson, *Shannon MacKinnon*	295
96.	One Last Thing, *M.D. Krider*	298
97.	We Dreamed a Little Dream, *Lori Chidori Phillips*	300
98.	The Climb, *Rob L. Berry*	303
99.	Tested, Not Arrested, *Kristi Woods*	306
100.	The Dream Dress, *Eva Carter*	308
101.	Feelings, *Monica A. Andermann*	312

Meet Our Contributors 315
Meet Amy Newmark 329
About Chicken Soup for the Soul 331

Chapter 1

Miracles Happen

The Christmas Diamond

Miracles come in moments. Be ready and willing.
~Wayne Dyer

I remember holding my mother's hand when I was a little girl and being mesmerized by the bands she wore on her right ring finger. The rings had belonged to my mother's mother, and her mother before that, and had been handed down through the generations. They were the only things remotely of value that any of the women had ever owned.

The engagement ring consisted of a small center stone surrounded by even smaller diamonds. I remember using one finger to gently trace the outline of that delicate gold band, so thin and frail from years of wear. None of the women ever had the means to have it repaired.

As a teenager, I used to beg my mother every single day to let me wear those rings, and she never would. Then, one sunny Saturday when I was seventeen years old, she gave in and let me borrow them to wear on a date. That very morning, my mother had announced that — after twenty-three years — she was finally filing for divorce from my abusive father. As she slipped the rings onto my finger, she made me promise that I wouldn't let anything happen to them, and that I'd return them to her the second I came home. Eager to finally have a chance to wear them, I gave her my word, childishly crossing my heart as I did so.

I never had a chance to keep that promise.

That night, while I was away, my father came back to the rundown rental house we had all shared, armed with a revolver. Without saying a word, he shot everyone in the house, killing my mother and brother and badly injuring my sister before taking his own life.

I wore those rings every single day for seventeen years.

Then, a few years ago while decorating the Christmas tree at work, I looked down to find that the center stone was missing from my mother's ring. For three days straight, I searched everywhere for the diamond. I swept the entire room where I had been decorating, pulling everything apart and retracing every step. I methodically sifted through every speck of dirt and debris, and checked every sequin, bead, and piece of glitter three or four times. The stone never did turn up, and finally I had to accept that it was just gone forever.

Thinking about the situation in the days that followed, I realized something. Although I had really hoped to find the diamond, I never felt desperate about the situation. The minute that I noticed it was gone, my very first thought was, *If you don't find it, you'll just have it replaced. No big deal.*

Had the same thing happened to my mother, I know exactly how she would have felt — we would never have had the money to fix that ring, and it would have been lost to her forever. These were her mom's rings, the only thing handed down to her, and they were probably the nicest things that my mom had ever owned. She meticulously cared for them and wore them with great pride. Knowing how much they meant to her, it would have been a huge blow, and she would have been frantic over the whole ordeal. I could picture the desperation in her eyes as she looked for that tiny stone, and I knew she would have been crushed when she didn't find it.

All that my mom ever wished for us was that we would have it better than she did. She wanted more for us. She wanted us to leave behind that poverty and desperation she so often felt. In many ways, that wish has come true, and I know she'd be proud that I didn't have to worry over that little diamond or anything else. So, even though I really hoped that I would find the stone that had been hers, I decided that I would have the rings repaired, and she would understand.

That Christmas, when it was time for the decorations at work to come down, I was in a terrible mood. It had been a chaotic several weeks, and I was busy and tired. I took the decorations from the tree and wrapped the ornaments for storage. But when it was time to put away the tree, I couldn't find the box anywhere. Agitated, I grabbed the tree by the base and dragged the entire thing across the property, outside and to the storage building fifty or so yards away from my office area. There, I threw it into the corner and slammed the door, leaving it forgotten for an entire year.

When the following Christmas season rolled around and it was time to pull out the tree and put it up, I found it exactly where I had left it. By then, it had been covered up with other discarded junk — empty bags, a broken weed eater, and a piece of water hose that had been chewed up by a lawn mower. I kicked all these items out of my way and dragged the pathetic artificial tree out of its corner and into my office. There, I began the painstaking process of shaping this battered and abused piece of junk into something that slightly resembled a pine tree.

While doing so, I thought about my mom — about those rings and the day that she gave them to me — and breathed a silent apology to her that I had lost her diamond. Suddenly, just as I had that thought, I got so cold that I physically shivered, and the skin on my arms broke out in goosebumps. All at once, as I pulled up one of the little branches of the tree, a sparkle caught my eye. It was a tiny diamond, just lying there, as if someone had put it on the branch of the tree, stood back and waited for me to find it.

Scarcely daring to breathe, I reached out with a shaking hand to pick up the stone. Gently, I laid the diamond in the palm of my left hand, convinced that I was imagining the entire thing, that I would blink and nothing would be there after all. But it was there.

Somehow, after having been up for the entire season the year before, after all the abuse that I had bestowed upon that tree, after having been pulled across a parking lot and abandoned in a pile of garbage for an entire year, the diamond was there. It just didn't make sense. How could that tiny speck of stone still be on the tree, perched on a branch without having fallen out anywhere? It was a miracle, plain and simple.

Miracles Happen

That day, I got the best Christmas present I ever received. It was not the diamond, although I am thrilled to have the same stone that my mother cherished back in my possession. No, the best present was the confirmation that my dear mom, whom I miss so much that it hurts, never left me at all. She is here, every second, watching over me still. I know it, as sure as I know that diamond was never in that tree until the second that I felt a chill come over me, and my mother laid it there for me to find.

—Candy Allen Smith—

The Interview

God has not taken them from us. He has hidden them
in his heart, that they may be closer to ours.
~Author Unknown

His name was Mark, and he was my first real boyfriend. He was a tall, blond hunk of a guy, with electric blue eyes. He was a senior and on the football team. He would walk me to class and grin at me as he dropped me off at the door. That sideways smile always made my heart flutter. When class was over, he would be there, casually leaning against the wall, books resting on his hip, and take my hand to walk me to the next class or to the lunchroom to sit and talk. He taught me to drive his car, me shifting gears as he pushed the clutch, sitting on the center console with his arm draped across my shoulders.

It was everything a first love should be.

Sadly, as many high-school sweethearts do, we drifted apart after graduation. He joined the Navy, and I moved with my mother to the West Coast to start a new life. We stayed in touch sporadically, but as the years passed, we lost touch with one another. Now and then, something would bring him to mind, and I would wonder how he was, and if he ever remembered me as fondly as I thought of him.

News filtered back to me that he was battling multiple sclerosis. A mutual friend saw him in our hometown and called to tell me that not only was he fighting MS, but he had been diagnosed with leukemia as well. He was struggling to get around with two canes, but apparently

Miracles Happen

his famous grin was still as bright and happy as it had always been.

I thought a lot about the young man I had known and the dreams we shared. When my workday was done, I looked up his phone number to call him and catch up. I am not a person prone to "stage fright" or shyness. For some strange reason, though, I could not dial the number. I sat there staring at the phone, seemingly at a loss for words. Finally, I decided I would wait a bit.

A week or so later, a girlfriend of mine from home sent me a message on social media that Mark had died. I was filled with such sadness that I'd not called to talk to him; it had been so unlike me to hesitate. It haunted me for weeks afterward, a chance I should have taken to connect with someone I had loved so much.

I have been lucky to make my childhood dream job a career. Being on air as a radio personality has been a great joy for me. As an avid book reader, I often do interviews with authors so that I can share my love of reading with my listeners.

One morning, I was scheduled to interview a famous psychic medium to promote her new book. As a rule, interviewers do not request personal readings — as a gesture of respect. We talked at length about some of her experiences in assisting the FBI and police on cases, and how her gifts affected her everyday life.

As the interview drew to a close, she suddenly stopped in mid-sentence. She asked if it would be all right for her to tell me the message she was receiving.

To be honest, I have always been a bit of a skeptic, but here we were live on-air, and I was curious.

She was quiet for a moment. Then she said, "It's Mike, no, Mark. Mark is here, and he wants you to know something very important."

I think I was holding my breath at this point, and she continued, "He wants you to know there was a reason you couldn't call him that night. He wants you to know that he stopped you and doesn't want you to feel sad anymore."

She explained that he had been in a deep coma that night, hovering between worlds. He had been drawn to me, sitting there. He had put a hand on my shoulder and whispered to me, "Wait," believing that if I got no answer and left a message, his not returning it would hurt me. He wanted me to know that he remembered everything in the same way I did, with a smile and with love. Our time had been important to him, too.

By now, the tears were streaming down my face. *How could she possibly know?* She asked me if this had relevance to me somehow, and I managed to confirm it. She told me he was no longer in pain, and that he would always be an angel watching over me.

Finally, as the time of our interview concluded, she hesitated and laughed a bit.

"He wants to know," she said, "can you still drive a stick shift?"

With that, she disconnected, and there I was, live on-air, and a complete mess.

That night, I called his mother, who was still living in our hometown. She shared with me about his son and the love he had for him. She told me of the coma that he had been in for several days and the night he passed, surrounded by those who loved him.

Some say these messages are just wishful thinking. Some say there are no such things as angels.

I can't help feeling that I have been touched by one, and I will never be the same.

— Cj Cole —

Knock, Knock

Don't believe in miracles — depend on them.
~Laurence J. Peter

I tried not to worry, but I was scared. The job I had lost was a good job, and I was good at it. It wasn't my fault that I lost it; it was just what happens when a government contract isn't renewed. I accepted my lot and filed for unemployment benefits.

My full-time job now was finding a full-time job. I searched diligently and tried everything I knew to find work, but without success. Weeks went by. If I didn't find a job soon, I wouldn't be able to pay the rent on my apartment — a modest two-bedroom in a four-story walkup. And then what?

It was the early 1970s, and job hunting was done the 1970s way. Print copies of your résumé. Peruse the Help Wanted ads in the local newspaper. Mark the jobs you think you might qualify for, even if you think they're long shots. Write a hello-I'm-wonderful cover letter, put it in an envelope with your résumé, and mail it to the employer. Tell everybody you know that you're available for work and ask them to help get the word out. Make phone calls and knock on every door.

One Saturday morning, the knock came on *my* door.

Silently grumbling, I arose and walked down the hall, temporarily abandoning my collection of Help Wanted ads and stack of résumés on the kitchen table. Why was it that every time I got my toddler settled down with her toys and started my job search, someone interrupted me?

"Hi," said a smiling woman in jeans when I opened the door. "I'm Melba. I just moved in upstairs. Can I borrow your phone for a minute? I'd like to call the phone company and ask them to turn mine on."

A neighbor in need — of course, I would help. "Hi, Melba. Sure, come on in. I'm Carole," I said, leading the attractive woman who looked about my age — early thirties — to the phone anchored on my kitchen wall. "Help yourself while I run into the other room and check on my little one."

Returning a few minutes later, I found Melba holding the phone to her ear and looking down at my résumé on the table. Apparently, the phone-company rep had placed her on hold for a moment. "Coffee?" I asked, holding up my glass coffeepot for her to see.

Putting her hand over the mouthpiece of the phone, she responded, "Yes, thank you." Barely glancing at me, she continued to look down at my résumé on the table.

Soon, her conversation was finished, and I invited her to sit down. She did and picked up one of my résumés. "May I look at this more closely?" she asked. "I gather you're looking for a job."

"Yes," I said, "and spending all my scarce money on paper, envelopes, and postage stamps."

"Well, your search is over. You're exactly the person I'm looking for."

I was puzzled. "What? What do you mean?"

A cup of coffee later, she had told me exactly what she meant. She was special assistant to the CEO at her company, and they had been searching for someone to fill a staff vacancy for which I was uniquely qualified.

Our conversation continued for several minutes as I elaborated on my experience. I answered her questions, and she answered mine. It was the most informal job interview I'd ever had, I would reflect later. I was happy that the company she represented provided a very needed service that I would be proud to support.

"Can you come in on Monday? I'll introduce you to my boss, but that's just so you and he can get to know one another. He has delegated hiring authority to me," she said, telling me the salary. "I haven't found anybody who is even halfway as qualified as you are for the job. How soon can you start?"

I was incredulous. "You mean, just like that?"

"Well, you'll have to fill out all the forms and pass the reference checks. But, yeah, just like that. I mean, if you like us."

"Like you? No, I don't like you," I replied. "I love you."

She laughed. "I'll slip one of my cards underneath your door as soon as I find one in the boxes I'm unpacking," she said, with one of my résumés in her hand as she walked to the door.

I let her out and leaned back against the closed door. What had just happened? Was she for real? Was this divine intervention? Perfect timing? Had I found a job without even leaving my apartment, making a phone call, or knocking on a door?

Yes, as it would turn out on Monday morning when I signed the official offer of a job that seemed tailormade for me. It would support my daughter and me for a couple of years until both Melba and I moved on to even better opportunities in our careers — but not until after we had built a friendship that endures to this day.

It was a fateful day. No, not the day I found a job. The day the job found me.

—Carole Harris Barton—

A Miraculous Departure

Out of difficulties grow miracles.
~Jean de La Bruyère

Parkinson's ravaged my wife Joan's body for four years. By the end she weighed eighty-five pounds, couldn't speak or move a limb, and could only communicate by blinking her eyes. She was also in excruciating pain. I called Hospice in to make recommendations on pain control and to aid with Joan's end care.

As was my habit for the two years of her nursing home residence, I arrived in her room at 9:00 A.M. and greeted her with a kiss. Then I massaged her rigid legs, and sat beside her to read. I had no idea whether she heard me reading to her or not, but I chose to believe she did.

The hospice attendant called me aside to tell me she believed Joan was very near the end and that I should call the children in to see her.

Our three children gathered around their mother's bed. Hearing their voices bidding their mom goodbye and declaring their love for her gave me a sense of finality — and profound sadness. They tried to be strong for her, but the tears on their faces told the truth.

Mrs. Deaver, the hospice assistant, was reading scripture aloud: II Corinthians 5:17: "Therefore, if anyone is in Christ, he is a new creation; old things have passed away; behold, all things have become new."

I lay beside Joan on the narrow hospital bed, held her as close as possible, and prayed for the Lord to receive her. My heart was breaking; a significant piece of me for fifty years was about to be taken from me. What would I do? How would I go on without her? I was experiencing total helplessness and gut-wrenching loss.

I noticed there was movement in Joan's rigid body; she raised both arms upward and was whispering. Mrs. Deaver and I exchanged looks of disbelief because Joan had been paralyzed for six months. But now she seemed to be greeting someone and welcoming that person. Her face glowed with joy.

"Joan, honey, what are you doing? Who is here?" I was stunned.

"I am talking to Jesus. He is here to take me to heaven, but first, I need to talk to you. Please do not interrupt me—just listen."

I sensed someone had placed me in a surreal suspension of time, place, and dimension; a profound sense of calm enveloped me. The experience was frightening yet beautiful, euphoric. And for the next twenty-five minutes, Joan reviewed our life together. She spoke of the good memories, accomplishments, the challenges we faced together, why she loved me, and what she expected of me after she went home to be with Jesus.

Then–she went home!

"Praise God," Mrs. Deaver and I declared in unison. We knew we had witnessed a genuine miracle.

I fell on my knees next to Joan's bed and thanked the Lord for His miracle. What a beautiful end for us both.

—J. Ross Archer—

The 115-Pound Miracle

Nothing has more strength than dire necessity.
~Euripides

"Hand me that wrench, Tammy."

I did what my Pappaw Luther said. I was about ten years old, and hunkered down near a car he had jacked up and was working on. A light gray one with a black top.

I didn't give his mechanic work a second thought. He'd lain under cars before, fixing them, and I'd seen him do it a dozen times. He lay on his back underneath in the gravel, only his head and shoulders visible. The rest of him, from chest down, was under the car.

It was a pretty summer day. Life on my grandparents' farm was quiet that day, with almost everyone having attended the funeral of a relative. My mother didn't want to attend, so she volunteered to babysit all the kids — my siblings and cousins. Usually the yard would be full of running, playing, laughing kids.

It was a one-hundred-acre farm, and my pappaw worked on the car in front of his house.

I liked hanging out with my pappaw once in a while. He was a man of few words, but when he talked, he liked to explain how things worked and what he was doing. He was a diesel mechanic and farmer, and could build or fix anything with his hands. I looked up to him

Miracles Happen | 3

and thought he could do anything — invincible.

That's why my brain was so frozen and stunned when the jack slipped and the car fell straight down onto his chest with a sickening thump.

He couldn't move, and the only sound was a slight gasp of "Get Dana," so I ran as fast as I could toward the trailer my mother, sister, and brother lived in.

My mouth opened to scream to my mother as I ran, but no sound would come out. My voice had frozen in my throat.

Finally I reached the door, and I screamed, "The car fell on Pappaw! The car fell on Pappaw!"

My mother and I ran back to the car, and he still lay as he had when I left — trapped under the car on his back.

My mother gripped the bumper of the car and lifted it, urging, "Scoot out! Scoot out!"

Pappaw scooted in the gravel, and my mother scooted the car over and set it back down.

My mother couldn't have weighed more than 115 pounds.

I couldn't believe my eyes. At ten, I knew something extraordinary had happened, but, on the other hand, it seemed like a perfectly normal thing for a person to do when a car crushes someone's chest.

My mother ran to the farmhouse to call an ambulance.

"I don't want to go to the hospital," my pappaw said. "With this hole in my sock."

Well, he did go to the hospital, and the doctors were amazed that he only had some bruises.

"It should have killed him," the doctor said.

At the time I thought of the incident as amazing, but now as an adult, I believe it was a miracle. Two miracles really. One, that my mom lifted the car and scooted it over. And, two, that Pappaw had only some bruises.

People claim adrenaline, and I don't doubt that. But the truth of the matter is, not everyone in a state of panic can lift a car, and not every person who has a car fall on his chest survives with just a few bruises.

All I know is that I witnessed firsthand the power of miracles that summer day so long ago.

— Tammy Ruggles —

Miracle in the Desert

Christmas is the day that holds all time together.
~Alexander Smith

His name was Benjamin Adair. His friends knew him as Bud and he owned a truck stop just outside Wickenburg, Arizona, "the dude ranch capital of the world."

The truck stop included a motel and restaurant. It was actually located in a tiny town called Circle City. Bud had converted the place into a ranch. He had built a corral and kept half a dozen horses in it for his own children and the neighborhood kids to ride.

I met Bud while working as a reporter for the *Phoenix Gazette*, Phoenix's former afternoon daily newspaper. Bud was a colorful character who loved to dabble in politics. He never won an election, but he ran for sheriff of Maricopa County, Arizona. and even once tried for the governorship.

Bud loved living in the desert, and he liked his neighbors. Each Christmas he would truck in a towering Christmas tree, decorate it lavishly with bulbs, lights, and ornaments, and invite the neighborhood kids in for a special celebration. The area supermarket managers would provide him with turkeys and Bud would dress himself as Santa and provide everyone who showed up with a plate of hot turkey and trimmings, as well as gifts.

The local news media liked Bud and we gave him ample publicity to make the Christmas party work. But one year it looked like it wasn't going to happen. Three days before Christmas, Adair called me and said, "We're not getting our turkey donations this year and I might have to call off the Christmas party."

I knew the previous year Bud had served turkey dinners to just under 2,000 children and adults. But the supermarkets he dealt with had made some changes in their policy and had placed a hold on any large-scale donations.

"So where do you stand, Bud?" I asked.

"Well, we've got the Christmas tree and hundreds of wrapped presents beneath it," he said. "But no turkeys."

After hanging up the phone I drove out to Circle City. Bud greeted me with a hot meatloaf dinner — he was famous for his meatloaf — and we sat down to discuss his gloomy prospects. Just as the sun was setting. a large semi pulled onto his parking lot. Steam was hissing from the truck and the driver stepped out and shook his head.

"My air conditioning isn't working and I've got a load of frozen turkeys that are going to spoil," he said.

Bud looked at me. I looked at him. We smiled.

We did some fast talking for the next hour or so. When we were finished, he called his boss. Then he shook Bud's hand.

On Christmas morning, Bud served more than 2,000 turkey dinners. He gave each of the kids a wrapped gift. And the truck driver — you guessed it — played Santa Claus.

— Geno Lawrenzi, Jr. —

The Voice

*When you get to your wit's end, you will find,
God lives there.*
~Author Unknown

My husband had been out of work for months. We'd borrowed money from family members for groceries, gas and utilities. Bill collectors were calling every day and treating us as if we were criminals. Stress was eating away at our family.

One day, as I was driving to work, enjoying the silence and the beautiful Vermont spring scenery, I heard a voice. It said, "Turn on the radio." Weird, but I did it. Then I listened as the voice on the radio told listeners about a contest the local shoe store was having. This was the last day to enter. They were also giving away free pieces of pizza. All you had to do was fill out an entry form and you could win a cruise to Bermuda and $25,000.

I decided to stop at the shoe store on my way home. My son would enjoy the pizza and I would enter the contest.

It was a busy day at work and I ended up forgetting about the shoe store. Then I heard that voice again: "Turn on the radio." I did, and I heard the same announcement about the contest. I had one hour to get there.

What were the chances that I would hear a voice twice in one day telling me to listen to the radio so that I could hear the same pitch twice? I actually said out loud, "Thank you, God, for the reminder." Then I drove to pick up my son. He was hot, tired and a bit cranky. He just wanted to go home, but he gave in when I told him about the pizza.

A storm was coming in when we got to the shoe store, and the radio personality who was conducting the contest outside the shoe store was packing up his equipment when we got there. I quickly filled out the form he handed me. Then I drew a cross in the upper right hand corner of the small white square of paper and said a silent prayer.

By that time, the pizza was all gone, my son was disappointed and it had started to rain. We drove home.

That night, as we were all catching up on how our days went, I mentioned what I had done on the way home. My husband was a bit perplexed, as I didn't normally participate in contests.

I explained about the voice and my family looked at me like I had two heads. I warned them, directing my comment to my husband: "When my name is called tomorrow, I won't be able to hear it as I will be walking across the street to my job. Would you be able to listen for me and let me know?" He had a funny look on his face and said, "When your name is called?"

I laughed, stunned that I had said that and used the *Angels in the Outfield* movie quote, "It could happen," in my defense. I didn't think any more of it.

My husband didn't call me the next morning, but a coworker excitedly ran over to me when she got to work and said, "Kris, the radio station just called your name — you won the cruise to Bermuda!"

I was floored. I don't win things. My life had been hard lately. I get seasick on boats. I didn't know what I was going to do with the trip. I didn't know if I was on a timer to call back, so I called the radio station to confirm they actually called my name and sure enough, I won the trip! Because I won for my local station, the station was entering my name into the second contest nationally to win a gift card for $25,000.

I didn't think any more of it. I didn't hear any more voices.

Two weeks later I was sitting in a meeting with someone I supervise and the phone rang. During meetings, I typically ignore the phone but I had the sudden urge to pick it up. I apologized. It was the DJ from the radio station. I had won the $25,000 gift card!

My coworker sitting across from me looked at my face and was worried. All I could say over and over was, "Oh my God, Oh my God!" My supervisee was worried something bad had happened and I gave her a thumbs up assuring her it was a good "Oh my God."

We were able to pay back my family and get the bill collectors off our backs. Stranger things have happened to others, I am sure, but I listened to the voice and was rewarded. I still get goose bumps when I think about this.

— Kristine Benevento —

The Palm Tree

> *When you live your life with an appreciation of coincidences and their meanings, you connect with the underlying field of infinite possibilities.*
> ~Deepak Chopra

We all heard her screaming for help, and the six of us turned to see where the screams were coming from. But that part of the Florida Everglades was so thick with jungle-like vegetation that seeing anything beyond thirty or forty feet was almost impossible.

It was late December 1972. While working with the police in Virginia, right outside of Washington, D.C., I had been attending a law-enforcement training program in Miami with four colleagues, just days after Christmas. We were planning to return to Virginia the next day, right before New Year's Eve.

But there were loud knocks on our hotel-room doors as the Miami police requested assistance in their recovery efforts due to an Eastern Airlines airplane crashing right into the heart of the nearby alligator-infested waters of the Everglades.

Within minutes, the five of us were dressed and running for the waiting patrol cars of the Miami Police Department. Not long afterward, we were assigned to a large airboat located in a staging area several miles within that endless swamp. The driver quickly started the motor, and the enormous propeller began spinning invisibly in the dark night.

We traveled at breakneck speed in and around countless tributaries, soon arriving at the smoldering wreckage of the enormous airliner. It seemed to cover a very large area of the swamp, perhaps a half-mile across, but it was still dark out and impossible to be sure. There were several fires still burning, and, with our motor turned off, we started to hear the shouts of survivors, some barely clinging to life.

Most of the passengers and crew had tragically perished in that awful crash, but, after almost twenty-four hours of searching, we and countless other airboat police officers had rescued more than sixty people, and we weren't about to stop looking. Rescue helicopters had been hovering above us for almost the entire time and airlifted countless survivors to area hospitals. But now, as it grew dark again, the numerous helicopters couldn't safely be flown in and out of the area.

Using our spotlights to see in the dark, we slowly scanned the entire area at one end of that enormous crash site, but we couldn't find anyone else. The police radio did confirm that a few other survivors had been rescued, and many bodies had been recovered. Our motor was shut off again, and we slowly drifted around in circles, hoping against hope that we would see or hear someone. The only sounds we heard came from countless insects, and we smelled the occasional odor of burning materials. As we approached the thirty-hour mark, and as almost all our cans of gasoline had been used up, we received a call over the police radio to cease our search and return to the staging area. Reluctantly, we did as ordered and were soon speeding back.

But then, when we were more than a mile from the crash site, we heard those screams for help. Her voice was so high-pitched! Our airboat driver instantly shut off the motor, and we drifted to a stop. The six of us turned to see where the screams were coming from. Using the spotlights again, we looked all around but only saw the thick vegetation.

"Hello!" one of my associates shouted, but there was no reply.

Using two oars, we silently drifted around but didn't hear anything else. Yet we had heard a woman's frantic cry for help, so someone was obviously alive, and we weren't about to give up.

"Hello!" the officer shouted again, but there was still nothing.

About twenty minutes later, as we drifted in increasingly large circles with our spotlights shining through the pitch-black darkness of the night, we came upon a tiny, raised mound of earth, almost like a small island no larger than twenty feet in diameter. And it contained one severely bent-over palm tree, the top of it almost touching back down to the water's edge.

On the upper half of the palm tree's limb was a young woman, maybe thirty years of age, and her arms were tightly wrapped around the trunk of that tree. Several alligators were in the dark waters close to the base of that tree.

"Help me," she said in almost a whisper. "Please, help me."

The driver stayed in the airboat, but two of us were quickly up that tree. While the other three stood underneath, we gently lowered her into their waiting arms. Within minutes, we had her safely in the boat with us as we sped back to the staging area.

We then helped the rescue squad carry her to one of the waiting ambulances.

"Were they still there?" she asked in a quiet voice.

"Was who there?" I replied.

She touched my left forearm and said, "The angels… the ones who put me up in that tree."

I was stunned, unable to say anything. She smiled at us as they closed the rear doors to the ambulance.

Several days after our New Year's Eve celebrations back in Virginia, we learned that the young woman had fully recovered and was uninjured, aside from being dehydrated. And I, to this day, believe that, for whatever reasons, she was carried by angels for over a mile from the smoldering wreckage of that airliner and placed safely up in that palm tree. And I also have to believe that the six of us in that airboat were placed there at that exact moment in time. I can't explain any of it, but I do believe it.

— John Elliott —

The Day Nanny Died

*We cannot banish dangers, but we can banish fears.
We must not demean life by standing in awe of death.*
~David Sarnoff

Nanny's body barely created a bump in the bed as she lay under the hospital sheets. I stood with my brothers and sisters alongside my mother as we gathered around her bed. The doctor held the do-not-resuscitate order in his hand. Mother was letting her go. Nanny's body could take no more. For the second time, she was paralyzed by a catastrophic stroke that affected her entire right side. We were there to say goodbye. My mother intended this to be a beautiful moment before she slipped away. But as it turned out, Nanny wasn't quite ready to go.

Nanny struggled to sit up and speak to my mother. A garbled sound came out. Nanny's irritation showed as her good hand flew in the air, waving wildly for Mother to move closer. She did. Nanny tried again. But with the right side of her face motionless, nothing she uttered was decipherable. Frustration showed on the left side of her face. She fell back in defeat.

Horrified, I cringed. Only sixteen years old, little things like school and dogs and elevators produced fear and trepidation in me. Withering bodies clawing for life scared me for real. Someone dying was a nightmare I had not encountered. Gillian, our dog, had died. Hit by a car. But he hadn't struggled. He hadn't cried.

I glanced around and saw my distress reflected in my siblings' faces. Death was in the room. I was frightened.

I watched as Nanny's good hand reached out, like a claw, and grasped my mother's arm. Mother leaned in as Nanny tried to speak again. A horrible rattle came out. She was drooling. Gone was my lovely, elegant grandmother who had played cards with us and taken us on fantastic cruises. In her place was someone I didn't know.

I tried not to recoil.

Mother grabbed a tissue and moved to wipe the drool off Nanny's face.

Suddenly, Nanny's voice cleared. She sat up, unhindered. All signs of her stroke were gone, but she was still clearly annoyed. She flapped Mother's tissue away and wiped her mouth herself.

She spoke. "Anita, I need you to listen. I'm trying to tell you where I hid Aunt Bess's diamond ring."

My jaw dropped. Now, Nanny was known as a great hider. She stashed dollars in jelly jars, rings in the sofa and her silver tea set under the bathroom sink. Everyone knew that. My mother was quite confident they would never find all the things she had hidden. Mother had spoken of "Nanny's stash" many times in frustration. She had tried to get Nanny to tell her where things were, but Nanny had always shooed her away, saying she would tell her when she needed to know.

Now, here Nanny sat, lucid and functioning, talking about her hoard. So bizarre. I swear, if Elvis Presley had walked in and serenaded us, I wouldn't have been more surprised.

My mother was shocked too, her eyebrows raised almost to her hairline. And she hadn't moved an inch. I watched as the tissue in mother's hand fluttered to the floor.

"Yes, Mother?" my mother said.

"I've placed Aunt Bess's ring in *Gone with the Wind*. I hollowed out the book." Nanny giggled, seeming pleased. "The book is on the third shelf in the library, left side."

Stunned, Mother nodded.

Nanny's giggle transformed to an expression of loving impatience as she turned and addressed an empty spot at the end of her bed. "Herman, I am not ready yet. Give me a minute."

Miracles Happen | 25

Herman was my grandfather, her husband and the love of her life. He'd died seven years ago, so I was surprised to hear her addressing him. Confused and still flustered, I looked to see if he was standing there. He wasn't, at least not that I could see, but I couldn't help but smile. I couldn't recall a time when Grandpa wasn't trying to hurry her up. He called Nanny "DD," short for his "Delayed Darling." She'd laugh and say she was never late for anything important. An inside joke. Everyone knew the only time she'd ever been on time was the day she married Grandpa. He told her he was not standing before the congregation and waiting for her. So she'd promenaded down the aisle before the flower girls and her bridesmaids, causing gales of laughter from all those who knew her well.

I always hoped to have a marriage like theirs.

Nanny turned back to my mother. "And you found my bracelet?"

Mother nodded again.

"Just a minute," Nanny said to the end of the bed.

"And the silver coins?" Nanny asked. Her voice had passed bossy and was right on its way to vexed, exasperated and demanding. Nanny shot my mother a look meant to burn. I'd seen that look before. Nanny believed that a quick switch on the butt made children more attentive. I was glad I was not in the hot seat with my mother.

Nanny's hoard of silver dollars flashed before my eyes. Great memories. Nanny used those coins as gambling money to teach us to count. We played 21, like in Las Vegas. By the time I was six, I could count better than anyone I knew. I loved those coins. I hoped mother had found those. I looked at her in time to see her nod.

Nanny looked relieved.

Nobody spoke. But everybody's eyes flashed around the room trying to assess if anyone else was seeing this… this… bizarre something we were experiencing.

By the look on everyone's face, everyone was.

"Good." Nanny lay back on the bed and closed her eyes. A contented look settled on her face. For a minute, she said nothing. Then she spoke again. "Okay Herman, I'm ready."

And she died. Right then, that very instant.

Silence. Then wild chatter filled the room as everyone started talking at once. A glint, something like an errant sunbeam, hit the window and caught my eye. It sparkled and then vanished. I wondered for a second, but dismissed the thought.

The doctor alone remained silent.

Finally, my mother turned to him and asked, "Did you see that?" She sounded rattled. "Have you ever seen anything like that before?"

"Yes," he said, taking a deep breath and letting it out slowly. "I see this more often than you'd think."

I looked back at Nanny, knowing she wasn't there. I'd watched her life pass to… to… I didn't know where. But, wherever Nanny and Grandpa had gone, they were together and happy.

Later, as we drove home, I realized one more thing. I was not afraid of death anymore.

— Karen Ekstrom —

Chapter 2

Divine Intervention

Miracle on Lake Travis

*Believe in miracles. I have seen so many of them
come when every other indication would say
that hope was lost. Hope is never lost.*
~Jeffrey R. Holland

In April 1995, my wife Debbie and I headed out with our three-month-old daughter to our favorite camping spot: a clearing on a large cove overlooking rugged beauty and awe-inspiring homes perched on seventy-foot cliffs.

Debbie, an avid reader, was happy to curl up under the majestic oak trees with her books. Our daughter was a delightful baby who truly enjoyed the peaceful, outdoor setting. I spent the mornings and evenings fishing. During the days, we took walks in the woods, swam in the clear, cool water, and enjoyed our idyllic time together. During the evenings, we cooked my day's catch of fresh fish over an open fire and then lay together in the hammock watching the stars.

As our week neared its end, Debbie decided to take the baby home and give me an extra day alone for a marathon of fishing. We packed up most of our gear, leaving me the bare necessities, and Debbie and Kayla left. I had no idea at the time that it might be the last time I would see them.

I hit the lake before dawn that glorious Sunday morning. The sun was shining brightly, and the fish were plentiful. After a long day of fishing and swimming, I was ready to head back when I noticed hundreds of crappie crashing against the west edge of the cove. I had to have one more shot at them! I started up my outboard motor and headed across the 2,000-foot-wide lake at full speed.

Then I felt something pulling at my leg. I glanced down and saw that my foot was caught between my fishing rod and the line. As I leaned over to free my leg, I hit the tiller handle on the motor, forcing the boat into a sharp turn. The jolt knocked me into the water. The motor was still turned, causing the boat to circle me. I tried to grab the side of the boat as it circled me, but it was moving too fast. I began to feel desperate, realizing that I was at least 1,000 feet from either side of the lake in 100 feet of water with no life jacket.

Suddenly, shockingly, the motor straightened out, and the boat took off down the lake, leaving me stranded. I tried not to panic and prepared to swim for the bank. The wind was blowing briskly, causing small waves to cover my head at times. I was in pretty good shape, but for some reason, I wasn't making any progress. I could barely move my left leg, and I was desperately out of breath.

About halfway to the bank, I realized I was not going to make it. I was exhausted. I couldn't breathe. I couldn't move my leg. The lake was empty. I slipped under the water, furiously fighting to stay afloat. Suddenly, I had the awful awareness that I could die. I slipped under the water again, praying to God to give me the strength to go on. It was no use. My arms and legs ached to the point that I could no longer move them. I knew it was the end. I said silent goodbyes to my wife and baby daughter and asked God to watch over them.

As I managed to break the surface once more, I was thrilled to see a boat speeding toward me. I was shocked when I realized it was my own boat. For a horrifying moment, I thought that it was coming back to finish me off, but then I saw two men on my boat, waving and shouting. With one last burst of strength, I shouted, "Help me!"

The boat pulled alongside me, and the men lifted me into the boat. I was gasping for breath. As we reached the bank, I finally noticed with horror that my shorts were shredded and barely hanging on my body. Three deep gashes were just below my hip. I realized that when I had fallen into the water and the boat had first circled me, the propeller blades had actually run over me, causing the severe wounds. The frigidness of the lake had kept me from bleeding out.

As we waited for EMS, my rescuers told me how they had come to my aid. George Miller and Grady Walker were construction workers who had been working on a new home on the cliff inside the cove. They had not been scheduled to work that Sunday, but they had chosen to anyway. Taking a break, they'd noticed my boat driving in circles, but they had thought someone was just playing around on the lake. Even after they saw me and realized I was in trouble, they knew they had no way to come to my rescue. That's when the true miracle occurred. George and Grady heard a crashing sound on the bank below. They looked down and saw that my boat had driven itself onto the shore!

After the boat amazingly straightened out from its spin and headed a quarter-mile down the lake, it made an unexplainable ninety-degree left turn into the country-club harbor, then drove itself past dozens of expensive yachts and pleasure boats without touching any of them, before turning to the left again, and finally crashing onto the bank below where the men were working. It was a miracle!

Taking advantage of this amazing opportunity, George and Grady dropped their tools, ran down the steep bank and hopped onto the boat. Quickly, they pushed it back into the water, hopped on board, and headed straight back for me, saving my life! George said it seemed that someone had been driving the boat. I said, "Yes! God was driving the boat!"

My wife met me at the hospital. She and the doctor were amazed by my experience. The gashes in my leg required nearly sixty stitches. There is no doubt that if the boat had not made its miraculous trip to the shore and the construction workers had not come to my rescue, I would have drowned in the lake.

A few days later, Debbie and I went back to Lake Travis to seek out my rescuers. Again, they told us their version of what had happened, and we all agreed that a miracle had taken place.

About six months later, I received a sad phone call from George's wife. She told me he had died of pneumonia. She'd found the thank-you note we had given him and called to give me the sad news. I said another prayer, thanking God for extending George Miller's life, allowing him to save mine before God called him home.

— Michael Evans —

A Voice in the Desert

*Angels deliver Fate to our doorstep —
and anywhere else it is needed.*
~Jessi Lane Adams

I was jogging around our base in Tikrit, Iraq. As I rounded the corner I could see the front gate and was glad the run was almost over. Then, as I headed for the final stretch, a voice in my head said, "Take cover behind the wall."

I looked up and did not see any imminent danger. There were no missiles in the sky, the alarm bell was not sounding, and everything was relatively quiet. I kept jogging, assuming that the paranoia of being on a battlefield had begun to take its toll on me. Then I paused for a moment as I got closer to the wall because my brain was screaming, "Take cover!"

Suddenly, I heard a bloodcurdling scream coming from the front gate. As I whipped my head around I saw a huge ball of flames, and then everything went black. When I woke up I was at the medical station with the medic staring down at me. I was confused about what was going on. The medic told me to hang on a minute and went off. He brought back one of the other medics with whom I had done a great deal of work during my deployment. Jim put his hand on my shoulder and said, "Ma'am, you were the only survivor. Do you remember anything that happened?"

I was stunned and couldn't speak. Jim told the others that I might be in shock. I looked at him puzzled and said, "All I remember is screaming, a large bang, and then a fire ball. The fire ball was about a mile across." Jim nodded and said that would make sense because it was a tanker full of explosives that detonated at the gate. I instantly felt sick. I knew there were always six guards stationed at the gate. I asked about them and Jim repeated quietly, "You are the only survivor."

And with that I became consumed with "survivor guilt."

Once released, I went back to my bunk, where I found glass had shattered all over my bed and belongings. My roommates greeted me enthusiastically and asked how I survived. I explained that I had heard a voice telling me to stay behind the wall and so I did though I did not know why. My closest friend, Kathy, said quite simply, "Well, you have a divine purpose; that much is for sure." I doubted her. After all I was a single person with no real purpose in life, so that could not be the case.

A few weeks later, I received an e-mail from Robin, the mother of a girl named Erica who I had been a "big sister" to for the past six years. Its message was simple:

"Linda, Child Protective Services took Marissa. Can you please get her back when you come home?"

Marissa was Robin's grandchild and Erica's niece. I knew her and had taken care of her on many occasions prior to my deployment. I was confused, though. I was a "big sister," a volunteer, not an official foster parent. When I went back to my bunk I sat staring off into space. Kathy came over to me and said, "What's up you?"

I told her about the e-mail I had received. Kathy and I had been friends for years, so she had met Erica and Marissa. She gripped my shoulder and stared at me intently. "Linda, don't you see? You survived the explosion to be a mother!" I shook my head in disagreement; after all foster care is temporary. But Kathy shook her head firmly and said, "No your purpose is to be Marissa's mother."

When I returned home I did in fact go through the steps to gain custody of Marissa. I learned she had a sister, Mary, who no one had mentioned, so I took her, too. After fostering them for two years, I adopted Marissa and Mary.

Kathy was right. That voice saved me for a very special purpose, to be a mom to two wonderful young girls.

— L. Thorburn —

My Interstate Navigator

Not everything we experience can be explained by logic or science.
~Linda Westphal

I was zooming down Interstate 80, heading east in Pennsylvania. The beautiful mountains covered with lush greenery loomed above both sides of the highway. Every few miles a farm appeared nestled among the rolling hills. It was a beautiful day with no weather issues and very little traffic.

But I couldn't really enjoy it. I was rushing to Lehigh Valley Hospital, where my mom had suffered a setback. She had called me at work just two hours before, crying that she needed me. As her daughter and a nurse, I couldn't ignore her plea. I left work and drove home to throw some clothes into a suitcase and let my husband know where I was going and why.

In an effort to calm my mother, I had promised her, "I'll be right there." What was I thinking? It was a three-hour trip.

Ahead I saw a large tractor-trailer laden with lumber. The load was held in place with multiple straps. As I looked at the trailer, I started to feel uneasy.

A voice said clearly, "Those straps are going to break."

"What?" I asked incredulously.

The voice elaborated. "The straps are going to break and that lumber is going to spill onto the road."

"Holy Mother of God!" I thought, panicked at what the voice was telling me. I was a few car lengths behind the truck and we were both moving at about seventy miles per hour.

The voice urged, "Pass him. Get away from him. Do it now!"

I obeyed, but when I pulled into the passing lane, the truck accelerated. This was creepy. I increased my speed enough to overtake the truck and kept an eye on the hazardous load.

Horrified, I watched as the straps holding the stacks of lumber in place started snapping, one by one, and twirling around uselessly in the air. Everything seemed to be happening in slow motion. When the third strap broke, the lumber started to shift.

The voice said authoritatively, "Pedal to the metal; get away from him as fast as you can."

I didn't question the voice. I floored it.

As my small sedan pulled away from that big truck, I watched the scene unfold in my rearview and side view mirrors. The stacks of wood rotated sideways and cascaded onto the road. The first pieces missed the back of my car by a few feet. I saw the truck slow down and could see the look of horror on the driver's face as he realized what was happening. He could clearly see the lumber slide off his truck onto both eastbound lanes of Route 80.

I safely pulled away and my speed returned to normal as I viewed the spectacle in the rearview mirror. I watched as the trucker brought his vehicle to a stop.

I offered up a prayer of thanks for having heard the voice. There was no doubt in my mind that God was my navigator on the interstate that day.

—Nancy Emmick Panko—

13

Lifted

Are not all angels ministering spirits sent to serve those who will inherit salvation?
~Hebrews 1:14 (NIV)

The bright headlights came straight at me. With my hands on the steering wheel, I stared at them but could not move. I had become like a passenger in the driver's seat, unable to turn, swerve, or get out of the way as my car sped down the highway.

The headlights came closer and closer, glaring into my tired eyes. Still, I could not move.

It had been a long day. Between working and client appointments, all I wanted to do was go to sleep. But as the mom of two teenage daughters who played on their school's volleyball team, I could not miss their away game that night. I was proud of my daughters and attended virtually all their games.

So it was that I found myself driving home late that night after a glorious victory. Riding in the church van in the lane to my right, the team was in a celebratory mood, and I wished I could have shared in the fun of their exuberant ride home. But the girls were required to ride in the church van with their coach, so I had taken my own car.

Entranced, I stared helplessly at the headlights that fast approached, wondering what they were doing straight in front of me. This was a four-lane highway, after all, with each pair of lanes going in a single direction. At a certain point, the highway would turn into a two-lane road, with traffic going in opposite directions, but we had not reached that point yet. Having traveled the road hundreds of times, I knew it well.

I kept staring ahead at the brilliant headlights that now blurred my vision. Closer and closer they came. Soon, they would be upon me, yet still I couldn't move.

Just as the headlights were about to overtake me, invisible beings lifted my car off the ground, carried it slowly through the air, and gently placed it on the grassy median at the side of the road.

Suddenly, I awakened.

All was still. I turned off the ignition and just sat there, stunned by what had just happened.

He gives His angels charge over you, to keep you in all your ways. Years before, I had memorized those precious words from Psalm 91 and had recited them regularly over my children, spouse, and myself. Now I had literally experienced their truth. God's angels had rescued me from a horrific, head-on collision.

From almost certain death.

With tears welling up in my eyes, I drew in a deep breath and thanked the Lord for His great mercy in sparing my life.

Soon, I heard the shouts of teenage girls running toward my car. "Mom, are you all right?" My daughters were the first in line.

"Dr. Diorio, are you all right?" the girls on the team asked. "We were so scared. We were praying at the top of our lungs that God would protect you."

Dazed, I looked at the girls. "What happened?"

Coach Debbie approached the driver's side window that I had rolled down. She laid her hand on mine. "Are you okay?"

"Yes, I'm fine." Deep peace had settled over me. "What happened?"

"You almost had a head-on collision. You were driving in the wrong lane on a two-lane highway."

A two-lane highway. How did I miss the changeover from four lanes to two lanes?

Coach Debbie's voice caught. "I kept blowing my horn to get your attention, but you didn't respond."

The seriousness of the situation dawned on me.

Coach Debbie's eyes glistened with tears. "The team and I watched God's angels lift your car off the highway and place it on the median."

I swallowed hard. "I must have fallen asleep at the wheel. Thank you so much for praying."

Coach Debbie smiled. "I don't think I've ever prayed so hard for anything in all my life."

She opened the car door, and I got out. Then, she and the team surrounded me and gave me a huge group hug.

"Girls," Coach Debbie said, "let's thank the Lord for this great miracle tonight."

With my two precious daughters close beside me, we all joined hands. Right there on the grassy median at the side of the highway, Coach Debbie led the team in a powerful prayer of thanksgiving for God's mercy in saving my life. His angels had protected me. And I would never be the same.

— MaryAnn Diorio —

Tsunami Survivor

The purpose of life is a life of purpose.
~Robert Byrne

When I was in third grade, my school principal allowed me to start my Winter Break early with the condition that I kept a journal on what happened each day of my vacation. Well, here's my journal entry.

It seemed like an ordinary morning on vacation. My family and I were vacationing in Sri Lanka (our country of origin) for the holidays; it was the day after Christmas. My parents and I were very tired in the morning, delaying our plans to head for the beach by two hours. Two hours that seemed meaningless, but ended up meaning the world to us.

My father and I washed and went downstairs for breakfast at the busy hotel restaurant while my mother decided to sleep in a bit longer. We tried to eat slowly so that my mother wouldn't have to eat alone, but in the end it was no use. We waited even longer; still no sign of her. And then we spotted my aunt and uncle, who were to drive with us to the Hikkaduwa Beach. We chatted for a while and then my mother finally joined us.

I was nearly as eager to go as my dad, who had spent his life by the sea and had so wanted to take me to the beach... but unfortunately (well fortunately, actually) my mother needed to take her asthma medication, which required her to eat first. Then once more we waited as my mother dashed upstairs to get her water bottle. She

Divine Intervention |

apologized for her tardiness and we all packed into my uncle's van, delayed by yet another half hour.

It was a two-hour drive down to Hikkaduwa Beach; we were shocked at what we found. People were running and screaming as the police blocked traffic. My mother told me to duck (she feared it was a shooting or a bombing) and I hid my head in her lap as the police officer explained to my uncle (who thankfully was driving) that there had been a tidal wave and that we should turn back immediately. My uncle was reluctant, but decided that since I was there (being only a mere child) we were to turn back.

I am thankful to this day that it was not my father driving, for he was in denial over the fact that his ocean was taking lives with the push and pull of its waves and he would have continued driving us straight to our deaths. I was nearly in tears as we turned around. People banging on the van and screaming, "Let us in! Let us in!" and wailing in agony. We had neither room, nor time, to spare.

So we drove back and my father stopped at a good friend's house to see if everyone was okay. After a few minutes he ran back and said that his friend was at work, and the wife was in hysterics because she couldn't find her mother (who had been praying at a temple), and that he'd tried to bring her to safety but couldn't get in a word between the shrieks. The danger seemed to be gone, but he didn't like the looks of the water crawling towards them. Besides, we were all still in the van that could easily be swept away by the water.

And so we drove for a while upwards, to the Holy Cross Church, where we could still see the ocean but were too high up for it to reach us. We weren't the only ones there. Many people crowded together on the point, some of them wet. I saw a young man carrying an elderly lady on the steps, another elderly lady holding nothing but a few saved belongings and a picture of Jesus Christ who couldn't find her son or grandson, a few young girls wailing for their families, and of course those who were by themselves,; and would remain so. I tried comforting the lady with the picture and some of the wailing girls… I was in a trance-like state of mind. We handed out crackers and tried to make sense of what would happen next. I gazed out at the ocean;

it was a murky brown, filled with debris.

Once we deemed it safe, we returned to the van. I was so exhausted; I couldn't take much more... and so I fell asleep. When I woke up we were going out to lunch as if nothing had happened. Had it been a dream? No, it had been a nightmare. My parents later told me that once we had turned around and headed for Holy Cross, the second wave had hit. It was that wave that had taken thousands of lives, and left many homeless. I have never looked at the sea the same way again. Also, about 200 cars that had not turned around as we did were swept away; some license plates were found in the Maldives, 767 kilometers away. It all came down to a minute or two that had saved our lives.

There must be a purpose I have to serve, a reason why I lived through that tragedy. I was witness to something that has affected the world.

— Sheoli V. Gunaratne, age 13 —

Miracle on Mott Street

*A guardian angel walks with us, sent from up above,
their loving wings surround us and enfold us with love.*
~Author Unknown

There are certain places on the planet where you can feel a connection with the spirit realm or a loved one. That's the way my mother, Terry, and I felt about Little Italy in New York City. The very streets brought us back to our roots that were planted before either of us was born. It's the spot where, on a hot July night in 1906, my grandfather Tony was born to immigrant parents. "I was born on the corner of Hester and Mott," he often said. Save for the clothes and cars, little had changed since that time period, making Little Italy almost a living museum.

Grandpa Tony loved to tell me stories about when he was a little boy running the streets of the neighborhood. As it turns out, he and my Uncle Dom were running a little too wildly for my great-grandfather's liking, and he soon moved his family to a then very rural town in New Jersey. Occasionally, Grandpa took us to New York for pastries and cappuccino and to walk around the streets, which sadly didn't span the vast neighborhood they once did. Little Italy was whittled down to one main drag, Mulberry Street, and two cross streets, Hester and Grand. The rest had become Chinatown.

Now it's important to note that New York City in the 1970s was nothing like the theme park it's become today. In fact, most parts were downright dangerous. All the trendy neighborhoods, such as Soho (South of Houston) and Nolita (North of Little Italy), were nothing but sweatshops and factories back then. Since those businesses were closed in the evenings and on weekends, the streets were dark and deserted. While it made for easy parking, it was still scary for two women walking them alone. Moreover, it had been reported in the news that gangs were running the streets of Chinatown mugging tourists. While it didn't stop us, we were on our guard when we ventured to Little Italy on Sundays for Italian food and shopping.

One Sunday, I felt lucky to find a parking spot on Mott Street, which was one block over from Mulberry. It was a busy street filled with sidewalk stands selling Chinese vegetables, fish, and fowl. We only had to walk down the street and around the corner to reach our restaurant. After a few steps, though, we saw people scattering. A gang of young men was coming down the sidewalk armed with baseball bats and who knows what else.

Panic set in. There was no time to return to the car. Besides, it really wouldn't offer any protection. Yet if we walked forward, my mother and I would come face-to-face with them.

"Come on." My mother grabbed my arm and pulled me into the vestibule of an old tenement house, which was, surprisingly, unlocked. With our hearts pounding, we hid in the stairwell until we heard them pass. When we walked back out, something struck my mother and she said, "Do you think this could be the building where Grandpa lived?" She took out a pen and wrote down the number.

It's odd, but neither of us remembered Grandpa showing us the house where he lived. It couldn't have been that he was ashamed, because the entire area was terribly poor even to this day. There's a wonderful old photo that's been made into a poster called "Mott Street 1906." It shows the pushcarts and peddlers and the clotheslines overhead covered with the residents' laundry. More importantly, after their precarious start running with gangs in the early 1900s, my grandfather and his brother went on to become very successful men. Grandpa became the first Italian-American man to join the local police force, solving the

Case of the Missing Corpse (the husband was buried under the new patio), and eventually becoming captain.

A few days later, my mother handed me a piece of paper. "Take a look at this." It was my grandfather's birth certificate. "Look at the address." She also had her planner where she wrote down the number of the tenement building we ran into on Mott Street. It was the same building. "Grandpa was looking out for us that day," she said. A chill ran through me as we stared wide-eyed at each other.

Was it a miracle or a coincidence? But isn't a miracle really just a glorious coincidence? We tend to think of miracles as great biblical events, but I believe that we should appreciate those tiny gifts that come our way. Seek simple miracles, and you will always catch a glimpse of heaven.

In any event, Grandpa Tony always loved a good time. If he decided to join us in spirit on our Sunday adventures, he would certainly do anything in his power to keep my mother and me safe, especially from the type of gang he used to run with. Maybe he was working off some old karma.

I'd like to believe he was there with us, and that it was a miracle—the Miracle on Mott Street.

—Lynn Maddalena Menna—

September 15, 1998

> *Sometimes, our grandmas and grandpas are like grand-angels.*
> *~Lexie Saige*

Some dates are etched into your memory. Your birthday, your wedding day, the birth of your child, or any other date that changed you are dates that are not only remembered but are usually celebrated. Some dates, though, go down in infamy. Those dates force you to relive what happened whether you like it or not.

September 15, 1998 was the latter kind of date. It was the day my daughter was reborn, in the spiritual sense. It was a day I was reborn, as well.

My husband and I had recently purchased a new car, and our daughter had only been driving for a short time, but we agreed she could use it to go visit her boyfriend. She left with a promise to be careful and to call when she got there. Everything would be fine, I told myself, as I fell into my easy chair to catch up on the evening news.

Half an hour after she left, the phone rang. When I answered, I heard what would send any parent into an emotional frenzy. I heard Jess scream. Then there was a brief silence before she calmly said that she had been in an accident. She was sorry and didn't want us to be angry that she had messed up the car. She asked if we would come to her.

My husband and I jumped into our other car. We headed toward the mountain road she had directed us to, but were surprised to see

Divine Intervention | 47

EMTs, firetrucks, ambulances, and police cars pass us. I worried there had been an accident on this route that could delay us from reaching our daughter. Then we saw all the lights. And our new car facing us on the wrong side of the road.

I couldn't get out of my seatbelt fast enough. My child was in that crumpled car. I ran toward Jess, only to be stopped by a police officer holding a clipboard.

I felt sick to my stomach. I could see her in the car, mostly hidden behind the exploded airbag, but I couldn't see much else. The officer assured me she was being taken care of and that a helicopter was on its way to take her to the hospital. I could barely focus on his words but I clearly heard him say the Jaws of Life. They had to extract her from the car before the rescue flight.

After I gave him some personal information, he told me to walk over to the car and remain calm while I talked to her. She had been in shock, and there were two EMTs in the back seat, bracing her neck and calming her down.

It had rained and the road was slippery. She had hit a van coming from the opposite direction head on. The other driver wasn't hurt, but Jess had hit his van so hard that the front end of her car was pushed in, the dashboard pinning her to her seat. She had blood around her mouth, and they had to wait to discover the extent of her injuries because they couldn't see past her upper chest area.

I remember going to the side of the road to throw up before I went to see her. I needed to be her mom.

I approached the driver's window and smiled. My whole body was shaking. There she sat, with a brace on her neck. She could move her eyes enough to meet mine. All I could think about was the first time our eyes had met when they placed her in my arms after she was born.

I told her in the calmest voice I could muster that she was going to be okay. That she needed to stay strong until they could get her out. She looked back at me calmly. And just like I will always remember the date, I will remember her words.

"I know I'll be okay, Mom. Grandpa was here. He helped me call you."

I stopped breathing for a second. What? I needed to be honest with her. They had told me to just keep talking until help arrived. "Honey," I replied, "Grandpa died last year."

"I know," she said. "He was here in the white golf hat and jacket we buried him in. He told me I was going to be okay."

I didn't respond. I only fought back the tears and smiled as I nodded. Then I was asked to stand back so they could cut my child out of the mangled metal. I thought about the first time she'd been cut out to save her life—when she was born by C-section.

We stood by for an hour and a half, watching, praying, pleading that she would be okay. The officer came back with more questions, but this time our answers were not what he expected. He asked how we learned there had been an accident. I told him about the call we had gotten from Jess. I mentioned the scream that didn't make sense, shared her explanation of what had happened and then added her request to come get her.

"That can't be," he said, shaking his head. "She couldn't have made the call. She's been trapped all this time. Look at her; you can't see her arms at all."

I stuck to my story. It was the truth. "Come with me," he directed.

He led us around to the other side of the car. As he pointed to the floor behind the front passenger seat, he showed us the cell phone on the floor, covered with the white airbag dust. It had clearly not been touched after it flew there during the collision. "You see? She couldn't have called you on that."

Then, without a doubt, her words replayed in my mind. "Grandpa was here." He had been. Oh my God, he had been.

After pulling her out of the wreckage, they flew her to the hospital where we drove, sobbing, and so grateful, so blessed to know she would be fine.

September 15, 1998. The day two miracles happened. The day Jess was spared, and the day that my dad was there to make sure she was okay.

—Kim Garback Diaz—

Frozen

Never drive faster than your guardian angel can fly.
~Author Unknown

I adjusted the car's visor and leaned forward, straining against my seatbelt. The aviator sunglasses I wore were no match against the intense sun. I gripped the steering wheel tighter as I attempted to follow the road's yellow line. The asphalt was worn so smooth in some areas that it served as a reflective surface. No matter where I looked — up and straight ahead, or down at the road — I was blinded by the sun. I took a right at the first stoplight, and in an instant I could see again.

I pulled into the local Dollar General and ran in for a few essentials. I was back in the car in less than twenty minutes. Thankfully, the sun would be at my back for the drive home.

I sat at the intersection and waited for the light to turn. The light turned green, but my body suddenly seemed to stop working. I was completely unable to move. I stared at the green light, fully aware I needed to take my foot off the brake and place it on the accelerator, but it was as if I had become frozen in time.

This is weird, I thought. *What's happening to me? Am I paralyzed? Did I have a stroke? Should I be alarmed?* But I wasn't alarmed. I felt bewildered, but at the same time peaceful. There was no fear.

With every bit of strength in me, I willed my body to move. My efforts sent my body lurching toward the center console in a jerky motion, and suddenly I had full range of motion once again.

I was easing out into the intersection when the unmistakable roar of a diesel engine filled my car. It sounded entirely too close, and it was coming from my left side. A blur of color filled my peripheral vision. I slammed on my brakes as a large truck narrowly missed my vehicle. The driver had blown right through a red light and never even slowed down. Perhaps he, too, had been blinded by the sun. Shaken, I pulled into the first parking lot I came to.

I sat there contemplating the "what-ifs" of my near miss. If I'd pulled into the intersection three to five seconds sooner, I could have been seriously injured or worse. I shuddered at the thought. That's when I looked up and noticed the building I'd ended up in front of; I was sitting in the parking lot of a church. As I focused on the large cross adorning the front of the chapel, I realized my unexplainable, temporary paralysis had lasted three to five seconds.

I grabbed my phone and called my husband.

"Hey, babe," he answered. "What are you doing?"

"Oh, not much," I replied. "Just hanging out with my guardian angel."

—Melissa Bender—

Chapter 3

Angels Among Us

Last Words

*Angels descending, bring from above,
Echoes of mercy, whispers of love.*
~Fanny J. Crosby

I have been a firefighter and paramedic for many years, and I know we take chances every time we respond to a call. We all understand we are testing fate every single day as we work to snatch people back from the jaws of death or disaster.

One particular day while working in Louisville, Kentucky we responded to an elderly woman who was having a heart attack. She was in her upper eighties and terribly ill. While working on her, I was talking with her, as I do with all my patients, about what I was doing as well as all kinds of subjects, whatever came to my mind at the time. I was down in the space between the bench seat — the long seat on the side of the ambulance — and the stretcher. This was a small opening not meant for people of larger sizes; luckily, I could still fit there.

As we were driving with lights and siren to the hospital, and I was busy working on the lady, a horrific booming noise came out of nowhere at the same time that I felt a huge pain in my side. Suddenly, our ambulance was on its side, and I was stuck in that small space, basically lying on top of my patient from the waist up. All this, I learned later, was the result of an elderly lady running through an intersection with her old Buick and T-boning our ambulance.

As we lay there, my partner, though injured, asked, "Are you okay?" I said, "Yes, do what you have to do." He exited the unit and started to care for the patient who hit us. While this was going on, I asked our primary patient if she was okay. She stated, "I'm fine, honey. Are you okay?"

I replied, "Yes," as I continued to work on her.

I couldn't move much because I was still trapped by the bench seat, but I continued to talk to my patient, reassuring her that we would have her at the hospital as soon as possible. This sweet lady said that she understood and urged me to make sure that I was okay. I advised her that I was and continued to work.

When responding ambulances and the fire department arrived, my colleagues began to extricate us. Due to the way our ambulance was positioned and how it had collapsed, it took a long time for them to cut us out. All the while, I was talking to my patient and working on her. As she was finally being removed from the unit, I apologized for this happening and told her that she would be at the hospital momentarily. She smiled and said, "Honey, it's not your fault."

I wished her well and told her I would pray for her fast recovery. She smiled and said, "Please make sure you are okay. I'm heading home. I'll be okay."

I was then taken for evaluation at the hospital. I was released with a clean bill of health — just bumps, bruises, and soreness. When I got back to the office, I was advised that my patient had passed away. I asked, "When did she pass? Did she make it to the hospital?"

My supervisor asked worriedly, "Bill, are you sure you are okay?"

I answered, "Yes. Why?"

He said, "Just make sure you put everything in your report. The coroner will need it as soon as you finish it."

While I was finishing my report, the coroner arrived at our station headquarters. We talked as I finished my report. He said, "She passed on impact."

I said, "I spoke with her through the entire event until she went with the other ambulance."

He asked, looking at me with concern, "Bill, are you sure you are okay?"

Getting agitated, I answered, "Yes. Why does everyone keep asking me that?"

He responded, "Bill, the other crew members, including your partner, confirmed that she passed on impact. When your partner asked if you were okay, he said it took a little bit for you to respond. Also, when he exited the ambulance, he checked you out, then checked out your patient, and then went to work on the patient in the Buick."

Again, I stated, "You all are crazy. She was talking to me, encouraging me, asking me if I was going to be okay."

Her autopsy confirmed that she did pass on impact. So, who was talking with me all that time?

I believe my patient told God, "Hold on, I'll be there in a minute. This boy who was watching over me now needs me to watch over him."

I was so blessed to have this sweet angel by my side who kept talking to me. Godspeed, you truly were my angel.

— Bill Hess —

Mechanic Angel

I am convinced that these heavenly beings exist and that they provide unseen aid on our behalf.
~Billy Graham

He was the biggest man I'd ever seen — tall, wide and solid. As he approached my stalled van in the Lower Ninth Ward of New Orleans, every horror story I'd heard about the neighborhood rushed into my mind.

His tap on the window was surprisingly gentle for such a big man. A compassionate smile filled his face with warmth. I rolled down the window an inch.

"Looks like you have a problem, ma'am. Maybe I can help, if you want." His basso profundo seemed to resonate within me, and my fears eased.

"The engine coughed a couple of times as I came down the bridge," I said. "And then it just quit on me. It won't start, but the gauge says I have plenty of gas. I don't know what to do. I'm just glad I was able to coast out of traffic." I thanked God for the steep slope of the Judge William Seeber Bridge, which gave me enough momentum to get clear of the flow of cars on busy Claiborne Avenue.

In those days, before cell phones, I was cut off from all the resources I might have utilized.

"Let's just take a look under the hood," he said. "You just stay there in the shade. I'll be back in a minute."

He popped the hood, and I heard his cheerful humming as he

examined the engine. True to his word, he was back in a few moments. I rolled down the window a little more to hear his findings.

"All your connections and hoses seem tight. Let's try starting it again, if you would, please."

I nodded and turned the key. He cocked his head toward the engine compartment and listened to the grinding of the starter.

"Sounds like it's not getting any gas. But you said you have plenty?"

"Half a tank, according to the gauge, Mr. James," I answered, using the name embroidered in red over the pocket of his faded navy-blue shirt.

"Well, maybe it's a filter problem if you got gas and it ain't getting through. Let me just check that out." He disappeared around the front of the vehicle again.

By now, my pulse had returned to normal, and I wasn't afraid of him anymore. When he came back to my window, I was able to return his smile.

"I'm going to need one of my tools to get that loose." He pointed diagonally across the street to a tiny service station. "I'll go get it and be right back."

I watched him cross the traffic lanes, the grassy neutral ground (the local name for a median), and then the traffic lanes on the other side. For all his size, he moved as lightly as a dancer. He disappeared into the shadows of the repair bay. A few minutes later, he emerged with a tool I didn't recognize in his hand.

When he returned to the van, he gave me another of those billion-kilowatt smiles. "We'll get this now," he assured me. He dove back under the hood, and I heard clinking noises as he worked. In a few minutes, he straightened.

"I think this is the problem," he said, holding up a cylindrical part. "Got some grit in it, like you got some dirty gas." Before I could respond, he put the part to his mouth and gave a mighty blow. He might have been a bugler sounding the charge for all the energy he put into it. One, two, three strong puffs. I saw a little cloud emerge from the opposite side of the part. Was it the particles he mentioned, a cloud of gas, or the vapors of his mighty breath?

Angels Among Us

"Let's try it now," he said, and vanished under the hood again. I heard another round of noises. In another moment, he called, "Crank her now."

I whispered a prayer, turned the key, and heard the sweet purr of the engine.

James slammed down the hood, ensured it was closed, and then walked to my window.

"You should be fine for now, ma'am, but I'd get that checked at a garage first chance you get."

"Thank you so much. You're a lifesaver. What do I owe you?"

"You don't owe me nothing. It was my pleasure to be able to help," he said, smile beaming.

"But your time and your tools. And your diagnostic expertise." I was flabbergasted at his generosity.

"No charge, ma'am. Just using the talents God gave me."

"Well, you're my hero," I told him. "A real angel. Thank you."

He gave a little salute with his tool and headed back across the street. I continued on my way home, another forty-five minutes away, but I couldn't get him out of my mind. How could he stay in business if he didn't charge people for his services?

My husband took care of the mechanical details, leaving me to ponder a way to say thanks to my angel. I made up my mind to go back and pay him something for his efforts. A week later, I had the chance to make the trip.

I pulled into the little service station, and a thin man came out to greet me. He was much shorter than James and probably 150 pounds lighter. His skin was much lighter, too, more a café au lait than James's rich ebony.

"Hi, I'm looking for James," I said. "He helped me out last week, and I wanted to thank him."

"Nobody here by that name," the man said. "Just me and my cousin, Billy. I'm Walter." He pointed to the name on his stained khaki shirt.

"But he came over here to get tools," I told him. "A big man with very dark skin."

"No, ma'am, he wasn't here. I don't loan my tools to nobody. Are you sure you're in the right block?"

I looked across the highway to the place I had coasted in my stalled van and confirmed to myself I was in the right place.

"This is the place. I'm sure of it."

"Can't help you, lady." He shrugged. "I don't know him."

"Well, I made a coffeecake for him to say thanks. Maybe you'd like it?" I picked up the foil-wrapped package from the passenger seat and offered it to him.

"Why would you do that?" he asked.

I thought back to my giant angel. "It's my pleasure," I answered. "Just using the talents God gave me."

— Mary Beth Magee —

The Garden Visitor

*Mothers hold their children's hands for a short while,
but their hearts forever.*
~Author Unknown

It was a new year, 1981, and spring was finally here! We had moved into our beautiful new home and acreage a few months earlier. We were looking forward to better days ahead since the previous two years had been full of challenges and sadness.

In 1979, soon after construction began on our house, loan rates soared to 16 percent when the oil industry collapsed, and work slowed to a snail's pace at the concrete plant where my husband Don worked, causing paychecks to be cut nearly in half. Those days were rough, but they couldn't compare to the sadness of losing Don's mom, Nita, to congestive heart failure in May of that year.

Don and Nita had been as close as any mother and son could be. She was his confidante — his "rock" — and her sudden loss was terribly difficult for him. He missed the daily visits with her for coffee, swapping stories about family and friends, and sharing their differing views on politics. There was never a day that went by without him thinking of her and wishing he could talk to her just one more time.

Although Don never shared his thoughts and feelings of depression and grief with me, I could sense his pain. But as the months passed, I could see his sadness slowly lift as he watched our house being completed.

By the time spring was approaching, Don's eyes began to sparkle whenever the subject of planting a garden came up—our very first garden, a symbol of hope and new growth. He had purchased all the necessary tools, including a rototiller, and enough onion sets and seeds for nearly ten acres!

Finally, the day came to put Don's garden ideas into motion. He had just started the tiller as the sun was appearing on the horizon. I could hear the tiller running and decided to look out the window to watch the progress.

As I lifted the blinds, while squinting through the sun's glare, I didn't see the tiller, but I saw Don standing at the edge of the garden. A woman was standing beside him, dressed in a black coat and wearing a head scarf.

That's odd, I thought. *Why would someone be wearing a coat on a warm morning like this? And the head scarf—that's strange, too. Perhaps she's a neighbor who is just curious about the garden. Oh, well, I'll wait for Don to come in and ask him who she is.*

A few minutes later, Don came in through the garage to the kitchen. I noticed that he had a strange look on his face.

"Who was that woman you were talking to?" I asked.

"What woman?" he asked.

"The woman who was beside you at the edge of the garden," I replied.

"I don't know what you are talking about," he answered.

"Look, I saw her! Now, who was she?" I said, my curiosity now turning to frustration.

I couldn't understand why he denied seeing the person whom I had seen. His denial was hurtful to me.

Suddenly, I felt tears welling in my eyes. I looked at Don's eyes, and they began to fill with tears, too.

"Sheryl, it was Mom! I saw Mom," Don revealed. "One minute I was tilling, and then all of a sudden, Mom was standing beside me. It seemed like time was standing still.

"She asked me, 'Donnie, what are you going to plant?'

"'Mom, I'm going to plant green beans, okra, tomatoes, squash and peppers,' I answered.

"'That's nice,' she said."

"And then, Sheryl, she disappeared, and I shut the tiller off," he said. "It was so strange. One minute, she was there, dressed in dark clothes, and the next minute, she was gone. I walked away thinking maybe I had dreamed it. But then, when I walked into the house, and you started asking me about her, I was shocked that you seemed to know about her visit. I didn't know how to react or what to say to you, other than to deny it. Then when you kept pressing me about her, I realized it wasn't a dream after all because you saw her, too. We both saw her!"

At that moment, we realized we had experienced the same vision at the exact moment in time! We held each other and cried.

We shared details of that special event with only a few family members and friends. We could tell that some of them doubted our story, but we didn't care. We knew it was true, and that's all that mattered.

Don believes his mom may have appeared for a reason—to let him know she was okay and to help mend his broken heart. As to why she appeared to me, I can only guess that it was simply for confirmation to Don that her visit was real.

From that day forward, Don became a happier person. He seemed to enjoy life and his family more and was hopeful for the future.

Now, many years have passed since that special spring day, but each time garden season rolls around, Don remembers that day with fondness and can't wait to plant those vegetables. Each seed he plants reminds him of the day his mom came to see his garden.

— Sheryl K. (James) Winbolt —

Leave Now

*The guardian angels of life fly so high as to be beyond
our sight, but they are always looking down upon us.*
~Jean Paul Richter

I was the third child in my family. My older brother Bill was of course the boss. He was always ordering everyone around and in charge of keeping us out of harm's way. Looking back, I am amazed at how many times Bill stepped in and kept us safe.

I vividly remember the day when I was nine years old that our horse, Midnight, got his saddle horn caught in the clothesline. He was wild-eyed and frightened. Nothing could calm him or stop him. He charged at me, and Bill yelled, "Leave now. Jump in the pond." I was terrified of the horse but even more terrified of the pond. Bill had always told us to stay away from the pond, as it had no bottom and would swallow us up. I froze and to this day I don't know how Bill managed to beat the horse to me; he shoved me into the pond and jumped in with me to hold me up. Scared to death, I was trying to tread water and hoping the horse would stop before it got to the pond. Thankfully my dad showed up and got the horse under control. Bill and I emerged from the pond unscathed.

"Leave now" was his famous order and it always stuck with me. Bill was killed while serving in Vietnam, but I never forgot that advice from him.

One day I had a business meeting with a client who needed to sign up some new employees at his repair shop for group health insurance. I always liked seeing Russ, the shop manager. He was a wonderful man and always cheerful and willing to help. The moment I arrived, Russ cleared his desk and told me to use it to sign up employees instead of trying to juggle my paperwork standing up. One by one, Russ sent in each new employee to be enrolled and brought me a cup of coffee just the way I liked it. "Strong and black." It was a standing joke between us that I would gladly adopt him if he promised to make my coffee every day. Russ was definitely a bright spot in an otherwise boring and routine stop that day.

Just as I was finishing with the last sign-up I distinctly heard my brother's voice from all those years ago say, "Leave now." It startled me so much I almost spilled my coffee, but it also gave me an uneasy feeling that I really needed to finish up quick and get out of there.

From there I continued my day as usual and returned home that night safe and sound. From time to time throughout the evening I thought of that strange moment in the day when I heard Bill's voice saying, "Leave now." As I got ready for bed I suddenly remembered it was the anniversary of Bill's death. How could I have forgotten? It was the first time in many years that the day did not send me into tears. I shrugged it off and decided Bill just wanted me to know he was still in charge and looking out for me. After drifting off to sleep, I was startled awake at midnight by the shrill ringing of the phone.

Half awake, I fumbled in the dark and answered the phone. My heart was in my throat as my father had been very ill and I was afraid something had happened to him. As soon as I said "hello," I heard the voice of Mitch, who owned the repair shop. Mitch blurted out, "Russ is dead. Someone came in the shop just after you left and shot him at his desk and fired at all the other employees. They managed to escape by the back door or dive into the repair bay pit." I was in complete shock and devastated at the loss of such a fine man.

Suddenly I knew my brother was with me as I had made my rounds that day. Bill knew the danger I was in, and that was why I heard him say, "Leave now." Even from beyond the grave my big brother Bill was still watching over me.

— Christine Trollinger —

Maybe, Under Some Circumstances

The angels are the dispensers and administrators of the divine beneficence toward us; they regard our safety, undertake our defense, direct our ways, and exercise a constant solicitude that no evil befall us.
~John Calvin

I will call my encounter a she. And you, if you wish, may call her an angel.

An angel? A ghost? A spirit? Or the residual energy that can connect us with another after the self is gone? I truly don't know. It's hard to determine absolutes in a story like this.

What I am sure of, however, is that she was a definite presence, that I was her emissary, and that she sent through me an indelible message that spared me the unexplainable, unnamable grief of losing a child.

She had no wings and no halo, no quivering air mass and no sound of bugles. Nothing of the stereotype — just a gentle, urgent presence that lifted me from my troubled vigil and sent me on one of the most contained, most important missions of my life.

For the first decade of my three children's lives, I was a single mom five days a week. My husband came home on Friday evenings and left again on Sunday after dinner.

Our home was large and old, a late-1800s masterpiece we were restoring as time and finances allowed. It was four stories and had a huge cement and stone cellar. The second level had hardwood doors, floors and trim in each of the large, spacious rooms as well as floor-to-ceiling windows throughout. The bedrooms, similarly large and spacious, and with floor-to-ceiling windows, were on the third floor. That floor also had a bathroom with an exterior door that strangely opened onto a porch along the front of the house. The fourth level was a full walk-up attic space where we were planning to create a loft.

It was magnificence awaiting restoration, but it was old and it groaned and shivered with its age. It was a very vocal house and I was not the bravest of young women. So during the night, as the creaks and whispers seemed to portend skulking intruders and all manner of beings with nasty intent, I tried to sit vigil with a book on my lap.

One night, I had fallen into a cramped, uncomfortable sleep on the couch. This was not something that I had done before. When fatigue won out, I always climbed the winding staircase, checked on my three little ones, and then, my heart and mind clenched in foreboding, slipped into a shallow sleep.

This night, however, as I lay asleep on the couch, I felt a gentle, persistent pressure—curing my normal nightly agitation and wrapping me in a state of perfect calm and silence such as I had never before felt. I lay hushed and unmoving, holding to the perfection of the moment. I was consumed.

And then, gently creeping under my awareness, I saw my name.
Robyn...
Robyn...
I rolled onto my elbow and my book slipped to the floor.
Robyn...
I could feel her message and I could see her message, but still there was no sound. There was only the perfect calm and silence.

"You will need a cold, wet cloth. Put it on the little one's head. Call for an ambulance. Strip him and wrap him in a fresh sheet and his blanket. Call Mary to stay with the others. You will have to follow the ambulance in your car."

I moved with an absolute certainty. I wet a cloth and, upstairs, I found Declan thrashing and rasping. His breath came in short puffs of agony; his little face glistened from an effort almost beyond his endurance and from the intense heat of his body.

I called 911 from my room, wrapped him in a fresh sheet and then telephoned my neighbour Mary. She answered immediately. "It's Robyn," I said. "Declan needs to go the hospital."

"I'll be right there," she said. "I got up a bit ago. I wasn't able to sleep."

I stood at the door with my son in his sheet and a light blanket, the cool, wet cloth draped across his head. There was no panic — just a calm, understood urgency. Mary arrived, as did the ambulance.

"I'll follow in the car," I said to my neighbour. I couldn't tell her how I knew that the rules prohibited me from riding in the ambulance.

In the hospital, I waited until dawn. "We were very lucky. Much longer and he wouldn't have made it. Convulsions..." The doctor shook his head. "Very lucky," he repeated.

Declan stayed in hospital for the next two days and then was released on a Friday. His father, Martin, who had driven home to be with us, collected him.

"Who's the Blue Lady?" he asked me.

"The Blue Lady?"

"Yes, Declan said that she swept the hotness off him with her broom. And she wrote him a letter."

"A letter? What about?"

"His name. He said that it was his whole name, Declan Liesen Gerland. But he's three. He can't read yet. Can he?"

I paused. "Maybe," I said. "Maybe. Under some circumstances. Maybe, just under some circumstances."

— Robyn Gerland —

The Doctor

All God's angels come to us disguised.
~James Russell Lowell

My dad paced the hallway, wringing his hands in despair. He had called the doctor's office and left another message with his answering service, but there had been no reply. My mom sat next to me on my bed trying to soothe my forehead with a cool cloth after another bout of vomiting had left me weakened and feverish.

The knock at the front door brought a man, medicine bag in hand, bundled against the winter's cold. It was the 1950s, and doctors made house calls. He introduced himself, explaining that he was filling in for our regular family physician that evening. My father quickly brought him to my room. After an exam, he announced that my appendix had ruptured and they needed to get me to surgery immediately. He told my parents to drive me to our local hospital and he would meet us there.

I was wrapped in blankets and loaded into the car, my younger brother in the front seat with my dad and my mother by my side in back. I remember the anxious look my parents shared as they drove to the hospital. When I arrived, the doctor was waiting.

My parents had walked through the same hospital doors just months earlier after the death of my older brother. A car had hit him while riding his bicycle home from school. Now, I saw the look of fear on my parents' faces as they watched me wheeled into the operating room.

Over the next few days, I would wake for short periods of time inside an oxygen tent only to see my mom or dad in a chair by my bed. A couple of days after the surgery, our regular doctor came into the room. The look he exchanged with my parents was one of shock and disbelief.

I would learn many years later that our family doctor had just returned from a trip and was given my dad's old messages. There was no doctor on call that night by the name given to us. No one from our small town hospital had heard of him either. He had told the staff that he had just joined our doctor's family practice and was filling in for him that evening. My parents, our doctor, and the hospital tried to find the man who showed up on our doorstep that blustery night to save my life. They never did.

— Catherine Kopp —

Bandit's Run

Dogs are miracles with paws.
~Susan Ariel Rainbow Kennedy

I was fourteen years old and lost in the woods. My hand gripped the steel handle of my father's pistol and I shivered from the cool of the coming night. I had fallen down a rocky ridge about fifteen feet above a deep valley and rolled into a dry creek bed below. I had a deep cut on my left arm and I was bleeding heavily. I didn't think too much of it, as I had cut myself on the sharp rocks many times before. I sat down hard on the stump of an old cottonwood tree and wondered what to do next.

Our family had been coming to the backwoods of Ozark country since I was born; my two older sisters, mom and dad, and now a baby brother. The little cabin sat against the hills near Lake of the Ozarks, and we would drive down from Kansas City, Missouri and spend every weekend fishing, swimming, hunting, and walking through the deep woods and rocky ravines that formed the landscape. This time, I had gone out alone. My father had given me the gun for squirrel hunting, or maybe a rabbit if one happened by, but now it felt like its purpose had become much more sinister.

Beyond the grove of dead elms, I heard the snapping of brush and the familiar low grunting sounds of wild boars. My father had warned me about them. He had come across a herd of them years before and barely escaped with his life. Now, here I was, lost, cold, alone. The sun had just gone down over the farthest hill and the woods were getting dark.

I pointed the gun in front of me and got to my knees. There was a pack of them, circling. Their yellow eyes cut a path in the darkness. The blood on my arm was thick and dry but they must have smelled it. There are too many of them, I thought, but I was suddenly unafraid as I heard my father's words: "If you ever get into trouble out there, stay calm and do what I've taught you to do. Survive."

The largest of the group charged me first, missing my arm by inches.

I rose to my feet, gun in hand.

They were all growling and grunting now, snorting and biting at each other.

I could barely see the coarse, wiry hair on their backs standing straight up, all the way to the dark red skin of their necks. I kicked at them and shouted.

I had three bullets in the gun. How many of the boars were there? Maybe six.

From behind me came a rattle of brush and then, one of the boars was on me, aiming for my neck. I fell back, and dropped the gun.

I brought my feet up to my chest and prepared to fight for my life.

Then suddenly, there was another growl. But it was a much different sound this time. It was lower than the excited half-squeals of the wild boar and it froze us all. I saw my chance and got to my feet, spotting the gun a few feet away.

As I went for it, I saw him. It was Bandit, my father's old coonhound. He lurched through the forest, his teeth all fury, showing no fear.

I picked up the gun and ran to him.

Two boars leapt on the dog's back, their golden eyes now green and focused. Bandit rolled, as he was taught to do.

They fell from his back and the dog was on his feet again, positioned in front of me.

I leveled the gun and aimed. I fired.

The shot was deafening in the still of night and roared up the sides of the hills, echoing through the ravine. The whole herd took off running with Bandit in hot pursuit. I called after him as I ran blindly through the woods, following the loud bawl of the old hound. I was up and over a small hill, into the next ravine. Bandit was getting farther and farther away but I kept on running, trying to keep up. Before I knew it I was in the clearing where I had first started the day, only about 100 yards from the cabin. I could hear my mother's voice calling for me and I ran to her.

My father was at her side, already putting on his jacket to come and search for me. I hugged my mother and burst out crying, trying to explain what had happened. I could feel my father's hand on my shoulder, he was telling me to calm down, everything was all right. I looked at him and said, "It was Bandit, Dad. He saved me. He came out of the woods, full speed, he..."

"Bandit?" my father asked. The look on his face was one of confusion and wonder. "David, Bandit's been dead for two years now, remember? We buried him up past those two hills, by that creek bed in the ravine. It must have been another dog, son."

I was going to tell him, tell them both, that I saw his face, I knew it was him, but something told me not to. As we all walked into the cabin together, I could hear a wail in the distance, coming from over the hills and down in a small ravine.

Or it could have been the wind.

— David Magill —

Father, Son, and Brother

Yet if there is an angel at their side, a messenger, one out of a thousand, sent to tell them how to be upright.
~Job 33:23

My son Mike and I had a rather tumultuous relationship ever since the day my ex-wife called and said, "Come get him. I can't do a thing with him."

I was thrilled to get my son back and looked forward to using my own parenting methods on him. Mike had gotten into trouble with the law on several occasions. On the day I picked him up, I told him I would not tolerate such things. If he got into trouble with the law while he lived with me, I would let the law handle it. Of course, being fourteen years old and knowing all there was to know about the world, he didn't believe me. After living with me for two months, he found himself incarcerated in a juvenile facility in our county.

This started a long string of events where he would promise to stay out of trouble and then go right back to his old ways. We had some great times together and some times of terrible grief. When he was thirty years old, he was working for a man who cut logs for a living. One night Mike took off in the man's pickup truck that had two chainsaws in the back along with some other logging equipment. None of us had any idea where he went. Word was put out to law enforcement agencies, but Mike and the truck could not be located.

My lifestyle had changed for the better, and I was traveling in a motor home and selling jewelry at various events to make a living. While I was selling at an event in Quartzsite, Arizona, I got word through a long grapevine that Mike had been killed in an accident in California. I found out he had married a woman who had two children, and they had another child of their own. The youngest baby had stayed with her grandparents while her daddy, mom, and two brothers went to the store. All four of them lost a battle with a train at an unmarked crossing on their way home. I had a granddaughter I had never met or even knew existed. And she was an orphan.

I was about seven hundred miles away from where my son was going to be buried, so I took off the next morning to attend the funeral. I got into the small town on the morning of the second day of my trip, arriving just forty-five minutes before the funeral was to start. A man met me at the door of the church and explained that he was an assistant pastor for the church and folks called him Brother Bob. He said my son's wife's family had requested that he help me through the whole process since I had never met any of these people and certainly didn't know them. I hadn't even known until three days before that my son had gotten married and was a father.

The coffins were in a side room off the main sanctuary of the church. They were left there so the family could spend some time alone with their loved ones before the main service. Brother Bob was a rather short, stout man, but he did manage to hold up my three-hundred-pound body when I almost collapsed at the first sight of Mike in a coffin.

He knew a great deal about Mike's past. The one thing I remember him telling me was not to beat myself up over everything that had happened in our relationship. There were many other factors that led to this moment, and all of them were not my fault. He quoted several passages from the Bible that were comforting, and he prayed with me. He got me seated in the sanctuary before the service started and then left to attend to some other duties.

After the service in the church, we all went to the cemetery for a graveside ceremony. After that, we returned to the church for a huge meal that had been prepared by volunteers. After I finished eating, I sought Pastor Paul Simmons and thanked him for the services he had performed. I asked him where I might find Brother Bob so I could thank him for his help. He got a quizzical look on his face. "Who?" he said.

"Your assistant pastor, Brother Bob."

"I'm sorry, but we only have one assistant pastor here, Brother Luke. He's a young, tall man with sandy red hair."

I went to each member of the family and asked if they had seen this man who called himself Brother Bob. I said he was short, stout and wearing a black suit, white shirt, and a black, string western-style tie. He was also balding. None could remember seeing him and none of them said they asked anyone to be there to specifically help me. I told all of them I was talking with him in the side room off the sanctuary before the service. Still no one remembered seeing him. I guess I was the only one, but he was as real to me as this keyboard I'm typing on.

On my way back to Quartzsite, I had a lot of time to think. I came to one conclusion. All of my son's in-laws had been friendly and helpful, but Brother Bob was sent especially to help me through this whole horrible process. I guess angels come in all shapes and sizes. They don't have to have wings or golden halos. They can be short, stout, and balding, but they can still be angels.

— Gary R. Hoffman —

Chapter 4

Random Acts of Kindness

Feeding a Family on a Prayer

Through the eyes of gratitude, everything is a miracle.
~Mary Davis

At nine years old, I had been through more than the usual amount of excitement and change for a girl my age. In the past few months, my stable and predictable life had been turned upside down when my father, who was a nurse, was laid off from his job at a local hospital. This set into motion a series of events, including my parents losing our beautiful Victorian home and forcing our family into a fifteen-foot pull trailer we had previously only used for weekend camping trips. My parents also withdrew me from my private school and began homeschooling my brother and me.

Life in the trailer was tough. I contracted scarlet fever and remember being sicker than I ever thought possible. We were incredibly crowded. I'll never forget the first time we sat on the tiny couch together, the one that served as my parents' bed at night. When Mom, Dad, my brother, and I all sat on the couch at the end of the trailer, the entire front end began to tip in our direction, forcing one of us to jump up and scramble to the front. This settled the trailer back on the ground. Furthermore, we were running out of options for places to park our mobile house. It finally got so bad that we had to park the trailer in our church parking lot.

Things were getting bleak. I remember my mom's shrieks as a gray mouse ran across the floor and under the stove. One day, she sat at the cramped table and made out a shopping list while the last of our food, fried chicken, sizzled on the stovetop. "We need to pray," she said aloud. "We don't have enough food to last the week." And so, we joined hands and asked God to provide not only food but all our pressing needs.

Then Mom got up and started putting the chicken on a plate for dinner. I opened the tiny door and let the smell of dinner follow me as I wandered outside to find my dad. He was working on our broken-down truck. As Dad leaned over the engine, I noticed a disheveled man walking up to our humble abode.

"Can I help you, sir?" my dad asked in his friendly way.

"I'm hoping you can," he said. "I'm hungry and was wondering if you had any food to spare."

I looked up at Dad, knowing we didn't have much.

"Sure!" Dad chirped without hesitation. He brushed off his hands and went inside, returning with a fresh piece of fried chicken wrapped in a paper towel. The man's grimy face lit up. He devoured the home-cooked food, and I happily listened to a friendly conversation between the two men. The stranger mentioned that he had some canned food that he couldn't use because he didn't have a can opener. Dad offered him our can opener, but the man refused, saying he'd bring the cans by later. Dad said that wasn't necessary, but the man insisted.

After dinner, our little family locked our dog and cat in the trailer and walked across the parking lot for Wednesday night service. Doing something we used to do, before losing our home, was a comfort to our family. The small congregation was warm and familiar. The evening activities consisted of all the things a midweek service should have: homespun music, heartfelt prayer, and encouragement.

When we returned to the trailer, we were surprised to see three brown paper bags near the drop-down step leading up to the door.

"Well, that man said he was going to leave us some canned food…" Dad's voice trailed off. Dad had left the conversation with the impression it was a few cans, not a few bags. Mom and Dad brought in the bags and began to unpack them on the table. About two bags in, Mom's eyes filled with tears. She grabbed her list from under a magnet on the empty, pint-sized refrigerator. Dad took it from her and began to cry himself, something I rarely saw throughout my lifetime. I glanced over his shoulder and saw it in black and white. It was a simple grocery list, written in Mom's fancy cursive.

"This is unbelievable!" Mom gasped. "Every item I listed, even down to the 'tuna in water,' is on our table! Milk, eggs, noodles, bread…" The list went on.

It was enough to get us through another week. Dad sat us down and thanked God for providing for us in such an immediate, specific way. Then he got out his big brown Bible and began thumbing through the thin pages until he found the book of Hebrews. "Chapter thirteen, verse two," he said in a shaky voice. "Do not forget to show hospitality to strangers, for by so doing some people have shown hospitality to angels without knowing it" (NIV).

From that day to this, our family has always referred to that man as an angel. Life got better for my family after that. Dad began working as a traveling nurse, and we upgraded to a thirty-four-foot Class A motorhome. This fit our new homeschooling lifestyle like a glove. We all recall the years spent on the road with great fondness, seeing just about every state west of the Mississippi. It was a time of bonding and memory-making that could never have happened in the Victorian house.

"Remember the angel?" my younger brother often said, which conjured up the memories. We would retell the tale of the day an angel visited a trailer and fed a family on a prayer.

— Hosanna Barton —

Giving Life to a Stranger

To know even one life has breathed easier because you have lived. This is to have succeeded.
~Ralph Waldo Emerson

Through my body surges the blood of people I've never met. An amalgamation of souls, hopes and dreams runs through me. The viscous red liquid creeping into my veins as these strangers share their life force with me when I can't sustain my own.

The first time, it scared me. I'd been having litres of luminescent yellow liquid pumped into me: chemotherapy—cytotoxic drugs—meaning "toxic to living cells." It kills off all your cells without discrimination, which is a terrifying thought. But it was specifically crafted by experts for that purpose: to kill the cancer growing within me, hopefully quicker than it kills the rest of me.

But blood is a force of nature, not something medical geniuses have synthesised. It's something older than humanity. It is personal, intimate. It is part of us, made for us, to keep us alive. To think that we can pull it out of one person and put it in another is mindboggling.

The first time that doctors hung a unit of dark red liquid above me, I watched it as they fiddled around, checking the blood type was right, checking my name and birthdate. When they hooked me up, my heart started to race as I watched the thick syrup creep toward my arm. The inches closed until it was centimetres, and then it was in. They had to take my temperature to make sure my body wasn't rejecting it. But my desperate, exhausted body welcomed it, as if it was always meant to be there. And in that moment, it became part of me.

I've now had more blood transfusions than I can count. Time and time again, strangers have saved my life. In the absence of being able to thank them directly, I send that gratitude out into the universe and down into my body. With each transfusion, I wonder what kind of person is flowing into me. Are they mathematical? Or a writer? A marathon runner? Do they have siblings? Are they musical? Are they a mother? Or are they a man? Could I have a man's blood in me? I wonder what music they listen to, what books they read. I weave stories around them as we become one. I marvel to think that the fabric of my cells is now made up of the kindness and generosity of others, and I feel those connections moving through me. Those people, who willingly donated their blood and its components, will be with me forever.

My soul is also made up of other people, even beyond a cellular level. I really feel that. I'm a combination of everyone I've ever met and loved. Everyone who has imparted wisdom, opinions, some hope, a smile — they're all part of me. It culminates in the person I wake up as every day, and I marvel at the behaviours and views I have picked up from others along the way.

I think of all the webs that link humanity, the connections we make and the effects we have, and I am eternally grateful for every ripple, every wave caused by another person that I have felt in my own life.

But, more than anything, I am grateful for the blood that courses through my veins that has been given freely by people who will never meet me. Without it, I would no longer be here. I cannot think of a greater gift to give someone: sharing a piece of yourself so that they might live.

—Jen Eve Taylor—

28

Secret Santa

Sometimes beautiful things come into our lives out of nowhere. We can't always understand them, but we have to trust in them. I know you want to question everything, but sometimes it pays to just have a little faith.
~Lauren Kate

I was scrambling again. It was Sunday, December 10th, my brother's fortieth birthday party, and I was struggling, as usual. The kids and I were trying to get out the door and on our way to this family celebration, but my mind was spinning a bit. Okay a lot. It was overflowing with worries and concerns about the upcoming holidays, and just how I was going to guide us through them.

Freelance employment sounds very appealing in theory, but the financial reality can frequently be daunting. I'd had very little work in the previous few months. We'd been on our own for about two years, having finally managed to escape a life filled with controlling abuse and violence. I had expected — or at least hoped for — life to be less challenging by now, but in fact, it had become overwhelming. I had been running on pure adrenaline for the last few years, keeping myself incredibly busy with family court, criminal court, lawyers and custody assessors. That was in addition to being busy with work, raising two beautiful children, maintaining a house and focusing on everyone else's struggles. I would find myself counselling friends, nursing sick or injured neighbours, finding employment for my peers and coming to the rescue of just about anyone I came in contact with. For some reason I felt a responsibility to help solve problems and ease the struggles of others. This made me feel good of course, but it also allowed me to avoid focussing on my own problems. Tending to others left me no time to think about myself, and that's the way I liked it.

This was an unusual day because my own challenges were finally consuming me. Work had slowed down and I wasn't even sure how I would pay the mortgage, let alone create a Christmas. As I was preparing to visit my family my thoughts were full of kids' Christmas lists, Santa visits, how I would pay my bills and even just buy groceries this month. Successfully leaving a destructive family situation with my kids intact had made me realize that I am much stronger than I'd ever realized, but on this day I was not feeling strong at all; I was worn down and very worried.

As the kids slipped on their boots and coats I opened the door to go start the car. And that's when I saw it. Stuck between my old wooden door and the storm door was a cardboard FedEx envelope. I hadn't heard anyone come to the door, so I peeked my head outside hoping the driver might still be out front. The street was quiet. I was not expecting anything, and I was trying to recall if FedEx even delivered on Sunday. I turned the envelope over to examine the packing slip. The sender had addressed it to my married last name (and misspelled it) but it was clearly meant for me. I noticed the sender's name listed as "Saint Nick from 'Northern Products.'" The return address was latitude 0.00 longitude 180.00, Baffin Island Post. Obviously this was a gag gift. The contents description read "Christmas making products."

I zipped it open and found two smaller envelopes inside. One, a small manila bubble wrap envelope, and the other a crisp white letter sized envelope that read "Merry Christmas Suzanne." The script was large, flowing and artistically beautiful. I didn't recognize the handwriting, but marvelled at the penmanship. I opened this envelope first and found a typewritten note signed "The Spirit of Christmas."

My Dear Suzanne,

Well, over the last year you have truly captured the market on giving to others, almost to a point that I did not have a job. Well, enough giving, it is now time to receive.

Your kindness and caring of this world around you and your family are exemplary. You need to know it does not go unobserved or unappreciated by those who receive your kindness but also by those who observe your unconditional giving.

In your heart and in your soul there exists such a priceless love for all, even though life's trials and tribulations sometimes can wear one down. The fact that you could stay true to your heart and do the best you could is an example of how special you truly are.

I hope you do not mind me dropping off your gift now, in order to help you do, what comes so natural to you — GIVING.

I know that with this gift, your first thoughts will be what you can do for those you love. Please, do what comes naturally and I hope you will.

However, there is one stipulation that goes with this Christmas gift and it is not negotiable! I know it may be hard for you to do, I know it will go against your natural spirit, but this Christmas, just this Christmas, I also want you to give to the most difficult person for you to give to, YOU!!

Wishing you, family, friends and all dear to you the very best and God's blessings in the year to come.

From The Spirit of Christmas

I was overwhelmed by these words. The writer was correct in knowing I was much more comfortable as a giver, and found receiving very difficult. I quickly opened the bubble wrap envelope and found a fistful of cash — much more than I had seen for some time. I did a quick count. Two thousand dollars. My mortgage payment. The kids had been standing with me through this entire experience. It felt like a long time, when in fact it had been only a few moments. The kids were confused. Santa had been here? My mind was racing. Who was this Spirit of Christmas? My family lived in another city and as we were on our way to see them, I knew it couldn't be from them. I have some beautiful friends, but none were in a financial position to be so generous. I do have a couple of people in my life in a position to do such a thing, but not only is it not in their character, I doubt them capable of writing from the heart the way this writer had done.

After the excitement of that day had passed, I spent many days trying to track down my Secret Santa to no avail. I was baffled. My family was baffled. My friends were baffled. Finally my mother's wise words made me stop searching. She pointed out how the sender had obviously gone to a great deal of trouble to remain anonymous, and it was not my place to take away his/her pleasure in giving by exposing them.

Realizing she was right, I put a public "thank you" status on my Facebook page. No explanation. Just thank you. If my Secret Santa happened to be a Facebook friend I hoped he recognized the message as being for him. I desperately wanted to thank my benefactor, for this person had truly made a difference in my life. Not only was I able to provide Christmas for my children without worrying about the immediate bills being paid, I managed to honour the condition to give to myself by — for the first time in my life — turning down work during the holidays so I could actually enjoy some family time. That was the best Christmas gift ever.

But in addition to those immediate and intended gifts I now carry this incredibly renewed faith in my fellow man. I have literally carried this symbol of faith with me now for six years. Both the handwritten envelope containing the heartfelt letter and FedEx packing slip go with me everywhere. If at any point I'm having an overwhelming day, I have only to look at the envelope or slip my hand in my bag to touch it and I feel better. It makes me smile. It reminds me to have faith. It reminds me to believe in the Spirit of Christmas, and of course to continue to share, with gratitude, my blessings with others.

— Suzanne Lindsay —

Faith in Humanity

> *Christmas is the season for kindling the fire*
> *of hospitality in the hall, the genial flame*
> *of charity in the heart.*
> *~Washington Irving*

On a Saturday afternoon three weeks before Christmas I got a call from my mom. "I made two hundred dollars selling my towels!"

"That's so awesome," I said, delighted that people bought the decorative kitchen towels she'd worked so hard to make.

For months, Mom had sat at a sewing table in the living room of her small, subsidized apartment, cutting, stitching, gathering, and appliqueing decorative towels to sell at the annual holiday craft fair in the lobby of her apartment building.

"They bought every single one," she said. "Now I have money to buy Christmas presents and some new puzzles for the girls on the fifth floor, so we don't have to put together the old ones again."

The heavy snow that had been forecasted for the weekend had already begun to fall that evening when Mom decided to pick up a ham at the grocery store. After brushing the snow off her car in the apartment parking lot and again in the grocery-store lot, Mom arrived safely back home and filled a simmering pot with the ham, potatoes, and rutabaga.

At 9:30 that night, I received a second call from her. She was sobbing.

"I lost my wallet and all the money I earned at the craft fair. My Christmas is ruined."

"It's okay, Mom," I said, completely unaware that she had gone out in the snow.

At eighty-seven years old, Mom often lost things, such as her reading glasses and cell phone. Sometimes, she even lost her teeth. So, at first, I wasn't overly concerned about it.

"I'll drive up in the morning," I said. "I'm sure we'll find it."

"No. It's gone. It was in my jacket pocket when I went to the store. But when I checked my jacket tonight it wasn't there."

She started to cry. "I searched the car and retraced my steps to the front door. And I drove back to the store to see if I left it. But it wasn't there either. I tried to remember where I parked, and I walked through the parking lot looking for it because it must have fallen out of my pocket. But it wasn't anywhere."

My heart broke at the thought of her out in the snowy, windy night.

"It'll be okay, Mom," I assured her. "We'll cancel the credit card, and we can replace all the rest of the things in your wallet." However, the thought of getting her a new license, along with bank, medical, and insurance cards, was daunting, even for me.

It took me several hours to drive to Mom's house the following morning, but I was overdue for a visit. Before I got there, she had already gone back to the store. With tears in her eyes, she shared her story about the money she'd earned from the sale of her towels with the store manager and asked if he could check any other places for her wallet — hoping against hope that someone might have found it and turned it in.

That, of course, did not happen, but what did happen was something that restored Mom's faith in humanity.

The store manager, who didn't even know Mom, kindly took her into his office where he searched through videotapes from the previous night. The tapes only showed Mom making her purchase and leaving the store. Wiping tears from her face, Mom thanked him for trying to help. But as she got up to leave the store, he reached for her elbow.

"Hold on a minute," he said.

Taking his wallet out of his pocket, he pulled out two one-hundred-dollar bills and pressed them into Mom's hand. "I would like you to have a Merry Christmas."

Mom shook her head, barely able to speak as she tried to push the money back. "No… I can't."

With a warm smile, the store manager squeezed Mom's hands around the bills. "It would make my Christmas if you would take this," he said.

Mom left the store in tears, and more tears fell when I met her back at her apartment. We called the police station to see if the wallet had been turned in, but no luck. I spent the night with Mom, and the police department called the following day. They had her wallet. Most of her money and all her cards were still in it.

Mom immediately drove back to the grocery store. With tears of joy this time, she gave back the store manager's money, thanking him wholeheartedly for a Christmas gift that was so much more valuable than money.

Since the manager already considered the money no longer his, he said he would donate it to a local charity that delivered baskets of food and Christmas gifts to families in need. Mom's holiday experience went from heartbreaking to heartwarming. And remarkably, thanks to a stranger's big heart and special gift, another family would have a similar holiday experience.

—Linda L. Koch—

A Mysterious Angel

I believe that prayer is our powerful contact with the greatest force in the universe.
~Loretta Young

It was nearing Christmas in 1987. I was a single mother of a teenager. I was on sick leave from a motor-vehicle accident, and no benefits had come in. There was very little food in the house, and I didn't know which way to turn. I had prayed for divine intervention but so far our situation had not changed.

One morning, I shed a few tears and then said, "Let go and let God." I knew that He could help me in this situation.

A few hours later, I heard a loud rap on the door. I opened it to find an old man with rheumy eyes and huge hands standing there. His beard was scraggly and unkempt. It was frigid out, and I wondered what he could want.

"Can I help you, sir?" I asked.

In a crackly voice, he answered, "Missus, do you happen to have a hot cup of tea and something to eat for a hungry old soul?"

"Well, sir, there isn't much food in the house, but I can offer you some tea and toast with peanut butter or jam."

"That would be most appreciated," he said as the water from his eyes ran down his cheeks.

I was leery about letting this man in the house, so I asked him if he minded waiting on the steps. He assured me he didn't.

I went into the house, prepared a cup of hot tea and four slices of toast with peanut butter, and took them to him. We sat on the porch as he ate and chatted a little about life and how hard it could be.

When he finished, I asked if he would like more, and he assured me he would. While the teakettle was boiling, I looked around for a pair of gloves and a scarf that had been my late husband's. With the items in hand, I took them to him, and he tried on the gloves.

"A perfect fit," he said. Tears rolled down his rosy, cracked cheeks.

We chatted a bit more as he ate, and then he politely thanked me and turned to go. When I went back into the house, I remembered a pair of boots that had been my husband's. I grabbed them out of the closet and ran outside, but there was no sign of the elderly man. I ran to the end of the block and looked up and down... nothing. I ran to the other end of the block... nothing. I jumped in my car and drove around the neighborhood. Again... nothing. Where had he gone?

Christmas Eve was just a couple of days away, and as those hours passed, the situation continued to be desperate. About 6:00 that evening, a rap came at the door. When I opened it, a man stood there with a huge box of groceries. Behind him, I saw a taxi.

"Delivery," he stated.

"From who?" I asked.

"I have no idea," he answered. "It was sent anonymously. I can tell you, I picked this up at the grocery store, and the man was old, scruffy-looking, and had huge hands."

I was stunned. The man he was describing sounded like the old man who had come to my door and whom I had fed.

With a wave and a "Merry Christmas," we parted. I took the box into the house. There was a small turkey and all the fixings for stuffing, as well as a bag of potatoes, vegetables and an apple pie.

We had a wonderful Christmas with lots to eat and gave thanks for the man, whom to this day I refer to as my mysterious angel.

— Mary M. Alward —

Fifteen Dollars

*Kindness can transform someone's
dark moment with a blaze of light.*
~Amy Leigh Mercree

"Wake up, Mama!" I felt a chubby, little hand on my face and reluctantly opened my eyelids. There was my son, ready to start the day. I also heard my baby and toddler awake in the next room. Ready or not, the day had begun!

I loved being home with my little ones, but I felt the weight of the world on my shoulders. My husband and I had just bought a house, and some unexpected expenses made our budget tighter than it had ever been. I was weary of pinching pennies. We weren't foolish with our money. We worked hard. We were doing all the right things. But we had had one financial disappointment after another.

I dragged myself out of bed and pulled on my faded jeans and sneakers that had seen better days. I only had one task on the to-do list for the day. I was going to pick up my kids' photo portraits from the studio at the local mall. Despite our small budget, it was important to me to have pictures of my children as they were growing up. The previous week, I had found a coupon and used some change from the car to buy a $7.99 portrait package, and today was the day I was to pick up the portraits. Since we were going to the mall, I decided to make it an outing and packed some sandwiches for us to eat at the food court.

After breakfast, I bundled everyone into the car, and off we went. After we parked, I unfolded the double stroller, put in the youngest two kids, and gave the oldest his instructions to hold onto the stroller and not let go.

We wheeled into the portrait studio at the mall, and I approached the counter. The young woman smiled. "May I help you?"

"Yes, I'm here to pick up our photos."

The woman asked my name and squeaked open her large filing cabinet drawer. "Schmoyer… Schmoyer… Ah, yes, here they are. Aren't they just so adorable?" She fanned out the photos, and the smiling faces of my kids warmed my heart.

"Yes, they are great. Thank you," I said.

She scooped up the photos to place in an envelope for me. Then she spread out additional photos of my kids that I hadn't ordered. I knew what that meant. The upsell pitch was coming.

"Would you like to purchase these extra portraits? They are only fifteen dollars apiece!" she smiled sweetly.

My face hardened, and my heart turned cold. "I don't have fifteen dollars." I took the photo envelope and wheeled away, with my cheeks red after my curt reply.

Next, we stopped at the ride-on cars in the mall's food court. There weren't any other kids there, which was good because my kids still didn't know that the machines took quarters. They just climbed on them for some free, stationary fun.

After a while, I corralled them to a table and unwrapped our peanut-butter-and-jelly lunches that I had brought from home. It was early for lunch, but we were hungry and the food court was mostly empty.

After we bowed our heads to thank God for our food, I lifted up my eyes and was surprised to find a woman standing next to our table. She stretched out her hand and pressed something into mine. She said, "Here. Take your family out for ice cream after lunch." I was surprised. I managed to mumble "thank you" as she turned and walked away. Then I looked down at what she had given me.

The crumpled bills totaled fifteen dollars.

Tears rolled down my cheeks as I quietly finished my sandwich. The doubts in my heart melted away and my faith was renewed.

— Rachel Schmoyer —

32

Angels' Food

Angels live among us. Sometimes they hide their wings, but there is no disguising the peace and hope they bring.
~Author Unknown

One rainy spring day, Mom became a single mother. My little brother was two, my sister was eight, and I was fourteen. Those first weeks were especially hard before our small monthly support payments began. Mom found work in a potato-chip factory, but didn't get paid right away.

That first Saturday morning as she left for work, Mom said, "I don't know what you'll cook for supper. My boss put a rush on my beginning paycheck so I'll have it Monday, but I'm out of money, and our shelves are as bare as Mrs. Hubbard's cupboards." She laughed, but tears filled her eyes. "I forget. Does that nursery rhyme have a happy ending?"

"No, but we'll do better," I said. "I'll ask Jesus to get us food today." My words sounded bold even to me. She shook her head and went to work.

I had planted a garden out back. The lettuce and peas were up, but nothing was ready to eat. I poked through the kitchen and discovered Mom was right. We had enough cereal for our breakfast but that would be the end of the milk. We had half a package of dry macaroni, one medium-sized can of tomatoes, and a quart of home-canned green beans. That didn't sound appetizing, but I could do something with it.

While my sister and brother played, I prayed and tidied the house. I was washing our front-room window when a cheery man in a blue denim shirt and narrow-brimmed hat wobbled past our house on a bicycle and turned into our driveway. He climbed our porch steps and rang the doorbell. Although I'd never seen him before, his big smile made me trust him.

When I opened the door, he asked, "Have you heard about the new grocery store a mile from here? Today's their grand opening."

I nodded. I'd seen their signs as I rode past on the school bus.

"They're giving away gift coupons to celebrate." He pulled three white cards from his shirt pocket and handed them to me. "The first is for a jumbo-size loaf of bread, the second is for a gallon of milk, and the third lets you choose a half-gallon of your favorite flavor of ice cream."

I stared. "Really? There's no purchase required?"

"None at all. These are free. Go and see."

I thanked him and watched as he got back on his bike and rode down the street without stopping at any other house.

Could it be true? We had to find out. I took my battered blue bicycle and put my sister on the seat behind me and my brother in the basket. We pedaled to the store, where colorful balloons still announced the grand opening. After I parked the bike, we walked inside and showed our cards to the nearest clerk. "It says these are gift cards. Is a purchase necessary?"

She peered down. "No. You have gift certificates. These items are absolutely free."

My sister, brother, and I could hardly believe it. We grabbed a jumbo-size loaf of Wonder Bread and a gallon of pasteurized milk. We went to the ice-cream section and agreed on Cherry Delight. We left the store with blinding smiles. I tucked the groceries in the basket around my brother and raced home before the ice cream could melt.

When Mom returned, we had nice plates, silverware, and food on the table. Our glasses held fresh milk.

"Where did you get this?" Mom asked.

"I prayed," I said. And then I opened our freezer to show her the ice cream.

"Really," she repeated. "Where did all this come from?"

I told her about the man on the bicycle while we ate one of the happiest meals of our lives. Even our vegetable macaroni tasted okay with a little extra seasoning.

She shook her head again, this time with a sense of wonder.

Monday morning at the school bus stop, I asked other kids up and down our street if a man representing the new grocery store had stopped by their houses.

"What man?" they asked.

I told them about the man on the bicycle and the cards he gave me.

"Free food? You're kidding. We would remember if we'd seen him."

But he had brought food for our table — maybe angels' food, including the Cherry Delight ice cream that is still my favorite. That day taught me to expect good things, even in hard times, and to keep my eyes wide open so I won't ever miss seeing the unexpected.

— Delores E. Topliff —

The Day I Met an Angel

*Each day offers us the gift of being a special occasion
if we can simply learn that as well as giving, it is
blessed to receive with grace and a grateful heart.*
~Sarah Ban Breathnach

I was a single mother of three in 1978, living through the recession. I lived close to my mother, so I didn't have to pay for childcare when the kids were out of school. I worked as a waitress for $1.05 an hour plus tips and managed to squeak out enough for the necessities, but as the recession worsened, so did my tips. I couldn't really blame the customers, but it sure made things tough.

Nonetheless, my faith kept me going. I knew that God had a plan, even if he hadn't let me in on it.

One morning in August, I sent the kids outside while I neatened up the house. I was thinking about the upcoming school year. They really needed clothes, especially my two boys, ages five and seven. My younger son, Dave, was wearing his brother's hand-me-downs, but they weren't new when his brother, Thomas, got them, and some of them were unusable now.

Suddenly, Thomas ran in to tell me that someone was outside waiting to talk to me. I wondered who it could be since we didn't get a lot of visitors. A new white Cadillac was parked in the street and a

Random Acts of Kindness | 97

slim, twenty-something woman with blond hair was on our porch. I greeted her, and she asked if I would accept some boxes of clothing. She explained that her son had recently outgrown them, and she was looking for somewhere to donate them when she saw my children playing in the yard. I agreed, figuring that if they were trash, I could just throw them away, but maybe I'd get a few things we could use. She brought in two big boxes of clothes. Before I could thank her or even get her name, she was gone.

We started looking through the boxes. None of the clothes looked worn — no holes, stains or evidence that any child had ever worn them. Everything was the size each boy needed. In the bottom of one box, we found three coats. The largest fit my daughter perfectly. It buttoned either way, so it could be worn by a boy or a girl. When my daughter put her hand in the coat pocket, her face lit up — she pulled out three silver dollars!

I will never know who this woman was or why she had two boxes of clothes that appeared to be brand-new and were perfect for my children. She may have just been a very kind and generous woman, but I will always believe she was an angel sent by God. Whether He sent her from heaven or from across town, I'll never know. Either way, she helped us when we needed it most.

— Jackie Eller —

Chapter 5

Comfort While Grieving

Miracle of the Green Tide

*When you open your mind to the impossible,
sometimes you find the truth.*
~From the television show Fringe

I'm a nurse. I always believed in science, not miracles. That is, until I experienced one of my own.

It happened one August day, walking the shoreline from Red Rock in Swampscott, Massachusetts, to the Tides, a restaurant in nearby Nahant. I had done this nearly every day that summer. But that day, dismal and gray, was different, sadder, for it marked the tenth anniversary of Dad's fatal stroke. With each step, I relived that pain.

Back then, I'd just returned home from errands and casually hit the answering machine. "Your dad has been rushed to Springfield Hospital. We found him on the floor." It was a neighbor of his. "I think he had a stroke."

I grabbed some things for the two-and-a-half-hour drive. Mom was away visiting family in Charleston, South Carolina. My brother lived in Texas, my sister in Myrtle Beach.

Dad, a vibrant seventy-eight-year-old, walked and played golf almost daily. He did all his household chores and was repairing the porch roof. Months earlier, he had cheered as I graduated as a nurse practitioner.

When I saw Dad, I knew it was not good. He had suffered a massive stroke, his entire right side paralyzed. He could not sit, speak, nor swallow. But he was alive and his eyes showed relief—his daughter, his nurse, had arrived.

Luckily, he understood me. "Daddy, you're going to be okay," I repeated, trying to hide the fear in my eyes. I phoned my mother and siblings. That night, and for most of the next fourteen, I stayed by his side.

Dad could not tell me what he wanted or needed, frustrating us both. Then, I gave him a pad and put a pen in his left hand. He scratched out a few words. Dad was still there.

Dad was so ill that he could not make his own health care decisions. The doctor explained that he needed a "health care proxy," to authorize someone to make health care decisions. "Dad, who should this be?" Slowly but clearly, he wrote, "Bonnie (my childhood nickname) is in charge."

Over the next few days, Dad seemed to improve, and that weekend, he rallied. With support, he sat up to enjoy time with his wife, children, and grandchildren. As we were leaving for dinner, he teasingly wrote, "Make sure Dick (my brother) picks up the check!" Dad always had a fondness for greenbacks. Surely he must be getting better, I thought, if he's thinking about money!

Dad still could neither eat nor swallow. A tube in his nose was giving him liquid nutrition, but it was only temporary. Now we had to decide if a permanent tube should be put in his stomach. Would Dad want that? I recalled our talks about his wishes. I carefully weighed the benefits and risks of such a procedure. My mom, brother, and I were uneasy about it. But my sister in Myrtle Beach insisted, "You just can't starve him to death!"

In the end, Dad went to the OR. After many long hours, he was rolled back on a stretcher, a permanent feeding tube in this abdomen. I looked at his face, the pain visible. His eyes spoke, "Why did you let them do this to me?" I was shaken. Had I let Dad down?

The next day, his condition worsened. He was burning with fever and was not responding to my voice. He could not sit, write, or communicate in any way. The antibiotics were ineffective. A brain scan confirmed that he'd suffered another, more severe stroke, with irreversible brain herniation causing all basic life functions to quickly fail. There was nothing more that could be done, the doctor said.

I thought about my grandmother. Dad had found her collapsed from a stroke. She died within weeks. Dad said it was "for the best;" she wouldn't have wanted to live "like that" completely dependent on others. Neither would he, he said.

I recalled our talks about the difficult end-of-life decisions made by my patients and their families. He'd listened, then had nonchalantly said, "When my time comes, you'll know best what to do for me." Nothing was ever written. It was understood then. It was understood now.

Being a devout Catholic, Mom consulted the priest, then calmly said, "We can't let Dad continue to suffer. We have to let him go in peace."

Dad's care now changed from curing to care, comfort, and dignity. The antibiotics and tube feedings, no longer helpful, were stopped. His only medications were for comfort. This decision was too excruciating for my sister in Myrtle Beach, who shrieked, "Who do you think you are, Dr. Kevorkian?"

But Dad was our focus. In his final journey, we chose the path of least suffering. He'd been there for me at my birth and I would be with him in his death.

We all had our final goodbyes. In the end, he left on his terms, in a brief peaceful moment, with Mom, his love, at his side.

Now, ten years later, I walked the shoreline recalling my sister's words and the anguish in Dad's face when he returned from the OR. Had I let Dad down? I softly sobbed.

All that summer, I'd walked the beach finding treasures: starfish, shells, sand dollars, a green bottle, an unopened green can of beer, and green sea glass. I even found a denture with inlaid gold initials, but never any money. So, being my father's daughter, I thought, Dad, if I did the right thing, please send me a sign? Let me find some real money!

Just then, sloshing through the area called the Red Tide (really harmless red algae) I looked down — a green one-dollar bill! "Wow!"

I chuckled. "But gee Dad, couldn't you do better? More like a $100?"

No sooner had I giggled, there it was, another green bill! I reached down; it was a $100 bill! Oh my God! This couldn't be real! Was it a fluke or was it the sign that I'd been seeking?

I shook my head in disbelief. Could a ship have sunk in the harbor? Not feasible. Could someone have lost his wallet in the surf? Not likely. Could someone have been robbed? Nothing about it in the paper.

I need to find one more dollar to prove this was real. I had to prove this was not just some strange coincidence. So I searched, turning over red algae; not another dollar appeared. I drove home stunned. Who finds $100 on the beach?

The next day, I walked the same shoreline, puzzled and uncertain. Then, as I passed through that red algae, there it was — another dollar!

This was no coincidence, I knew then. The red tide had turned to green money, a sign from Dad that I had not let him down. From that moment, I felt at peace.

I still believe in science. I'm still skeptical about many things. I still think of my father and miss him. But now I am a nurse who believes in miracles.

— Barbara A. Poremba —

The Messenger Daughter

Faith is like radar that sees through the fog.
~Corrie ten Boom

"Go home!" the voice in my head commanded. I heard it as clearly as if someone were standing next to me. I didn't recognize the voice, and yet it was authoritative enough to make me rethink my schedule.

Again, the voice demanded, "Go home. Go home!"

I apologized to my friends who had made luncheon arrangements to celebrate my upcoming wedding, explaining that something urgent had happened. I had no clue what to expect as I raced home, but I knew something was wrong.

My dad was home recuperating from the amputation of his right leg, so I was imagining the worst. Despite his faith and his indomitable spirit, his diabetes was slowly taking its toll.

He never complained. He was a proud man, a hard worker, the best father, and someone who always lent a helping hand. He never made much money, but we always seemed to have whatever was necessary to make us happy and comfortable.

I saw my father's face in the front window as I pulled into the driveway. He looked good, but now I felt a little sick. Did I just imagine this voice? Was this some kind of mind game or pre-wedding panic?

After all, I was getting married in two weeks.

As I walked through the front door, my dad looked surprised. "What are you doing home?" he asked. "I thought you were having a special lunch with your friends."

I didn't want to upset him, so I said that I hadn't really felt like going. He accepted my story as part of "wedding day" anxieties. I was relieved to find him well but still confused by the power of the haunting voice I heard earlier.

"Well Dad, let's have lunch," I said as I made my way to the kitchen.

"Sounds like a plan," he responded. "Let's split a sandwich. I'm not too hungry today!"

He rolled his wheelchair to the table as I made our sandwich. As we ate, I noticed how good he looked, with clear eyes and good skin color. He was as handsome as ever. We talked about my wedding and his plan to use his prosthesis to walk me down the aisle.

He wanted to wear a white suit instead of the gray tuxedos the men were renting. "I just see myself in a white suit. Would it bother you if I didn't wear gray?" he asked.

"Dad," I said, "you can wear whatever makes you comfortable." He gave me one of his big smiles.

And then, for some reason, I blurted out, "Dad, do you ever fear dying?"

It was a question totally out of context. Yet, he answered without hesitation: "No, never. I've had many close encounters with death throughout my life, but I've lived long enough to see all four of my children grown and capable of taking care of themselves. I've had an incredible job, not much money, but I've traveled all around this beautiful country and made so many friends. And then, there is your mother, my best friend and lover of forty-one years; she is my lifeline and we are blessed to share an incredible love."

He paused and smiled. "However," he continued, "the most important reason I don't fear death is that I will see my mother again. I was only nine months old when she died. They say she held me in her arms as she took her final breath. I never got to know her, but I know when I take my final breath she will be there holding me again."

That will be some reunion!"

Trying to hold back tears, I thought how blessed I was to have such a treasure of a father. With a hug and a kiss, I quickly cleaned up our dishes and headed back to work. I was thankful that I had that quick lunch with my dad.

That Friday night, my whole family was running crazy. Mom and my younger brother rushed out to pick up a pizza and get a car from the repair shop. Mom and Dad blew each other kisses as she hurried out. My sister and I were home with my father, talking on the phone with my older brother.

My dad pointed to a wedding gift that had arrived for me from a dear friend who loved to play practical jokes. The box was huge, and as my sister and I began unwrapping what seemed to be reams of brown paper, we were interrupted by a snoring, gurgling, awful sound. We looked up and saw Dad slumped in the chair, unconscious. My sister called 911 while I ran frantically up and down the street for help. One of our neighbors, a nurse, attempted CPR without success.

I went in the ambulance with my dad and I noticed, with concern, that we were moving slowly and with no siren. That told me he was already gone. The medics did take him into the hospital though, and it took another forty-five minutes before a doctor came out and told me what I already knew.

There lay that beautiful man, with one hand still open, inviting me to grasp it. It was then I remembered the voice that ordered me to "Go home!" Now I understood why. Miraculously, I had that conversation with him over lunch, when he revealed that he was not afraid of dying and that he believed he would be reunited with his mother. I would be his messenger for the rest of the family. I closed my eyes and saw my father dressed in his white suit, his mom embracing him, and I knew Dad had heard a voice calling him to go home, too.

— Lainie Belcastro —

Dragonflies

*The dragonfly brings dreams to reality
and is the messenger of wisdom and
enlightenment from other realms.*
~Author Unknown

"Send me a dragonfly, honey. You know how I love them." Fifteen minutes later, three dragonflies hovered over the tall golden reeds along the shore of the mountain pond. I smiled, looked up into the beautiful cobalt sky and whispered, "Thank you."

I feel a blend of sorrow and joy when I see dragonflies, especially at the pond by the old pine known as Michael's Tree. It is where my husband played and fished as a child and is across the street from where we lived. His ashes are buried beneath this tree. It is a lovely and peaceful spot. I first saw the dragonflies at the pond six years ago during our private family memorial service.

Michael and I met at a local coffee shop on Valentine's Eve. His long brown hair, sky-blue eyes and sly smile caught my attention from the moment he walked through the door. Obviously, he was attracted to me, too. He bought us a couple of coffees and sat at my table. We talked for three hours. Three weeks later, we were engaged.

We were middle-aged and had been married before. It was out of character for either of us to enter so swiftly into a marriage commitment. Our family and friends didn't know what to think. But we both "knew" that first evening. We got married more than a year later, but we were inseparable from the time we met.

We celebrated our eighteenth wedding anniversary nine days before Michael died. Since he was in the hospital at the time, I planned an impromptu surprise party. I called friends and family, inviting them to come that evening. I arranged with the hospital staff for a private conference room and ran around town picking up balloons, flowers, and a card. A friend kindly bought a cake. Now and then, I'd pop into Michael's room, placating his irritation that I was neglecting him on our special day.

That evening, when the nurse wheeled him through the door of the party room, his face lit up to shouts of "Surprise! Happy anniversary!" The pangs of guilt I'd felt earlier were worth the joy of the occasion. None of us knew it would be the last time most of them would see him alive.

Michael and I loved spending time with one another. We had only been apart a total of six weeks during our nineteen and a half years together. Most of those times were when we'd go visit family. We didn't like being apart, and we finally promised never to leave one another for more than a day or two again. I even stayed with him every night in the hospital, sleeping on a rickety chair or hard cots during the nine months he battled pancreatic cancer.

On the morning of his final day, he assured me that even though he was going Home, he would still be with me and take care of me. He has given me many proofs of that promise. One of those signs is dragonflies. I've always known of Heaven and felt that our spirits go there when we die, but I never really believed the stories I read or heard, even from my grandmother, of visions or signs from departed loved ones. The day of Michael's memorial changed my belief.

One of Michael's favorite hymns was "I Walk in the Garden." His grandmother sang it to him as a child. It held special memories for him. I located the song on a CD and played it after the opening prayer. Within seconds of the song's beginning, more than two dozen iridescent blue dragonflies flew to the shore and hovered over the pond in front of us. Blue was Michael's favorite color, and these ranged in beautiful shades from sky-blue to indigo. Then, as soon as the song ended, they all flew away. We each knew we had received a message from Michael that he was still with us in spirit and would remain in our hearts and memories.

I've heard it said that dragonflies are messengers from Heaven. I don't know if that's true, but I have seen a dragonfly glide beside me as I walk a beach, fly in front of my windshield when a favorite song of his brings tears to my eyes, and hover near me when I'm sitting along a river thinking of him. Many times over the years, blue ones have flown back and forth along the pond while I am at Michael's Tree. During those times, I sense his joy and feel comforted. I smile and say, "Thank you, honey."

—Carmen Myrtis-Garcia—

Listening to The Boss

*I think miracles exist in part as gifts and in part
as clues that there is something beyond
the flat world we see.*
~Peggy Noonan

My wife Betsy was always a Springsteen fan. When we were first going out in 1983, she stopped by my house unexpectedly one night to drop off a book, and my mom told her to go upstairs to my room. I had Springsteen's *Born to Run* album on the stereo, and the song "Thunder Road" was playing when she came through my door and scared me half to death. She smiled brightly, tossed the book on my desk, and sang the last line loudly. She said she didn't know I liked Springsteen, and it was the best of many signs from the Universe that we were "meant to be" and would be together always.

We saw Springsteen (aka The Boss) in concert four times, her favorite being the first in July 1984. A guy standing next to us yelled at the stage, "Bruce! You're the only Boss I listen to!" She'd often reference this line when we disagreed, and she'd remind me how she was the only boss I should listen to.

Betsy and I were married for thirty-one years when she died of liver cancer on August 4, 2018. We'd had many adventures together over the years — exotic journeys like traveling through Egypt, and many far more modest like getting rid of a large hornets' nest or hiking with the dogs through the woods—and I felt lost without her.

I woke up the morning after she died feeling as though I'd died myself. Our twenty-three-year-old daughter, Emily, had come home, but the house still felt enormously empty. That day dragged on slowly as I cleaned the house and tried to start planning the funeral service. Emily was a huge help and family members came by, but I still felt completely alone. I could not see how I would ever feel any differently.

Betsy always made me feel better when life knocked me down, and I celebrated every victory with her. We literally finished each other's sentences, and at least once a week one of us would say something when the other would respond, "I was just about to say that exact same thing." How was I supposed to go on living without her?

That evening, Emily's friends Krista and Heather came over. They were in the living room when I went into the kitchen to wash the dishes. As usual, I put on some music while I was cleaning up, and that night it was this "Music Through the Years" CD, a compilation of songs that Betsy had made for us years ago. This was an anthology of tunes we had loved from 1980 onwards on multiple CDs, and I put on one she always especially liked from June 1990. As I was listening to the songs, Monty the dog had to go out, so I hit Pause and went outside with him.

When I came back and hit Play, I should have heard the next song on that CD, which would have been Leslie Phillips's tune, "Answers Don't Come Easy." Instead, I heard Bruce Springsteen's "Backstreets." I was confused and reached out to hit the Forward button, thinking that the CD had gotten stuck, when I realized that this version of "Backstreets" wasn't on this CD, and it wasn't the song that had just played before Monty showed up. I stood still, just listening, and felt a tingle at the back of my neck and goosebumps running up my arms. When "Backstreets" ended, it was followed by "Born to Run." I stood in the middle of the kitchen just staring at the stereo on the far wall.

As the song played, I half-stumbled into the living room and said to Emily, Krista, and Heather, "You've got to hear what's happening in the kitchen."

Emily said, "That's okay. Springsteen's not our thing."

I said, "No, you don't understand. I'm not playing these songs. She is." I quickly related what was happening, and they were suitably freaked out.

I went back into the kitchen, and "Born to Run" was followed by "Jungleland" and then "Thunder Road." Two of those songs are not on that CD at all. In fact, "Jungleland" isn't on any of the "Music Through the Years" CDs.

The four songs that played that night were Betsy's four favorite songs on the *Born to Run* album. Betsy used to sing "Thunder Road" to Emily when she was an infant and asked me to play the *Born to Run* CD in just that order so she could finish listening by singing "Thunder Road" to Emily, acting out the song in dance and pantomime.

When "Thunder Road" ended that night, the machine stopped playing anything. As I said, this is a multi-album-length CD with many songs on it, and something should have come on after that song ended. The machine was working perfectly. I put in another CD to test it. Then I put the "Music Through the Years" June 26, 1990 CD back in, and it played the songs it always had.

I can't explain how those Springsteen songs played that night out of nowhere, but I know how they made me feel: I wasn't alone anymore. I knew I wouldn't be waking up the next morning to make her breakfast and we wouldn't hold hands as we walked the dogs or finish each other's sentences as we watched TV anymore. But I felt her presence in the room that night, and I knew that, even if I couldn't see her the next morning, she hadn't left me. She'd told me, that long-ago night when she burst into my room, that we were meant to be together always. And, the night after she died, she came back to let me know that not even death could change that.

—Joshua J. Mark—

The Gift at the Grave

*No matter where I am your spirit will be
beside me. For I know that no matter what,
you will always be with me.
~Tram-Tiara T. Von Reichenbach*

The first challenge of this emotional day was to find the gravestone with my father's name. The field was massive and peppered with nearly identical markers — rectangular, dark gray stones that lay flat on the ground.

I was twelve years old, and this was the first time I had visited his grave since his funeral the year before.

I didn't see my father as much as I would have liked since my parents divorced shortly after I was born. Despite that, my father knew about my deep interest in frogs. I can't remember a time that I didn't love frogs. My father always gave me little gifts that were frog related: a seashell with a frog painted on it; a frog figurine; a necklace with a frog charm.

After trekking through the maze of gravestones on a sunny day, there it was — the stone marking my father's final resting place. I gasped — not because I was seeing my father's name etched on a gravestone for the first time, but because a tiny green frog was sitting on the stone, right by my father's name.

I was astonished and happy and sad at the same time, and I started to cry. I crouched down to get a closer look at the frog, half expecting him to hop away, but he didn't flinch. The frog was calm and unbothered by my presence, as if he were expecting my arrival.

I scooped up the little creature and held him in the palm of my hand. We looked at each other as if we were having a silent conversation that only he and I could understand. When I finished crying, I set him down gently. It felt like the right time to say goodbye.

The frog hopped away, disappearing into the blades of grass, knowing his job was done. My father had given me his final gift… and I was at peace.

I whispered, "Thanks, Dad."

—Amanda Mattox—

A Message Delivered at the Museum

The love of a mother is the veil of a softer light between the heart and the heavenly Father.
~Samuel Taylor Coleridge

"Come see this oil painting," I called out to my sister. "It so reminds me of the beach landscape, you know the one with the beautiful lighthouse Mom painted years ago."

My sister was busy studying a sculpture across the room. She turned her head, and as she approached the painting, her eyes grew wide. "My goodness, it certainly does," she exclaimed.

It was early on a Saturday morning, and the two of us were wandering through a museum waiting for an art-appreciation workshop to begin. Weeks prior, my sister had seen an advertisement in the local paper for the workshop. We decided to register and attend together in loving memory of our mother, a talented artist who in her lifetime did more than dabble with paintbrush and palette. Her works of art were true masterpieces and prominently displayed on the walls of homes far and wide.

I struggled tremendously with the loss of our mother. My heart ached to hear her voice once more, to feel her caress, always gentle and reassuring. I found it challenging to remain focused on simple tasks. Recurring thoughts about heaven and the existence of an afterlife weighed on me. I wondered where my mother was and if she was okay. Daily, I prayed for a sign.

My sister and I meandered a bit more through the museum's exhibits and stumbled upon a fascinating artifact collection. Then we heard an announcement that all registered participants should report to Room 125. The workshop would begin in ten minutes.

Upon entering the room, we were greeted by a man who introduced himself as the workshop instructor. He invited us to take seats anywhere we chose. The seats were arranged in a horseshoe shape. My sister and I selected two seats next to each other, placed our purses on the chair backs, and comfortably settled in.

As other participants entered the room, I was curious as to their personal motivation to attend the workshop. Some arrived with notebooks tucked under their arms. Others held laptops, and a few carried tote bags with easels and sketch pads protruding. The instructor loudly cleared his throat, welcomed the class, shared his credentials and stated that he would begin the workshop with a lecture, and then take questions, followed by a twenty-minute break.

The instructor was undoubtedly passionate and knowledgeable about art history. He was interesting and engaging. However, I found myself suddenly no longer captivated by his PowerPoint presentation. Instead, I became completely mesmerized by an older woman who sat directly across from my sister and me. Her petite frame, delicate features, and flattering pageboy hairstyle with wisps of white bangs that softly framed her face immediately reminded me of my mother. I was completely astonished by the striking resemblance.

Our eyes eventually met. I initially felt more than a tinge of embarrassment at my staring, but I quickly found comfort in her response: a smile, a nod and a gentle wave. I nudged my sister and whispered, "Does the older woman in the pink cardigan…?" Before I could finish the sentence, my sister responded, "She most certainly does."

I continued to hear the instructor's voice, but to me his words were a string of garbled sentences as I was completely inattentive. I had drifted far from Room 125, overcome by waves of emotion, flooded with memories of my mother.

Comfort While Grieving

At one point, I heard the instructor ask if there were any questions. I quickly regained focus. Hands were raised. I looked at the older woman and desperately hoped she would raise her hand, ask a question, and share something about herself. I wanted to hear her voice. I wondered if it would sound just like my mother's or possess the same soothing and sweet cadence.

She never did raise her hand. The instructor answered the last question and announced it was time for the break. He encouraged the class to look around at some of the exhibits, visit the coffee shop or stroll the museum gardens.

My sister and I, both outdoor enthusiasts, decided to explore the well-manicured museum grounds. We discovered a bench directly under a dogwood tree in full bloom. Its pastel pink petals were breathtaking. I turned to my sister and was about to say, "Mom loved dogwoods, especially the pink ones."

Before I uttered my thought aloud, I heard a voice say, "Hello, girls." I turned my head, and my heart raced. It was the older woman in the pink cardigan! I was speechless.

My sister responded, "Good morning. Are you enjoying the workshop?"

A smile graced the older woman's face. "Oh, I most certainly am. It is wonderful." Her voice was as melodic as my mother's. She continued, "By the way, girls, my name is Eileen Patricia. What do you girls think of the class?"

My heart raced even faster. I could feel beads of sweat on my forehead. My sister, much more composed than me, eloquently expressed our complete shock. She said, "My goodness, my name is Eileen." She turned and looked at me and said to the older woman, "This is my sister, Patricia."

The older woman smiled, nodded and did not seem surprised by our shared names. It was as if she knew. But how? No nametags, no formal introductions. Since childhood, my sister and I had always called one another "Sis," so it was unlikely she had overheard our names. My sister proceeded to ask her why she had signed up for the workshop. Her eyes, just as blue as my mother's, sparkled.

Comfort While Grieving

"Well, girls, I used to paint landscapes, portraits, and still life, but I became ill, seriously debilitated. I was in horrific pain, but you see, girls, I no longer am. I am painting again and happily pursuing all my passions. I am free; the world is now mine to roam."

The older woman then looked down at an old Timex watch, tapped on it and said, "Oh, look at the time. The workshop will resume shortly." My sister asked if she would like to walk back with us. She responded, "No, thank you. I'd like to sit here a bit longer under my favorite tree. Isn't it lovely? No worries, girls, I am not far."

As my sister and I walked back to the museum, a steady stream of tears rolled down my cheeks. I managed to say aloud, "My prayers have been answered, Sis."

We returned to Room 125. The instructor began to lecture, and once more I was distracted, anxiously waiting for the knob to turn and Eileen Patricia to enter. She never did return. But her message was indelibly painted on my heart.

— Patricia Ann Rossi —

She Found Me

*The wings of angels are often found on
the backs of the least likely people.*
~Eric Honeycutt

I didn't open an independent bookstore in a small Mississippi town for the money. I opened the store to save my sanity five months after my son Perry was killed in an automobile accident. An avid reader my entire life, I always found comfort in books.

One rainy Monday, however, I found peace in that bookstore — not from the books — but from a source far beyond my wildest imagination. I spotted an elderly woman standing in the rain right outside the water department office across the street from my store. I assumed she had gone in to pay her bill and was waiting for someone to circle the block and pick her up.

But I was perplexed as to why she didn't take a couple of steps back and wait under the awning of the building rather than stand there in the rain. After several minutes the rain was literally dripping off the end of her nose and I couldn't stand it any longer. I feared she was senile or suffered some form of dementia and had wandered away from home. I grabbed my umbrella and hurried across the street.

As I approached her she gave me the sweetest smile. "Ma'am, are you waiting for someone?" I asked.

"No," she said simply. That was even more disturbing. She was just standing there in the rain on a city sidewalk?

"Would you like to come with me to my shop and maybe I could call someone to come pick you up?" She agreed without hesitation and, sharing my umbrella, we darted back across the street.

As soon as we entered the shop she said, "Oh! This is nice. There's a book I've been looking for." She seemed unconcerned that she was practically drenched, and though she seemed perfectly lucid I doubted very much that she had been looking for a particular book or, if she had, that I would happen to have it on my shelf.

She went straight to the religion section. The gray in her hair had fooled me but now I realized she wasn't nearly as old as I had thought. To my surprise she quickly made her selection and came to the counter to purchase the book. I remember it was a very thin volume on prayer.

I had meant to ask her if she needed me to call someone for her but I suddenly felt foolish. She was trim, her posture erect, her speech clear and precise, and her gaze seemed to see into my very soul. This woman didn't need anything from me.

As if we were discussing the weather she began to tell me about her daughter who had died. I struggled to offer my sincere sympathy but all I could think was *Please — not now. Not today.* This was one of those days I was weary of the pain and just wanted to wall myself away from it. I didn't want to share my own story and relive the trauma.

Her daughter had died of a brain tumor. She told me in great detail about the final twenty-four hours of her life. Perry's cause of death from the accident was a severe head injury. They had kept him on life support for about twenty-four hours. The account of her daughter's last twenty-four hours was almost identical to what I had experienced with Perry. How could this be!? I began to tremble with emotion yet she continued with her story relentlessly, her words slowly loosening the iron grip I had on my emotions. At this point I just wanted her to leave. I did not feel like reliving this right now and, quite honestly, I felt angry with her. Suddenly I burst into tears.

There was not one flicker of surprise on the woman's face. As she reached and took both my hands in her own, her exact words were, "Ah. So I have found you." To this day I cannot think of her saying those words without goose bumps rising on my arms. A warm rush of energy seemed to course through my body.

Without hesitation I surrendered to the wonder of her otherworldly presence. I laid my head down on the counter between us and sobbed as she gently stroked my hair. I remember being acutely aware of every drop of rain that fell outside my window and I was sure that heaven was weeping for me. It was no time for questions; all I could do was bask in the amazing feeling of love and peace that enveloped me. When I finally composed myself she asked if she could pray with me. Her prayer was brief and profound. After she left I could not remember a single word of that prayer but I will never forget its power. I only remember that her words were simple and seemed a little strange compared to all the prayers I had ever heard. It was not a prayer for comfort for my loss but a prayer for guidance in my spiritual journey.

She left, walking right back out into the rain as if it did not matter at all. I don't know how long I sat there. The shattering pain I had felt for months was lifted as I seemed to float in a space where I felt nothing but a powerful healing peace. Slowly I became aware of my surroundings and considered my encounter with this amazing woman. It was only then I realized I had never spoken a word to her from the moment I began to cry—never even told her why I was crying. She never asked because she didn't need to ask. "Ah," she had said. "So I have found you."

—Carolyn C. O'Brien—

A Golden Gift

Isaiah answered, "This is the Lord's sign to you that the Lord will do what he has promised."
~2 Kings 20:9

While my husband Doug and I were vacationing at a timeshare resort in Alabama one summer, the chlorine in the pool sent us shopping for protective swim goggles. Fortunately, there was a small sporting goods store at a little strip mall ten miles away. Luckily, they had two pair, one for each of us. As we were leaving the store, I felt compelled to go into a little jewelry store at the other end of the mall.

It was highly unlikely for me to be drawn to that type of store because I hadn't shopped in a real jewelry store since the long ago day we had purchased our wedding rings. Doug urged me to follow my whimsical impulse. It was totally out of character for him to want to shop, or to want me to shop. But, since we were on vacation, had no time constraints, and were on an adventure, we lightheartedly headed for the jewelry store.

Upon entering the quaint little shop, I was immediately attracted to a rotating display case that held gold earrings. I certainly didn't need another pair of earrings. I couldn't believe how I instantly spotted an adorable pair shaped like dolphins swimming in a circle. I smiled fondly remembering how our son Jay was always fascinated with dolphins, from the time he was a little boy to manhood. Sadness welled up in me as I contemplated the approaching anniversary of our beloved

Jay's death.

"Why would a store hundreds of miles from an ocean carry a pair of dolphin earrings?" I wondered out loud to Doug. Seemed like serendipity to me, so I rationalized why I wanted the dolphin earrings; they would be a fond reminder of Jay, or possibly a birthday present to myself. Maybe the earrings could be considered a reward for all the hard work I had been doing in physical therapy to recover from my recent serious back surgery. If those weren't good enough reasons, I would simply purchase them as a vacation souvenir.

When the clerk showed us the pricey sales ticket, I quickly returned the unreasonably expensive gold dolphin earrings to the showcase and put the thought of purchasing them out of my mind. Doug was relieved.

Our mood returned to "we're on vacation" and we realized we were wasting daylight and swimming time. We headed back to the pool to put our new goggles to good use.

A vigorous workout provided us with a peaceful rest that night. I was slowly awakening at dusk, in a blissful state of semi-consciousness, startled by a voice. It was a familiar voice that sounded like Jay. I strained my eyes, but couldn't see where the voice was coming from.

"How ya' doing, Mom?" The unmistakable greeting shocked me; that was the way Jay always greeted me when he came home for a visit. "I want you to know I'm really happy here," the voice continued. "I want you to buy the dolphin earrings for your birthday."

Jay's voice persisted. "Use the money in my wallet in my briefcase behind the boxes in the workroom closet. Then, when you wear the dolphin earrings, you will be happy like I am."

The voice was gone as suddenly as it had come. I felt disconcerted, confused, yet warmed by what had just transpired.

I was reluctant to tell Doug about this extraordinary encounter because I wasn't quite sure myself what had happened. It was so precious, yet too unbelievable to share.

I reasoned that he would attribute it to my understandable stress at this time of year. I made the firm decision not to tell him, and felt relieved.

And then, before I knew it, the tale of the unusual experience

Comfort While Grieving | 123

poured forth uncontrollably. Taken aback by the outpouring and obviously skeptical of my story, Doug carefully assessed the situation with his trained legal mind and asked me very specific probing questions.

Satisfied that something miraculous had occurred, he calmly and assuredly said, "God often does amazing things in the lives of faithful followers to show them His love."

My levelheaded hubby reflected that the mysterious event might have been the delivery of a special love note from God and Jay.

Unbeknownst to me, Doug said he'd hidden Jay's briefcase in the back of the closet soon after his death eight years ago, without looking inside it. Doug reminded me that at the time of Jay's death, I was too inconsolable to deal with his belongings, so he put Jay's property out of sight. The briefcase had long since been forgotten.

Then, my usually frugal hubby suggested an extravagant plan. He wanted us to go back to the jewelry store and purchase the dolphin earrings with the understanding that if there were any money in Jay's wallet, it would help offset the cost of the purchase. I felt loved and warmed by Doug's thoughtful gesture.

That afternoon, the day before the anniversary of Jay's death, we returned to the little strip mall jewelry store and made our golden purchase. Surprisingly, the next day, as I wore the beautiful earrings, I realized that for the first time in eight years I actually felt warmed, peaceful and happy on the anniversary date of Jay's drowning.

When we returned to San Diego after our restful vacation, Doug and I headed straight for the workroom closet. There, behind some dusty old boxes, was the briefcase. We cautiously opened it together. Jay's battered brown leather wallet was in there, inviting our visit. We opened the cash compartment and removed the money.

I held my breath as Doug counted out the bills.

The total of the cash equaled the exact purchase price of the shiny gold dolphin earrings! Instant tears of gratitude stung my eyes for my miraculous posthumous birthday gift from my son.

— BJ Jensen —

Chapter 6

Amazing Coincidences

The Boomerang Bible

Coincidences are spiritual puns.
~G.K. Chesterton

One of my favorite pastimes is shopping at yard sales and flea markets. I never know what kind of treasures I'm going to find, whether it's toys for my grandkids or a blouse with the price tag still attached. But one memorable summer day, I came home with something better than a bargain — I came home with a miracle.

I was at a popular flea market in my Wisconsin hometown where I was looking for some good deals on books. When I came upon a stall filled with shelves and shelves of books I was in heaven. There were so many — big books, little books, old books, new books — but something guided me to a specific one: a compact book, with a protective cover made from a brown paper grocery bag. I smiled, thinking back to all the schoolbooks I had covered with brown paper bags as a child. It was a fall tradition, sitting at the kitchen table with scissors and tape and the bags my mother had collected all summer.

Both the spine and the front of this book had a cross drawn in red marker. I slipped the brown paper off and admired the black leather cover with "Bible" stamped in gold. It was just like the Bible I had as a parochial school student. Intrigued, I started flipping through the pages. I came to the very first page of the book — a blank page that came before the title page. There, in the shaky cursive writing of a young elementary student, was my maiden name: Judy Torgerson. It

Amazing Coincidences

took a few seconds to sink in. This didn't just *look* like my Bible; this *was* my Bible!

My amazement quickly gave way to being mystified. Where had my book been for the last thirty or so years? What road had it traveled from parochial school to flea market?

Unfortunately, the bookseller did not have any information for me. I have warm memories of sitting at my school desk, following along as my teacher read us Bible stories. I hope that somewhere in those intervening years, the Bible helped another child's faith grow the way mine had.

My husband was initially speechless at my find. At most flea markets, he sees me coming with my arms full of finds, ready to check out, and tries to talk me out of buying most of them. But that Bible was one purchase we both agreed on. It was the best deal of my whole life. For just a dime, my Bible was returned to me.

We've dubbed it the "Boomerang Bible." I'm not letting that book out of my sight ever again! It has become a treasured family heirloom and a part of new family traditions. A few years after being reunited with my Bible, my daughter Cassandra was married, and instead of carrying a bouquet of flowers, she carried our special Bible.

—Judy Fleming—

At Last Sight

*Deeply, I know this, that love triumphs over death.
My father continues to be loved, and
therefore he remains by my side.*
~Jennifer Williamson

When my father died, it was a relief. He had struggled with lung cancer and it had been so hard to see him unable to breathe. I didn't cry when he died, because I knew that living longer would have only prolonged his suffering.

So I remained dry-eyed even though I no longer had someone to rescue me when I walked into the pool convinced I could walk on water. I no longer had someone who said he loved me even though he had to listen to the horror of me playing the flute. I no longer had the clever man who only pretended to hold up my bike as I rode it on my own without realizing it.

I didn't cry when I picked out that God-awful black hat and marched up to the altar to share my recollections of the man he was. I didn't cry when I bent over his casket to say goodbye. I didn't cry when my mother refused to allow my precious stuffed monkey to be buried with him.

There were no tears when I had to get a job because my father had been the breadwinner, and there wasn't much bread to be won after death.

No, I saved all of my tears for my second year in college. By that time, my friends had forgotten about my pain. They remembered vaguely that I was without a father. And I did my best to ignore that fact, too, preferring to imagine him at home 500 miles away with my mother and brother.

He couldn't call me, I lied to myself. He was too busy. There were lots of babies born in August and September. He was home. I was at school.

I didn't cry until my sophomore year when I saw him for the first time since his death.

Medical Ethics 101 was one of those classes that sound amazing in a departmental write-up, the kind of class one envisions will entail lively discussion on the pressing issues of the day.

It was anything but.

The conversations were stilted. No one wanted to share. The discussions were as uneventful as a middle-school dance with boys on one side and girls on the other. But there were no gender lines in Medical Ethics, just those who wanted to debate and those who didn't. And the professor sat firmly on the latter side.

It was just an average Friday of biding my time in a class I was hoping would produce an easy A to balance out my C in Econ. My curly-haired, ex-hippy professor slogged through yet another uninspiring topic, sidestepping the potential for lively debate by showing a video of a medical conference. My mind was on spring break and how, while all my friends were off to warm locales, I would be venturing home to a house now occupied by (only) two other people — hardly somewhere I wanted to be.

I was starting to doze off. The last thing I wanted to do was watch a video in which middle-aged medical professionals talked about end of life. But then, three rows behind one of the panelists from Jefferson Medical College, I saw my dad. He wasn't taking notes like everyone else. Instead, he was staring directly into the camera.

The video switched angles and another panelist was shown, but I continued to watch intently. For the next hour, I saw my father twenty-seven times. Most of those times, he looked directly into the camera like he had looked at me hundreds of times over breakfast right before flashing me a smile.

That class gave me something nobody else could—one more hour with my dad.

Years later, I would tell this story to my twin sons, who would ask if I ever told the instructor and whether she had given me a copy of the video. I shook my head with tears in my eyes.

They may not understand, but to bring my professor into it and to ask for the video might have shown me something I didn't want to see. Maybe it wasn't my father. Maybe it was just some other middle-aged guy with white hair in a suit. To ask might've pointed to a reality I didn't want to accept.

So I saw it for what I wanted it to be. I chose to believe.

For one final hour, I was in the same room as my dad again.

—Christina Metcalf—

Face-to-Face with a Miracle

Life is funny... We never know what's in store for us, and time brings on what is meant to be.
~April Mae Monterrosa

It had rained all summer. The fields were soaked, the basement was damp, my flowers were beat up, and I was weary. Fortunately, my husband of thirty years and I were leaving on a flight for the sunny beaches of Los Angeles.

Being farm people who didn't fly too often, we had arrived two hours early for our flight. As we waited, my attention was drawn to a woman sitting in a yoga pose. She was beautiful — with a fresh manicure, sparkling diamond ring, fashionable platform sandals, and a red carry-on bag. Her facial features seemed familiar to me — the lips, the structure of her nose, the color of her toned skin. I started to shake slowly from the inside out, wondering silently if she was the birth mother of our twenty-six-year-old daughter. The adoption had been private; we had been blessed to be the ones chosen.

She closed her laptop, packed up her belongings, and headed to the ladies' room. I knew it was her, as only a mother knows. I turned to my husband and said, "I'd swear that is our birth mother." He went to talk to her, and confirmed that she was indeed our daughter's birth mother!

Then our flight started boarding. My legs were shaking as I went through the motions of moving forward because I really wanted to stay with the woman. We were about to board the same plane and would likely be separated by rows and rows of seats. And we had a lot to talk about.

We boarded and discovered that we were, indeed, seated quite far apart. I wondered if I should try to find an empty seat next to her. Or perhaps she would come back and seek us out? On the other hand, maybe she didn't want to talk to us at all!

I was so eager to be near her and thank her, to fill her in on the last twenty-six years. But I did nothing. I tried to reassure myself. If it was meant to be, she'd reach out to us when we landed at LAX.

Soon, the announcement came for landing. We were trapped in the back of the plane, stuck behind all the people slowly disembarking ahead of us. It was so frustrating. What if we lost our chance?

But when we emerged from the jet bridge, there she stood, waiting for us. Emotions flooded all of us, and she rested her shaking hand over her mouth. I remember asking if I could have a picture with her and promising not to share it on Facebook. As we clung to each other, fighting back tears, a sense of love clouded my thoughts and vision. I don't remember many of the details of the conversation that followed. I do remember saying "thank you" repeatedly.

She insisted on giving us a ride to our hotel. Before I knew it, a car was edging through the traffic and making its way to the curb. Oblivious to what was happening, a young gentleman jumped out to open the trunk. She introduced him as her fiancé, David. Then she proceeded to tell him that she'd offered to take us to our bed and breakfast. He was agreeable, but looked a bit perplexed. I'm sure he must have been thinking, *Where did she meet these two?* We merged through rush hour and set off for the unknown again.

At this point, she said to him nonchalantly, "Do you remember the baby I told you I gave up for adoption?" He nodded, and she said, "These are the parents who adopted my baby!" With that, he darn near drove off the road as he glanced to the back seat where Jim and I sat cozily. He started asking questions.

"Where did you find them?"

Amazing Coincidences

"How did you know it was them?"

And again, we all concluded, it was meant to be!

I don't remember the route to our destination. In fact, I had to pinch myself to make sure I wasn't dreaming.

It was time to say goodbye, but we'd had an encounter that I will cherish the rest of my days, as I stood with this brave woman who had changed the course of my life. I had come face-to-face with my miracle, and now it was time to move on. We hugged. We cried. We thanked each other. We shared a most perfect love story in the form of our daughter.

—Denise Wasko—

The Night Santa Claus Cried

Every day holds the possibility of a miracle.
~Author Unknown

Four-year-old David was giddy with excitement as we drew near to the front of the line to see Santa Claus. He stood on his toes to see over the shoulder of the taller boy in front of him. "We're next, Mama," he said, grabbing my hand and pulling me forward.

Santa gently patted the back of the little boy who scrambled off his lap and turned to us. He held his hand out to David, barely giving me a glance. "Come, sonny. Tell Santa what you want for Christmas." He smiled indulgently as David rattled off an impossibly long list of toys he'd seen advertised on TV. "You know, son, I have many boys and girls to bring gifts to. I may not be able to bring you everything you want, but I think I can bring the things you'd like most."

David looked puzzled. "How will you know which things I want most?"

Santa gave a low chuckle. "Santa knows." For the first time, he really looked at me. The twinkle left his green eyes, and he swallowed. He turned to Mrs. Claus, who was passing out candy canes to the kids as they left. "I think I need a quick break."

Something in his face made her react quickly. "Boys and girls, Santa will be back in a few minutes. He just needs a little break."

Santa gently slid David off his lap and stood to follow Mrs. Claus. Although he tried to turn his head away from the kids, I was standing right in front of him, and I saw the tears in his eyes as he hurried away. I saw him grab Mrs. Claus by the arm and say something to her just as I was turning to leave. She looked back at me and motioned me to come forward. For a moment, I was too stunned to move, wondering what was happening and how it could involve me. She gestured again, this time almost frantically.

I grabbed David's hand and followed them into a small storage area in the rear of the store. Without saying a word, Mrs. Claus abruptly left the room. Santa stood staring at me, his green eyes glistening with tears that he somehow managed to keep from falling. I knew that if David had not been there, this man would have been sobbing. But why? And what did he want from me?

"Beth?" he whispered hoarsely. "You are Beth. I know you are." He swallowed. "I've looked for you for years, honey." He saw the confusion on my face, and he took the cap off his head and tore the fake glasses from his nose. "My hair and beard used to be red, but they turned snow-white quite some time ago. I'm your daddy, honey."

I reeled back on my heels. Daddy was an alcoholic, and Mama left him when I was seven years old. I saw him once in a while for the next few years, whenever he managed to stay sober long enough to come for a visit. Then Mama was transferred to another state with her job, and I never saw him again. He was always good to me, even when he was drinking, so I missed him terribly. But Mama was bitter toward him, and she never let him know that we were moving.

As I stared at the man in front of me, I began to see remnants of the father I once knew and loved. I especially remembered his green eyes that always seemed to shine when he looked at me. My own eyes were filling with tears, but I couldn't speak past the huge lump in my throat. I had resigned myself to the fact that David would never know his grandfather, yet here he was standing in front of us in a Santa Claus suit, of all things. But I had some of my mother in me, too, because I instantly doubted if I wanted my son to grow close to an alcoholic grandfather or not.

Amazing Coincidences

As if he could read my thoughts, he said in a rush of words, "I've been sober for ten years, honey. I started playing Santa Claus when I worked for the mall during the Christmas season one year to make extra money. The man who usually had the role got sick, and they couldn't find a replacement. My manager looked over at me and said, 'Joe, you'd make a good Santa with all that white hair and beard. How well can you do a ho, ho, ho?' I found that I actually liked it, and I've been doing it ever since."

He swiped at his eyes to knock back a stray tear. "Honey, I've searched for you everywhere. But I never dreamed I'd look up and see you in one of my lines." He looked down at David, who was utterly perplexed and not understanding anything that was being said. A huge smile spread across his face, and dimples that looked exactly like David's creased his cheeks. "I'm a grandfather," he whispered, reaching out for me.

I stepped into his arms, and as we embraced, I could smell the familiar scents that I had forgotten until that moment. The clean, familiar smell of his soap and after shave filled my senses as I clung to him.

David, eyes big with surprise as Mama and Santa embraced, stepped forward and put one arm around Santa's waist and one arm around my waist. Santa and I both laughed. David didn't yet know it, but he was meeting his grandfather. Ten minutes ago, I thought that my son would never know this man. But as I watched him place a big hand lovingly on David's head, his eyes sweeping over the boy as if he couldn't get enough of him, I instinctively knew that this man was in our life to stay.

I invited Dad over for dinner. David was overjoyed that Santa would be having dinner with us. I had a lot of explaining to do, but as I watched the small boy and the man in the Santa suit grin at one another, I knew that everything was going to be just fine. I could already see the beginning of a bond between them. Dad's green eyes shone when he looked at David, just as they always did when he looked at me when I was a girl.

When we got home, my husband, Glen, was making spaghetti for dinner. "Did you two have a good time?" he asked.

David ran to him and jumped into his arms. "Daddy, guess what! Santa Claus is coming for dinner tomorrow."

Glen looked at me over the top of David's head, his eyes full of questions.

I laughed. "I'll explain later," I said.

— Elizabeth Atwater —

The Painting

*When two people are meant to be together,
they will be together. It's fate.*
~Sara Gruen

Abstract paintings adorned the walls of the student union during my freshman year of college. Each was a unique expression by one of the art students. But one painting stood out for me. The vibrant yellow, the movement of the red and orange, the calming violet drew me in. I couldn't explain it. My fellow students knew that was my spot on the couch in view of the painting. It was there that I studied for sociology, statistics, history, and health. No matter the class, that painting exuded comfort.

Abstract art was not my thing. I preferred van Gogh or Monet — starry nights and water lilies. I couldn't explain it, but this painting was special. I tried to buy it, only to be told it wasn't for sale. Then, at the beginning of my sophomore year it was gone, replaced by something that was not memorable.

Five years later I had a job, an apartment, and more than one breakup behind me. I was finished with love. My sister told me to quit being dramatic. She insisted that I go Christmas shopping with her and her friend. I didn't know it was a blind date.

Frank was sweet and funny. However, he was a single dad with two kids under age six. What was my sister thinking? I really liked him, but did I really want to go there? A date or two wouldn't hurt. But if I was going to risk my heart ever again I needed a sign. A big one.

Frank wanted me to meet his children—they were a package deal—and he invited me to his younger son's birthday party. A birthday party for a kid wasn't a date so I agreed to go. I arrived early and met his two little boys who were bouncing here and there, so proud of their Christmas tree. They led me to the den area. As I entered the room, the twinkling lights of the tree faded for me because hanging behind Frank's couch was my painting.

"How did you get this?" I was amazed. "The lady in the art department told me it wasn't for sale."

"That was you?" He gave a little smile of disbelief, shaking his head. "How did you get it?"

He looked at me and grinned. "It's mine as in I painted it."

I had no words for a moment, so he continued.

"Do you like mythology? It's Andromeda in chains." He pointed to the yellow. "The Kraken is coming to take her, but Perseus is there. He's rushing in to break the chains and save her."

And he did save her. Not Perseus, but Frank saved me.

That was more than thirty years ago, and here I am, still married to Frank—now we have four grown kids. I'm still sitting by the painting even though I had to marry him to get it.

—Lisa McCaskill—

The Gold Ring

The older I get, the more I believe in what I can't explain or understand, even more than the things that are explainable and understandable.
~Lillian Gish

My father proudly wore his 1968 University of Michigan class ring until his death in 2012. It was a bulky gold number with a deep blue stone. Yet it was his plain gold wedding band, or lack thereof, that garnered the most attention. My father lost his original band almost twenty years after he wed my mother in 1968. Then he proceeded to lose the replacement wedding band my mother purchased for him, too.

For the remainder of his marriage, my father wore my maternal grandmother's gold wedding band, a ring my mother inherited after her mother passed away. My father's inability to hang onto his wedding band always stirred conspiracy theories, especially since his class ring stayed in place. Ultimately, I chose to accept that my father was absentminded and lost wedding rings.

Little did I know that my father's proclivity to lose wedding bands would affect me. In July 2016, my husband and I were visiting our children during parents' weekend at their camp in New York. We began our long trek up the steep one-mile road that led to the camp. I looked down to avoid tripping over a rock or stepping into a pothole. I wasn't looking for anything, just staying safe. Yet, for some reason, my gaze locked onto something hidden in the dirt of the road. It was not shiny, remarkable, or even interesting. Yet I absolutely had to touch it and hold it in my hands. I was drawn, compelled by some inner force to bend down and pick up this thing.

The item was terribly muddy and unimpressive; it resembled an old washer or a similar disc-shaped item normally found in a toolbox. My husband was anxious for us to continue our walk up the hill and remarked that I was wasting time picking up trash. I ignored him because I felt a weird connection to this weird item. I rolled it in my palm for a few seconds and saw that I was holding a ring.

I thought it was odd that someone had lost a ring, and I wondered if the owner even knew it was missing or had tried to find it. I wiped away the caked-on dirt from the ring. It was in remarkably good condition, save for one little nick along its edge. I took my time savoring the beauty of such a simple yet elegant gold ring. Then my heart stopped. I saw an inscription: "Zwinka '68." In that brief moment, everything made sense. Time stood still, and the world around me became instantly illuminated and perfect. Without a doubt, this was my father's original wedding band, engraved with my mother's nickname and their wedding year. This had been my camp, too, and my father must have lost his ring here thirty years ago, perhaps when he was attending a parents' weekend just like this one.

My husband's eyes opened wide with shock. In contrast, I closed my eyes and felt an overwhelming sense of peace. I zipped the ring into my jacket pocket, ready to give it to my widowed mother.

When we reached the top of the hill, I called my mother and shared the astounding news. She was speechless, overwhelmed by the unbelievable announcement that I had found my father's wedding band. Over the years, my mother had often expressed anger and sadness that the ring was lost, surely never to be found again. My parents married in New York City and had moved to numerous states. Long ago, they had abandoned hope of ever finding my father's ring.

Many questions swirled in my mind, although answers were irrelevant. It did not matter how a gold wedding band survived three decades on a dirt road being buried under upstate New York snowstorms, pounding rains, and messy mudslides. It did not matter how a ring survived the physical impact of decades of marching campers, massive tractors, and heavy food-service trucks climbing up and down the rocky hill. It did not matter how the band's Florentine finish survived three decades of erosion and weathering.

After all, the ring was not just surviving… it was waiting for me. I was destined to find this ring and reunite it with my mother. It was an overwhelming, sensational feeling to process, and a huge, beautiful responsibility to fulfill.

Later that evening, I drove an hour to deliver the ring to my mother. She removed her wedding ring and placed it inside my father's ring. They belonged together. My mother and I spent the remainder of the night talking about miracles, fate, symbolism, and coincidences. Together, we conjured various theories about why it took thirty years for the ring to be discovered, how I was the "chosen one" who found it, and the role of the deceased in our everyday lives. We talked about patience, faith, and never giving up hope. Ours was a long, lovely evening of sharing thoughts, tears and laughter.

The night ended when my husband shared his own analysis of the day's events. He said simply, "That ring is love." At a time when our marriage was troubled, he pointed out that just like the ring found on the ground, covered with dirt and eroded by time and neglect, love will get dirty and tarnished. Love will take a beating with heavy burdens and hardships. Love will be walked all over and taken advantage of. Love is sometimes hidden and dormant, but not dead. Love is never forgotten, lost or abandoned. Love can withstand separation, deterioration, and weathering. Love is like the ring; it will resurface and prevail.

— Andrea Lebedovych Bilaniuk —

Love You Forever

I cannot forget my mother. She is my bridge.
~Renita Weems

No one is ever ready to say goodbye to a parent, and I was no exception. When my mother suddenly passed away at the age of fifty-five, it was devastating. The only way I knew how to cope was to write. When it came time to write her eulogy, I welcomed the chance to honor her. After reading the eulogy at her funeral, I folded it neatly and tucked it between the pages of her favorite children's book, *Love You Forever*. When it was time to pay final homage to her, I felt satisfied as I placed my only copy of the book in her arms and helped to lower her casket.

Shortly thereafter though, I broke down. I could think of nothing but my mother. I missed her with every cell in my body. But most overwhelmingly, I could no longer grasp the concept of where she had gone. I found it impossible to believe that she was watching over me. If she were, I thought, then she would surely make her presence known. I pleaded with the Heavens to show me she was there, that she was still sending her love, and keeping a watchful eye. No such luck.

Weeks went by. I became depressed and broken, unable to fulfill simple tasks and care for myself. I stayed home. People came in and out, checking on me at all hours of the day. Family and friends tried to coax me out of the house, but all I wanted to do was hide. I wanted to hide from my harsh reality: I would never see or hear from my mother again. Finally, those who cared about me had had enough.

One night, my best friend and her partner came over with a plan to get me out of the house. I debated with them for over an hour, pleading for them to leave me alone. Two hours and a million excuses later, we finally compromised and I allowed them to take me on a quick trip to Target.

As we walked through the aisles my feet dragged. I didn't want to be there. I didn't want to be anywhere. Nonetheless, we perused the make-up, electronics, and home goods aisles. They were there to offer me an outlet, and I was only there to placate them. After several more minutes of mindless meandering I was done. I told them I had to go back home, that I needed to get out of there.

"Alright, but first we have to stop by the candy section. A little sugar will give you a pick-me-up," they reasoned.

I swallowed my pain and continued. I picked out a piece of candy just to avoid my friends' concerned stares. At the checkout, we dropped our items on the conveyor belt and waited in line. I looked at the merchandise arrayed at the checkout. At the top of a shelf, on top of the candy, hair ties, and hand sanitizer, sat a book, a copy of *Love You Forever*! I snatched the copy and skimmed the pages, enjoying the pictures of a mother cradling her child. Tears welled in my eyes.

"Ma'am? Ma'am? How would you like to pay for this?" the cashier asked.

I snapped back to reality, but ignored her question. "Why is this book here?" I demanded to know.

"I'm not sure, ma'am. Maybe someone was planning to buy it but chose not to in the end? They were probably just too lazy to put it back… It happens all the time, unfortunately. Thanks for pointing it out."

I felt compelled to know more, and am still not sure why I asked my next question.

"Where are the rest of the copies of this book?"

"Wow. You sure love that book. The rest are probably in our book section, but I'll scan it just to make sure. Sometimes when a book is on promotion it is moved."

She scanned it. The machine made a loud, shrill beep.

"Huh. That's weird. It's not scanning. Let me see…"

The few moments I waited felt like eternity. A ball of excitement mixed with anxiety formed in my stomach.

"I'm sorry, ma'am. This book isn't scanning because we have no other copies in-store. In fact, we haven't for a while. It says the last time we had this book in stock was two and a half years ago. I'm not really sure why it was sitting there… If you'd like to buy it ma'am, I apologize because I guess it's not really available for purchase. But… I mean… I guess you can… Just take it? It's not really ours to sell."

My heart fluttered as I gingerly took back the book. I cradled it in my arms and as I did, I felt a sense of security envelop me. I knew this was a message from my mother. It was a message of love, support, and understanding. It was her way of saying, "I will love you forever, no matter what." And I've never doubted that since.

—Amy B. Chesler—

Miracle Cat

Miracles are not contrary to nature, but only contrary to what we know about nature.
~Saint Augustine

Everyone has their superstitions about black cats. Some say they are bad luck and some say they are witches in disguise. Never has an old wives' tale been so disproven as in the case of Jinx and the love she showed our family.

October is the time for jack-o'-lanterns and witches on broomsticks. It was also a lucky month for a small, shy black cat. I was looking at a local shelter for a companion cat for my other fur baby, Onyx. I walked up and down the rows of kittens and cats, all of them purring or mewing to get my attention. All except for one were jumping at the chance to get a new home. The name tag on the reticent one's cage said "Angel." It also stated that this was her last day. Halloween was coming soon and the shelter would stop adoptions of all black cats. By the time the hold on the black female was to be released, her fate would be sealed. A stroke of bad luck turned into good because I could not turn away from her.

"May I see her?" I asked a shelter attendant.

"You don't want that one," she said. "She has been the meanest one in here yet. A real firecracker."

Not discouraged, I took her out of the small cage that had been her home for twenty-nine days and held her close. A faint purr emanated from deep inside this "mean" cat. Then to everyone's surprise, she

146 | Amazing Coincidences

licked my nose. From that day forward, Angel truly was a wonderful addition to my small family. Jinx, as I renamed her, was there for the birth of my daughter, and the deaths of Onyx and my horse Clover. She welcomed a new Poodle puppy named Winnie into her home and heart without any hesitation.

At the age of four, Jinx was diagnosed with cancer. The vet's words hit like a ton of bricks. So young and full of life; how could life be so cruel? I cried all the way home from the vet. I made up my mind not to worry about when she would leave us, but to focus on how much fun we could have while she still was here. Jinx spent the next year playing with gallon milk jug tabs and hair ties, and devising a plan to capture our fish. She tormented Winnie and let the Poodle chase her time and time again. After their sport, they would curl up next to each other and rest.

The moment came late one night when we had to say goodbye. Jinx went from bad to worse in less than a day. As I held her in my arms for the last time, I told her what a great cat she was and what an amazing friend she had been. As the pink liquid seeped into her veins, she sighed and was gone. No more pain for my baby Jinx.

While my husband and I were burying her in a beautiful wooded area, I said, through a flood of tears, "I don't think I could ever accept another cat in my life. She set the bar too high." Then I added, laughing with the absurdity of it, "Unless it's all white, the exact opposite of Jinx. Plus, it would have to have one blue eye and one gold eye."

Two days later we were at my mother-in-law's house and Winnie started whining at the sliding glass door. My husband said, "Take that dog out so she stops whining."

I walked to the door and saw, sitting on the porch with her tail curled around her paws, a pure white kitten with one blue eye and one gold eye. Gabby is a healthy, bouncy, mischievous little kitten who dried our tears and let us know that miracles happen. I believe that Jinx wanted us to love again. Her little message from the Rainbow Bridge reached our doorstep and our hearts. Jinx was truly an "Angel" after all.

— Angela Marchi —

Cold Goldie

What we see depends mainly on what we look for.
~John Lubbock

It was a bitterly cold morning.

When I left the house, I had to think where I had parked the car. The usually empty parking spots in front of the house were taken when I came home the night before, so I parked on a side street half a block away. I tucked my chin low inside the collar of my coat, ineffectively trying to cover what I could of my face against the cheek-numbing air and walked to the car.

Mercifully, the car started.

As was my habit, I let it warm while I tied my tie, which I had draped around my neck under my coat. Then I just sat, listening to the radio, watching two thawed spots appear on the driver and passenger sides of the windshield. Slowly they grew, as heater and defroster overcame the biting cold.

At first the spots were small, and I could see little outside. Out of the small thawed spot in front of me, a bit of the world appeared — the top of the car in front of me, the second story of the apartment building at the end of the block, and a poster on the telephone pole next to the apartment building.

The hand-lettered poster had been there for more than a month. I had stopped to read it weeks ago.

Lost Golden Retriever
We miss him greatly
Reward. Call…

We lived in a busy part of the city with much traffic. Lost dogs and cats seldom fared well here.

As the windshield cleared, more of the outside world became visible. I noticed that at the base of the telephone pole where the sign was posted lay a Golden Retriever.

I squinted and looked harder. "Naaaa… give me a break, no way," I said out loud to myself.

The dog just lay there, curled up tightly against the cold.

The internal debate began.

"You have to go check out the dog," said my better half.

"What? Are you crazy? It is below zero. The sign has been there a month. No way could a dog last in this neighborhood, living outdoors for a month," said my colder and lesser half.

"But you have to check."

"But staying warm would be so much better."

"Go on, go check it out."

"Let's get to work. Remember, you were going in early to get some extra things done."

That was the clincher. Who wants to rush to work?

So I got out of the car and walked towards the dog. As I crossed the street, the dog raised its head and watched me warily. As I got within fifteen feet, it stood up and began to move away. I stopped, squatted and held out my hand, calling to the dog.

"Here boy, come on, here boy, here boy. It's okay…."

I stood up and took several steps towards the dog, holding out my hand, but it kept its distance. So I squatted again and called it, reaching my hand out as I did.

I kept calling, moving towards him, and he would back away, never letting me get within ten feet. The cold began to penetrate even

Amazing Coincidences

my heavy coat and I imagined the conversation the police would have as they pondered my squatting, hand extended, frozen body. The dog, having more common sense than I, would have been long gone to someplace warm.

The dog had no distinct markings—just a typical, overall golden color. Judging from the near gray on his muzzle, he was an older dog. He did have a collar, and a red rabies tag, but I could not get close enough to see the engraved numbers on it. It looked like there was a shred of blue cloth hanging from the hook that attached the tag to the collar. I wondered if he had once had a bandana around his neck, and had caught it on something, ripping it off in the process.

So I rose, and returned to the car, grabbing the sign from the pole on the way. Fortunately, the car was wonderfully warm at this point.

I decided to call the number on the sign later that morning. "Did you lose a dog a month ago," I asked the woman who answered.

"Why yes, we did. It was six weeks ago when we were visiting friends in the city," she said. "Why do you ask?"

I told her my "Golden Retriever under the 'Lost Golden Retriever' sign" story. She sounded dubious, especially given the length of time that her dog had been gone. I told her what little there was to tell about the dog—the collar, the red rabies tag, and the shred of blue cloth.

"Oh my God!" she said. "Our dog was wearing a blue bandana around its neck when we lost him." She said she would drive down and look in the neighborhood.

She called back later that afternoon, and indeed, had found her dog, thinner, but in amazingly good shape for living six weeks outside.

I have often wondered how they taught that dog to read.

— Daniel James —

Chapter 7

Messages from Heaven

Not Forsaken

God could not be everywhere, so he created mothers.
~Jewish Proverb

The baby hadn't moved. I should have been concerned, but I was nauseated, hot, and in desperate need of a nap. As I sat on the couch, nodding while the sounds from the television began to fade, Grandma Maudie's voice called out to me. "Kathy Pollard, I know you're not sleeping sitting up like that. Get your tail to your room and lie down. Give that baby some breathing room."

I slowly opened my eyes so I could fully view my grandmother, sitting at her sewing machine with a cigarette dangling from her mouth. On a good day I would have sat up and argued with her, maybe tell her to mind her own business. But I was thirty-eight weeks into a pregnancy I was more than ready to see come to term, and with all of the vomiting and general discomfort, I didn't have the energy to partake in any kind of dispute. "Okay, Grandma," was all I managed to say. Besides, I knew I would be asleep as soon as my head hit the pillow.

As soon as I lay down, the air in the room seemed to split from ceiling to floor and open up, allowing a breezy wave to break through the gap. I eyed the peculiar phenomenon and then saw my mother. She looked like she was surfing on that wave of air, and she was coming toward me. I should have been excited, curious or even awe-struck over seeing her. However, my mother had died three years earlier — shot to death by my stepfather — and I had not forgiven her or God for leaving me behind. I frowned and turned away to show my discontent. I did not care if she would be hurt by the dismissive gesture; she had wounded me first, reneging on a promise to always be there for me.

I felt her presence hovering by the bed and trembled because, after all, she was supposed to be in Heaven doing afterlife things, not standing in my bedroom as if she wanted to have a chat. I remained tight-lipped, hoping she would get the hint and leave. However, she would not move. She would not vanish, or do any other ghostly thing except shimmer and sway. Annoyed by her dogged determination, I turned to look up at her. "Why are you here?"

"Are you okay?" The sound of her voice soothed all of the hurt I had carried in my heart the past three years, and I realized how much I missed my mother. Nevertheless, I was stubborn and I gave her a contemptuous frown. "Why do you care?" I wanted her to sass me and to say something like, "I care because I'm your mother and I asked you a question," but instead her face molded into sympathetic love.

"Are you okay?" she repeated as she stood waiting on that breeze, her body gently flowing up and down with the swaying of the wave.

My mother's patience disturbed me and I wanted her to vanish from my sight. I did not want her to see my shame from my being short with her. "Yeah, I'm okay," I whined.

She looked at my stomach and worry lines formed across her brow. "Are you sure?"

I thought about the baby. He still hadn't moved. But, I hadn't forgiven her for leaving me. I tightened my lips, narrowed my eyes, and clenched my jaw. "Leave me alone," I said.

My mother tilted her head and looked at me with eyes so full of love and compassion, I almost wept. "Okay, Kathy." She shrugged her shoulders, turned and rode away on the wave of air.

I watched my mother float away until she was a tiny speck of light. When that light vanished, I sat up in bed, threw my legs over the side and rubbed my belly. The baby still did not move. I stood, stretched and decided I would eat some leftover chili. Maybe the spiciness would energize the baby.

Grandma looked up at me as I walked by her on the way to the

Messages from Heaven

kitchen. "I thought you were sleepy."

I could barely hear her over the whir of her sewing machine and I spoke a bit loudly so she would hear me. "Mama came to visit."

The whirring stopped and Grandma jumped from her chair. "What did she want? What did she say?" She grabbed my arm and pulled me toward the couch. Then she forced me to sit down. "Tell me everything."

I yanked my arm away. "She looked at my stomach and asked me if I was okay," I said, rubbing my wrist.

Grandma drew her hand to her mouth and gasped. "Has the baby moved today?"

I shrugged. "No." I frowned at her, mainly because I was ashamed of not responding to my baby's lack of movement. I felt abashed because even my dead mother knew enough to break through the boundaries of life and death to check on her unborn grandson's status, and here I was acting nonchalant.

The next few minutes were a blur. Before I could do or say anything, Grandma had woken my grandfather from his nap, rushed us all into the car, and commanded my grandfather to "hightail it" to the hospital.

The visit at the hospital was also a haze of events after the initial tests of heart rate, reflex and breathing were done on the baby. A team of doctors and nurses raced to revitalize my lethargic son. After a whirlwind of injections, probing, more testing and monitoring, the doctors finally gave the baby a thumbs-up. They released me later that night, telling me that if I had arrived just a few minutes later the baby might have died.

During the car ride home Grandma scolded me for allowing a whole day to go by without movement from the baby. "Lucky for you your mama was there. Lucky for you she is still looking out for you."

The next week Brandon was born a strong and healthy boy. On the night of his birth, I held my newborn in my arms and cried for my mother in ways I had refused to the past three years. I cried because I loved her. I cried because I missed her. I cried because even in death she had not betrayed me. I also asked God's forgiveness for ever doubting His provisions and I thanked Him for my son and my mama, the angel who never stopped watching over me.

— Kathryn Y. Pollard —

Feathers from Heaven

What greater thing is there for human souls than to feel that they are joined for life — to be with each other in silent unspeakable memories.
~George Eliot

Winter flakes fell, wet and heavy. It had been snowing all day. Up to eighteen inches had been predicted. I groaned at the thought of clearing the driveway and sidewalks. Shoveling and handling the beast of a snowblower had been my husband's job until I lost him to cancer.

Bruce would have been out there already, getting ahead of the storm, wearing his famous red-and-black woolen hat with the huge bill and earflaps. I'd tease him mercilessly about the plaid monstrosity and then get to work preparing hot cocoa and muffins to warm him after he'd come in red-cheeked and tired.

But he was gone now, and I was left alone in the big, empty house with no reason to fix cocoa and muffins anymore. It wouldn't be the same without him. I missed him more than ever with the anniversary of his passing coming up. "It takes time," my grief counselor told me. *But how much?* I wondered. It felt like God didn't care, almost like He left when Bruce did. They both felt so far from me.

My spirit sagged, heavy with loss and a sense of abandonment. I needed a sign more than ever. For weeks, I'd asked God to give me one, something to let me know that Bruce was okay. But none had come.

I picked up my mug, sipped some coffee and stared out the picture window into the yard. Bruce and I spent many hours by this very same window, sharing our passion for birdwatching, marveling over the vivid sapphire of a blue jay or the eye-popping yellow and orange of a Baltimore oriole. Still, it was the cardinals we loved the most. It seemed one of them was always appearing to mark any occasion in our lives. It could be for something as special as an anniversary or as ordinary as the two of us barbecuing a slab of ribs together.

It was those precious moments that endeared the regal bird to us, and somewhere along the way the intuitive cardinal became our bird. The proud crest, the vivid red—the color of love, our love. I could feel my lips softly curve at the bittersweet memory.

How I wished one would appear now. Despite the winter storm, the yard was a beehive of activity. I'd never seen so many birds. But there wasn't a cardinal in sight; only finches, chickadees and sparrows pecked at the feeders. The moment a perch became empty, a new bird would land to fill it. It was quite a sight to see. Bruce would have run for his camera and snapped a dozen pictures—if he were still here. *Why, God?* I asked for the millionth time. *He should be here with me.*

The snow continued to fall from leaden skies, coating the wooded landscape. I drew my sweater tighter around me, staring out the window, listless and alone. Tiny wrens nestled in the soft, sheltering needles of a weeping blue Atlas cedar, while mourning doves padded underneath. No matter how much I yearned to see the bright flash of red wing, there was no cardinal to cheer me.

I swiped a tear, longing for Bruce. *Lord, please let me know he's okay.* It was no use. What could He even do to assure me? My husband was gone and I had to accept it. But how? It was too hard. Unable to pull myself away from the window, I realized that everything beyond the glass was Bruce. He'd created the sanctuary. He'd planted and nurtured each shrub, chose each rock for the waterfall he made, and hung all those bird feeders. All of them were gifts for me, except the two I'd bought for him.

Just as I reached for a tissue to dab my eyes, a cardinal swooped past the window. Another one landed on the patio, and a third on the branch of our elm tree. I watched in astonishment as the sky opened to release still more. My heart soared. It was raining cardinals! I swallowed hard and tried to count them all, but there were too many to keep track of.

The cardinals darted and weaved, landing to rest here and there, and then winged in and out of the woods. It was a miraculous display of brilliant red against a backdrop of pure white. I stood rooted to the floor with my nose pressed against the cold windowpane, not wanting it to end, willing them to stay, and smiling through grateful tears.

My heart sank when they lifted off. All but one. He flew over and landed on a sprig of pine right below the window where I was standing. He was so close I could see every detail, the way his little feathers fluffed and then lay in a perfect silken row as if they'd been combed. His deep, dark eyes were looking right at me. Then, he flitted away in a blur of scarlet. A sweet peace settled over me as I watched him fly over the trees.

"Oh, Lord," my voice quivered, piercing the silence of the empty house. The sign had finally come. God had sent His angels, not on wings of white but vibrant Valentine red. He'd sent an entire host of feathery cherubim. My prayer had been answered. My broken heart could finally mend.

—Susan A. Karas—

One Last Visit Before the Light

Life is eternal and love is immortal;
And death is only a horizon,
And a horizon is nothing save the limit of our sight.
~Rossiter W. Raymond

I was driving home from work and I felt troubled. I was thinking that we should have gone to Phoenix on Memorial Day, but I had just started a new job so we hadn't gone. My mother-in-law had been diagnosed with breast cancer shortly after our wedding and given six months to live. But with good doctors and care in Phoenix, she was still alive three years later. Natalie, at sixty-three, was a tiny four-foot-something, gentle, loving woman. Her favorite poem to quote ended with, "Love in your heart wasn't put there to stay. Love isn't love 'till you give it away." She loved her three grandchildren with every fiber of her being. She was thrilled when I had Nicholas; she just couldn't get enough of him.

My in-laws made a habit of summering in San Diego to escape the Arizona heat and to be near us, except this summer. Natalie instead asked us to bring Nicky to Phoenix over Memorial Day weekend. She didn't tell us how sick she was, not wanting us to worry. But if we had known, we would have gone.

It was 4:45 p.m. I had stopped briefly at home and was about to go to the sitter's house to get Nicky when the phone rang. It was my sister-in-law.

"Lisa, I'm glad I caught you," Helaine said in a voice choked with grief. "Mom just passed away at 4:30. Marcia and I were with her at the hospital. Can you guys come?"

"Sure," I reassured her. "I'll call the airline and get the baby. We'll be there as soon as we can."

Minutes later, I arrived at the babysitter's house. Dee-dee, a Navy wife, ran a home day care to keep busy while her husband was away at sea. It was a perfect place for Nicky. Dee-dee was sensitive and caring, treating her day care kids as her own. But today, Dee-dee was pale and visibly shaken when she answered the door.

"What's wrong, Dee?" I asked as I stepped inside. I felt an immediate tingling of panic for my son.

"It's Nicky. He did something strange a few minutes ago," Dee-dee replied nervously. "He was sitting out back in the sandbox, playing with his favorite truck. All of a sudden, he dropped it and looked up — at nothing, just up at the air, the sky, for a minute. And he said, 'Bye-bye, Grandma. Bye-bye, Grandma. Bye-bye,' three times, just like that.

"Then, I got the eeriest feeling," she said, rubbing her upper arms with her hands. "I felt like I was being watched by something. I ran out there and picked him up and brought him inside."

I felt a flush of heat rush over my body and face.

Dee-dee continued, "I knew you were probably on your way because I looked at the clock there in the kitchen and it was 4:30. But why he was saying 'Grandma', I don't know."

"Oh, Lord," I said, rushing over and grabbing Nicky off the floor. "My mother-in-law just passed away in Phoenix. I just got the call before I drove here."

Dee-dee put her hand on the wall to steady herself. She was a devout Baptist and regular churchgoer. "Praise Jesus, Amen!" Dee-dee shouted. "Praise the Lord, Jesus! It was her spirit!"

It was obvious early on that my son was gifted. I know most parents think their kids are gifted, but Nicky always hit his milestones before he normally should. By eighteen months old, he was fully conversational. You could ask him questions and get complete, coherent answers.

I sat the tiny boy on the sofa in the living room. Kneeling beside him, I asked Nicky why he said goodbye to his grandmother. He matter-of-factly explained that she had come to see him because she was going away. He said that she told him she loved him very much and wanted to see him.

I asked him where Grandma was. He pointed, indicating the backyard. "She was outside, over there, floating in the air."

Then I asked if Grandma did anything. Nick said, "Grandma talked, but not out loud. She talked in that little voice inside my head. She said, 'I love you,' and she wanted to kiss me, but she couldn't."

"Why?" I asked.

"Because, she had blood on her mouth," he said. "And then she went up to the clouds."

Dee-dee blanched. I tried to keep a calm exterior, not showing the alarm I felt. I didn't want Nick to cry; I wanted answers.

"And what did Grandma look like?" I queried further.

Nick explained in his "big man" voice, "She was wearing a dress with little flowers all over it and she had wires on her arms."

Dee-dee and I were dumbfounded. Natalie so much wanted to see him before she passed over that she came to him before going to the Light. I believe that distance and time are immaterial for the spirit once it leaves the body. She wanted to see her grandson and let him know of her love.

My husband and I got to Phoenix later that night. We were at my father-in-law's home with my husband's sisters. I recounted the story about Nicky and Natalie. A stunned silence fell over the family. Helaine said that at the time of death, her mom was wearing a hospital gown with tiny blue flowers on it and she had intravenous tubes in her arms. A therapist took her respirator out, tearing her lip slightly in the process. "She had a little trickle of blood on the corner of her mouth," Helaine said, stunned. "But how..."

My father-in-law realized how Nick knew. Nine years earlier, Bob had a massive cardiac arrest and near-death experience. He spent years reading about and researching these experiences, and taught us all about the spirit's ability to travel and the Light of God that one crosses into at the time of death. Bob made us firmly believe, "Death is the gate of life. It's not an end. The soul goes on." And Natalie showed us that.

— Lisa Wojcik —

54

The Beauty of Rubber Bands

*The love game is never called
off on account of darkness.*
~Tom Masson

We saw it at the same time. It was a sunny, blue-sky day in June, and my daughter Jamie and I were wearing beautiful dresses and walking on a small, paved path on a golf course. We were just a few feet behind a photographer, my new husband Nick, and Nick's two daughters. We were heading to an old, stone bridge for more wedding photos when Jamie and I saw the big, thick rubber band in our path. We stopped, looked at each other, and smiled.

I tucked that rubber band into my bouquet, and we moved on to take more photos and celebrate the joining of our families. It had been twelve years since her daddy had died, and I had waited for just the right partner. I had no doubts about the new adventure we were beginning. Still, that rubber band made my heart swell with happiness. I knew Mike was giving us the thumbs-up, letting his girls know it was okay to move forward.

My late husband Mike used to have a job in which he encountered hundreds of rubber bands a day. What did he do with them? He shoved them in his jeans pockets and brought them home. At first, he just emptied his pockets and left piles of rubber bands on the counter when he walked in the door after work. Then, after much complaining from me, he started putting the rubber bands in brown paper bags and saving them.

"What," I used to ask him, "do you need all those rubber bands for?"

"You never know," he used to say.

I gave up the battle and accepted the fact that our closets would be filled with brown paper sacks stuffed with thick rubber bands.

Just two years into our marriage, when our daughter was not even a year old, Mike was diagnosed with cancer and unable to work as much. The bags of rubber bands dwindled. When he died, I actually missed those rubber bands — even the piles on my counters and in his jeans pockets. Eventually, I put the bags away, far out of sight. I couldn't bear to see them anymore, but I couldn't bear to throw them out, either.

About three months after Mike died, I found a big, thick rubber band just like the kind he had brought home from work so many times. The rubber band was lying on my bathroom counter, but there was absolutely no reason for it to be there. It made me think of Mike and smile, and I laughed out loud for the first time in a long while.

A few weeks later, I found a rubber band hanging from the knob of the cabinet above the stove. I was flabbergasted. I had no idea how it had gotten there. I still don't.

Since then, rubber bands have popped up in my path in the most unusual places. In a clothes hamper. On my mom's dining-room table. On my desk at school after summer vacation. On the deck of a cruise ship in the Caribbean. On a street in New York City.

I found the New York City rubber band a few years after Mike died when I was crossing a busy street in Times Square with two colleagues. We were there for a conference, but had been in the hotel watching the Ohio State/Michigan football game. I'm a die-hard Buckeyes fan, even though I had married a rabid Wolverines fan. Ohio State was losing, and I couldn't stand to watch anymore, so my friends and I left the hotel. When I jumped with glee over the discovery of the wet, dirty rubber band smack-dab in the middle of the crosswalk, my friends thought I was nuts. I explained why finding that rubber band was so thrilling to me, saying that I thought Mike left it so I would know he was watching over me in New York City. My friend Kara commented with a laugh: "Yeah... or maybe he's rubbing it in that his team is beating your team!"

To anyone else, rubber bands are second only to duct tape in the myriad ways in which they can be utilized. They are useful. They are practical. They hold things together. To me, rubber bands are beautiful. They are magical. They held the pieces of my broken heart together until it was healed enough to love again. And now, rubber bands remind me that even though people die, love never does.

— Julie Rine Holderbaum —

Snow Angels

*Snowflakes are snow angels blowing
kisses from heaven.
~Author Unknown*

I grew up in a family of six children. Regardless of the temperature, we learned to make our own fun outdoors. We enjoyed making impressions on the freshly fallen snow. We would lie on our backs and move our arms and legs in a sweeping motion. When we stood up, we were careful not to disturb our creations — our snow angels.

Years after I married and moved away from my childhood city, I still made snow angels. My husband Brian and I would search out fresh snow, unmarked by our dogs, and lie down side by side, just far enough apart to move our arms and legs. Afterward, we would stand and look down with pride at what we had created.

After thirty-nine years together, Brian lost his battle with cancer less than nine months after the diagnosis. I lost my sparkle and the desire to go outside and make snow angels.

Months later, I purchased a cedar bench and had it erected on the walking path through the wetlands park near my home. The bench was inscribed in memory of Brian. Two weeks after the bench was finished, winter arrived unexpectedly. I was surprised when I looked out the kitchen window and saw the tree branches drooping under the weight of wet snow. The sun was just peeking out from behind the clouds, and the trees looked beautiful, glistening with ice crystals.

I love photography and was anxious to go outdoors and capture some photos before the sun had fully risen. It would melt the overnight snow, and the glory of what I was looking at would be gone. With a fresh cup of coffee in my hand and my camera tucked under my winter jacket, I stepped outdoors. The crisp winter air bit at my exposed skin. I quickened my step. Snowflakes were still drifting down slowly. A peaceful calm enveloped me.

During the summer, the wetland pond was alive with waterfowl but now the pond was silent. All I could see were the deer tracks across the ice.

It was absolutely silent as I walked, and it was easy to get lost in my thoughts. The only sound was the crush of snow beneath my feet. As I approached Brian's bench, mine were the only footprints. No one had walked before me. And yet, I saw two perfectly created snow angels, side by side, just a couple of feet from the bench. I wondered who could have created them. Snow was falling steadily now, yet the impressions were clear.

I turned and looked toward the pond. The bulrushes still stood tall, covered in a crisp ice frosting. The snow leading to the pond was pristine. I looked backwards from where I stood on the path. The only blemishes were the marks my own boots had left. There were no other footprints. I glanced around and realized the snow was totally undisturbed everywhere around me.

My attention turned back to the angel impressions. There was no reason for someone to lie down so close to the bench to create the angels with so much open area just a few feet away. As I stared at the angels, a realization slowly dawned on me. I smiled inwardly, knowing this was a sign from heaven. The angels were my husband's way of letting me know that he was here with me in this moment. I felt a swell of emotion building, but instead of letting the emotion push me to sadness, I embraced the blessing that our life together had been.

I captured the images with my camera. Then I brushed the snow from the bench and sat down. I leaned back and closed my eyes, thinking about the hundreds of times that Brian and I had made snow angels. It seemed a silly thing to do at our age, but whenever we stood up, we were proud of the angels we had created.

I can't explain how the snow angels appeared or why the angels were so close to Brian's bench, but it doesn't matter. All that matters is that it brought me comfort.

Years have passed since that day, and never again have I found snow angels. I believe that Brian knows I have learned to live without him, and time has healed my loneliness.

I plan to resume making snow angels in the winter–for both of us.

—Wendy Portfors—

Walk Me Home

There's no other love like the love for a brother. There's no other love like the love from a brother.
~Author Unknown

I sat at my kitchen table for two hours, working on something that should have taken me a quarter of that time. Writing usually comes easily to me, but writing my brother's eulogy was complicated.

Casey had died in a car accident. He was with his roommate, Kyle, a friend of ours, who also died. They were both twenty-eight. I happened to be working that particular evening.

I'm a firefighter, and we respond with the ambulance to medical calls. I wasn't on the first unit to respond, but we were asked to assist. As I pulled up to the scene, the ambulance carrying my brother to the hospital sped past us.

As I got the details of the accident, I suspected my brother was in that ambulance, and I went to the hospital to confirm. From there, I had to place the call to my parents.

My parents, my brothers Matt and Tom, and a few other family members made it to the hospital before Casey died. He was still technically alive when they arrived, being worked on in the ER, but with little hope of survival.

When it was over, we gathered in the room to pray and say goodbye. I went home to wake my fiancée and our two-year-old daughter. I didn't want to wake her to this news over the phone; I wanted to do it in person.

We went up to my parents' house and gathered in the way the immediately grief-stricken do — sitting around in their living room, talking, laughing, crying, stunned. Eventually, we went home in the early morning.

As we left, I remember the sound of my mom crying from the back of the house. It was barely human, like a wounded animal, the saddest sound I'd ever heard in my life.

The rest of the week was a blur, leading up to Kyle's memorial service on Thursday, with Casey's funeral Mass to follow Friday morning.

I had made up my mind not to bother with a eulogy. I thought it would fall to me by default, being the oldest. Our youngest brother, Matt, asked us if he could do it, though, and I had no objections, happy to be free of the burden.

At Kyle's memorial, I cried openly. Kyle was the youngest of four, with three sisters. Each of his sisters spoke at his service, and that more than anything changed my mind. I would have to get up and speak, along with Matt and Tom, for Casey's service the next day.

So I sat at my kitchen table and tried to transfer what was in my head to the page. It was going slowly, though. I knew exactly what I wanted to say, but it was so hard to physically write it down. It was just another thing that made it all real, and not some bad dream. But that awareness didn't make it any easier to push through.

Eventually, I did finish, somewhere around 1:00 a.m. I had to be up early to get ready in the morning, and I had some minor errands to take care of. Getting to sleep quickly was a major priority. I knew that if I went to bed right then, though, I'd lie awake for hours. The only night I'd been able to fall asleep at a decent time had been the first night after Casey's death, and that was the day I spent getting drunk and feeling sorry for myself. I didn't think that was a great option at this point.

So I went for a walk around my neighborhood. I strolled down the middle of the street, aimlessly, trying to wear out my mind and body so I could lie down at peace for just a few hours.

I was roughly three-quarters of the way through my walk, headed back toward my house, when I came to a particularly well-lit spot. I saw my shadow, looming, elongated in the distance. Then, two distinct shadows appeared on either side of my own shadow. I don't want to make this into more than what it was, but it was beautiful, pure, and filled me with emotion.

My shadow, in the middle, was definitely and clearly my own. The other two, though, were not. They didn't look anything like mine, and they didn't react like mine. Together, it looked like a group of three people was walking and laughing. This lasted the final two blocks I had to walk home.

I didn't want to let go of that moment. I just wanted to keep walking and stay in that bubble. I knew that this was all I was going to get though, and it was going to have to be enough. Feeling overjoyed and completely content, I went inside and fell asleep within minutes. And for the first time all week, I slept peacefully.

I got up the next day and made it through the funeral. I gave my eulogy, and I think it was pretty damn good. I thought about telling that story, but I didn't. I held onto it, wanting to keep it for myself at that time. I shared it with my cousin Sean that night at the reception. And later on, I told my wife, because that's the kind of thing husbands share with their wives.

My brother and my friend are both dead, and I'll never see them in this lifetime again. But I know that we'll see each other eventually, and we'll finish that walk.

— Dan Boyle —

My Miracles and Me

*It only takes a thought and your angel will be there...
for although you may not see them,
you're always in their care.
~Author Unknown*

It was the weekend after Thanksgiving, with three weeks left in the first semester. Like many high school seniors, I looked forward to skating through the second semester, filled with fun times with my friends and family.

As any kid from a small town will tell you, hanging out in parking lots, driving around back roads, and munching on fast food are peak activities for students with plenty of time on their hands and little money in their pockets. On this particular night, my friends and I climbed into my 1997 Oldsmobile Cutlass Supreme and headed for the Valdosta mall to grab some pizza. After eating we headed to a small playground outside of our school's football field. We talked, laughed, and joked together until it was time to head home.

On our way home, the car ran slightly off the road and before I could correct the steering, the right tire hit a pothole that ripped the front end from under the car. The Cutlass began to spin out of control and we hit the concrete railing of a bridge. The air bag deployed, knocking me unconscious and permanently blinding me.

I was not wearing a seatbelt and was thrown from the car after it flipped. I landed among trees, bushes, and vines. The vines actually softened the impact, preventing further damage to my body.

Then a miracle happened.

My grandfather, whom I called Papa, had died several years earlier. But there was Papa right in front of me. He told me with genuine love in his face, "Bubba, now it ain't your time to be here, so you just get back down there. You'll be all right son, now don't you worry, God ain't finished with you yet."

Leaving Papa and returning to my broken and bloody body I heard bushes shaking and someone calling my name. I managed a grunt and the searchers eventually found me. Before I passed out again, I said clearly, "Tell my mama that I'm going to be all right." I was confident in that statement because Papa never lied to me and he'd just told me God wasn't done with me yet.

My parents got the phone call no parent ever wants to receive. My mama quickly threw my little sister into my grandma's arms and rushed to the hospital where I was being airlifted. She was told there was no way that I would be alive when I arrived but she told the doctor, "Well you ain't God and He is the one that decides life and death."

When my mama saw me for the first time in the hospital, she leaned over me and said, "I'm not leaving your side until I carry you home with me. We are stuck together like super glue." Over the next couple of months, we faced many trials and tribulations. I had setback after setback, but we kept holding on.

I spent seven days in Phoebe Putney hospital in Albany, Georgia. Due to the damage from the air bag, I was unable to take breaths as normal, so a breathing tube was placed in my airway. At one point, it slipped and no one was aware for several minutes. I was told later I went for almost ten minutes without oxygen and yet I did not suffer any brain damage.

It was another miracle.

Later, a common antibiotic used to treat infections caused me to run a fever so high that I had to be put in an ice bath. It turned out I was allergic to that medication.

After a few weeks, I was taken to Children's Scottish Rite Hospital in Atlanta. Since my trauma was so severe, the doctors decided that it was best to keep me in a medically induced coma to prevent more damage, manage the pain, and keep me calm. Then the surgeries began.

To rebuild my facial structure, a titanium metal plate was installed, the bridge of my nose was repaired, and several eye surgeries occurred. My jaw was tightly wired shut and I was put on a liquid diet, causing me to lose a significant amount of weight. After a particularly hard night, a kind nurse named Kim came to change my bedclothes. As she turned me in my bed, my trach slipped again and I began to suffocate. Once again I saw Papa. Shaking his head, he simply pointed behind me and said, "I done told you that it ain't your time. Now get back 'cause you worrying that nurse something bad." Following Papa's instructions, I came back to my body and shook nurse Kim's arm to alert her to the problem.

It was yet another miracle that I did not suffer any brain damage despite the lack of oxygen.

By the spring, I managed to attend my senior prom with the girl who was also in the accident.

I am eternally grateful for the paramedic who found me in those woods, the doctors and nurses who cared for me at Phoebe Putney and Scottish Rite Hospitals, the Life Flight crews, and my family who stayed by my side throughout this journey. I thank God no one else was injured that night. And I thank my Papa for sending me home, twice.

— Richard Bennett —

A Stop on His Journey

Grandchildren are the dots that connect the lines
from generation to generation.
~Lois Wyse

Grandpa Macdonald arrived at my mother's house with a battered suitcase and little else. In his eighties, he stood barely five feet tall. My mother said he used to tell people he was 5'4" before he got old and shrunk, but that wasn't true — she said he'd always been about the same height.

He had a soft Scottish brogue that he denied he had. I found it enchanting. His strongest drink was tea, and he liked it well steeped. Cheese? He'd never tried it because he didn't like the way it smelled.

I liked him immediately.

My grandmother had died when I was about four, and until Grandpa came across the country from Seattle to live with my mother in Maryland he'd been only a faint shadow in my life. While I was growing up, my father was in the Foreign Service and we lived on the East Coast or overseas in India. Grandpa visited us once when I was ten; we went to the White House but then he left to go back home.

That was the story of my life. People came and went, but no one ever stayed. Friends I had overseas returned to their home countries, and I never saw them again. I went to nine different schools before I graduated high school. Nine times I adjusted and made friends, and

Messages from Heaven

nine times they were gone.

So I was happy when Grandpa Macdonald came to stay, even though by then I was in my thirties, married, and on my own. I finally had more than just my immediate family; I had a link to the past.

After a year with my mother, Grandpa was diagnosed with cancer. He had an operation. When I visited him in the hospital, he said he'd had "hallucinations." In one, he'd been back in the Scottish Highlands. In another I'd brought him fresh cookies I'd baked. I smiled, glad I was part of something pleasant.

When the hospital released him, he was temporarily sent to a nursing home for additional care. When I arrived for a visit, I hardly recognized him. He had aged years in just days. The bed engulfed his small body, and the wheelchair the nurse put him in barely held him up. We talked for a couple of minutes and then I pushed him into the social area, away from his institutional room.

"You can watch TV here with other people," I said as I set the brakes on the wheelchair and pointed to the others sitting quietly in wheelchairs.

He shook his head. "I don't want to watch TV. I'm getting too old for this. I don't want to be here."

I smiled, hoping I looked reassuring and cheerful. "It won't be for long. I'll be back tomorrow." I felt terrible for abandoning him, but fled nonetheless.

That night I woke up about 3:00 a.m. Grandpa Macdonald sat next to my bed.

"I'm leaving," he said.

For some reason, I knew what he meant immediately. "No. I don't want you to die."

"It's time. Life's too hard. I just can't do it anymore."

"Please…" I begged.

He shook his head. "I'm tired. It's what I want."

Somehow, somewhere deep down, I knew this was the way it was supposed to be.

I wanted to reach out, but I didn't. I just nodded, accepting that he would be gone. Before I knew it, I was asleep.

The next morning the phone rang. It was my mother. "The nursing home called. Grandpa died during the night."

Ordinarily I would have felt a terrible emptiness because yet again someone had left me. But while I was sad, I knew in my heart it was okay. Grandpa and I had discussed everything in the early morning hours, when he came to me to say goodbye.

— Michele Ivy Davis —

Chapter 8

Let Hope In

Turned Messenger

The key to life is accepting challenges.
~Bette Davis

Every sense in my body was on high alert with sheer terror. I stood fully frozen, unable to look away while I watched a dark, monstrous wall of water coming toward me. I was in a building of some sort with giant windows. Maybe a hotel?

People I cared about were with me, but they were nameless. My feet betrayed me, frozen so that I couldn't turn and run away from the tidal wave. I stood there stunned, watching the water come and knowing I'd soon be pulled under.

Suddenly, I was awake, sweating, with my heart pounding and my mind racing.

The tsunami had first occurred in my dreams in high school. Though I can't remember that first nightmare, I remember that the waves came back to me uninvited throughout my teens and early twenties. Each time, I'd startle myself awake, trembling. The details were always a bit different, but the foreboding tidal waves that left me paralyzed were the same.

Somewhere along the line, I realized that dreams might hold meaning. They could be messages emerging from the subconscious to be interpreted. So, I sorted back through what I could remember, realizing that sometimes they had come just before the start of a new school year or other milestones, or when big work projects had loomed. The interpretation was obvious. The waves represented my feelings of

Let Hope In

fear and uncertainty when I was overwhelmed or stressed.

Every year or so, the tidal wave would come back for me. I'd find myself once again standing in some sort of a shelter with large glass windows or on a beach with buildings just behind me. It always felt sudden, like the light turned to darkness without warning, without a hint of storm clouds. I'd turn around from eating or laughing with some fuzzy yet familiar faces to see that giant wave suddenly appear.

When I entered working adulthood, the dreams came a few more times. My faith and self-awareness had deepened as I weathered the normal storms of life. Even still, I never thought much more of them than as a sign of stress. They were just something funny to share when a leader asked about recurring dreams during a group icebreaker.

Then, one time when the dream came back I decided to analyze it. What I unlocked was a sweet and weighty realization. I'd felt all the negative emotions but had missed a very important fact.

Those colossal waves had never actually overtaken me. Not once.

Though the dreams were scary and recurring, they never went past a stunned awareness that all that awful water was coming for me. Never was I washed away. Never did the dream end with me bobbing wildly, sinking, or gasping for gulps of air in rushing water. Never did I feel even a drop of water. Never once did I run.

That awareness left me with a whole new understanding: In hard situations, I needed to balance my feelings with facts. The fact of the dream was that though I stood before something powerful and potentially overwhelming, the bad ending never came. And the fact that I stood there frozen? That was a good thing, not a sign of weakness. I was merely recognizing that I couldn't fight off every hardship or stressor. To properly deal with them, I must face them first — with courage.

I felt a profound faith lesson. In this life, I might have to feel all kinds of uncomfortable feelings, but I'd never be overcome.

As it turned out, those scary waves held all kinds of wisdom for me. From then on, I viewed those walls of water as a gift. They reminded me to balance out my feelings with facts. They encouraged me to deal with challenges by facing them. And they reassured me that no matter what comes, I'll never be overcome.

I haven't had that dream in years, but it stays with me still, a nightmare turned messenger.

— Rebecca Radicchi —

Balloons of Hope

In your unfailing love you will lead the people you have redeemed. In your strength you will guide them to your holy dwelling.
~Exodus 15:13

"Okay. One, two, three, let them go!" I shouted. Sue's three young children, Stephanie, Kristen and Billy, released the purple balloons covered with messages of love.

It was a cold March afternoon. A misty rain fell as we stood in Sue's driveway to mark the second anniversary of her passing. The dismal weather reflected how I felt in my heart, but I mustered up a smile for the children's sake. My twin sister Sue, just forty-one years old, had died suddenly, leaving behind her children and her husband Bill.

Just yesterday, while chatting with my friend, I mentioned Sue's upcoming anniversary. Mary, who knew firsthand the heartache of loss after the passing of her ten-year-old son John, offered me an idea.

"For John's birthday we write messages to him on balloons. Then we release them."

I headed for the store and bought three purple balloons, since purple was Sue's favorite color.

Now here I stood watching the balloons leave the little hands that held them so tightly. Privately, before liftoff, I read many of the messages. They tugged at my heart. *I miss you, Mommy. To my loving wife, all my love. We love you Aunt Suzy.* And the one I added, using her nickname: *I miss you Twinpop!*

Filled with anticipation, we watched as the balloons were released. Immediately, they drifted down onto the driveway. It was too cold. Realizing my mistake, I thought I should have waited for a nicer day. I prayed, "Please God help us!"

Suddenly, the wind kicked up. I held my breath as the balloons slowly lifted. Two floated up past the trees to the sky, but the third wedged itself between two branches. "Uh oh," Sue's youngest, Billy, exclaimed. "It's going to pop!" Sue's husband, Bill, and I looked at each other.

"Oh boy," he whispered. Again I prayed, "Please God don't let them pop!"

The kids began to cheer for the one lone purple balloon. Slowly, it began to creep out of its trap, bobbing along the prickly branches until it made its way to freedom. "Go! Go! Go!" the kids shouted. We let out a collective sigh as we watched the balloon finally edge its way around the trees, miraculously not popping. It then took off to catch up with the other two and sailed out of sight. "Thank you God," I offered silently. I looked around at all the smiles and I knew somewhere in heaven, Sue was smiling too.

A week later, my youngest, Caroline, was upstairs. She looked out her bedroom window, then called to me, "Mommy, there is a purple balloon out back. Is it the one we sent Aunt Suzy?"

I glanced out the kitchen window and spotted a purple balloon bouncing on the grass. I walked out the back door to take a closer look. As I approached, the balloon took off through my neighbor's yard, with me in my pajamas chasing after it. Finally, I grabbed the purple balloon. It looked identical to the ones we sent, minus the messages. Hmm. What a coincidence. I brought the balloon into our house. Caroline asked, "Mommy, did Aunt Suzy send you that balloon?"

"I wouldn't doubt it, Caroline," I answered with a smile.

That same spring my mom became very sick. After a series of mini strokes she was weak and confused and could no longer live alone. She soon developed dementia. I prayed daily as I placed Mom's name on several nursing home waiting lists. I knew they could care for her in a way I could not physically do.

Months passed and my mom continued to decline. It had been a frustrating afternoon of phone calls to nursing homes, agencies and family. After one particular phone call ended with an abrupt "no," tears filled my eyes. I was exhausted. Between dealing with the loss of my twin sister and now the concern I felt for my mom, I was overwhelmed emotionally, physically and spiritually. Wiping away my tears, I grabbed my coat and called to my kids, "I am going for a walk."

It had started to snow. As I walked, the snowflakes mingled with my tears. I talked to my sister and prayed to God. "Please God, help me! Sue, what am I going to do?" I thought about the past two years and wondered how much more I could handle. Where would I get the strength to continue?

As I turned the corner, I noticed the snow and wind beginning to pick up. But it was not all I noticed. On my neighbor's front lawn, one purple balloon gently bobbed up and down in the snow. I could not believe it. My heart lifted. The purple balloon again. I knew the days ahead would be tough but I was encouraged knowing I was not handling this alone.

On Christmas morning, my mom had a seizure and was admitted to the hospital. Ten days later, she was stabilized and scheduled for discharge. She was now blind in one eye and could no longer feed herself or walk. In addition, she was confused most of the time. Mom needed round-the-clock care. The hospital found a temporary placement for her fifteen miles away. After she was admitted, I gradually realized it was a terrible nursing home.

Once I found her asleep with her face lying in a full plate of food. She often looked disheveled, unclean and isolated. At first I thought, "Maybe they are just understaffed today. Or perhaps the staff is still getting her into a routine." But soon it became clear I had to get her out of that place.

I was filled with guilt; I could not physically care for her myself. At this point I couldn't even lift her. I begged God, "Please find her another place. Sue, watch over her." Then I began my futile search for a new nursing home.

On my birthday, I drove over to see my mom. I thought back to happier days and all the celebrations my mom, Sue and I had shared on this special day. Turning into the parking lot, my joyful birthday memories were soon clouded with concern for Mom.

Saddened, I entered her room. There underneath her shabby metal-framed bed, was a purple balloon. I was stunned! "Mom, where did you get that purple balloon?" I asked in astonishment.

"I don't know," she answered. "Someone gave it to me this morning." I smiled.

A few weeks later, at work, my boss asked, "How are things with your mom?"

"Not good," I responded. "She is still on waiting lists for a better nursing home."

"My grandmother lived at Pembrooke for years. It was great!" a coworker chimed in.

I had never heard of Pembrooke, but I made a call. Miraculously a room was available.

My mom was being transferred by ambulance. I planned to be there when she arrived. Driving up the pike, I was so nervous. "Is this a nice place, Lord?" I kept watch for the new nursing home. But it was easy to spot.

Tied to the post just across from the Pembrooke sign was one lone purple balloon.

— Donna Teti —

Blessed Bloom

*There are always flowers for those
who want to see them.*
~Henri Matisse

Green thumbs run in my family, on my mother's side. It shouldn't be a surprise, I guess. Her father used to operate a greenhouse.

We kids grew up playing on lush green Ohio grass, lined with long, colorful rose and iris beds that separated the back yards in our neighborhood. When Mom planted something, it usually grew.

The acorns didn't fall far from that oak, and we children turned out to love the earth and growing things in it, too. As adults, we appreciate all our mom's labor-intensive gardening work, applaud each other's gardening successes, and commiserate about the frustrations of chipmunks that eat our strawberries or deer that strip our lilies.

All four of Mom's children are also remarkably healthy, just as she was. I have a theory that gardening is good for people. Working outside and putting our hands in the dirt to help plants thrive is therapeutic. Nurturing others (things and people) is symbiotic and, in turn, nurtures us. A vase of fresh daisies on the kitchen table, raised and picked right outside our door, is good for the soul.

I have always been the healthiest person I know, along with my mother. And grateful for it. While others come down with pneumonia or need knee surgery, I just get a light cold once every four or five years. I had perfect attendance at school and work most years.

That was until last year, when my good fortune hit a wall. A biopsy confirmed a small stage-1 lump. It was caught early and, luckily, removed in a lumpectomy (although it took two surgeries). But, to prevent it from coming back, the doctors recommended both chemotherapy and radiation. These kept me in treatments and drugs for six months and left me devoid of hair, white blood cells, and strength. But there was nothing to do but put one foot in front of the other, take one day at a time, and pray that it would all go away. I was well aware that millions of women have had to deal with the shock and trauma of breast cancer. You have to try to stay positive, even when it seems impossible, I decided.

But between the surgeries and the first chemo treatment, a sudden shocking diagnosis of type 2 diabetes landed me in the emergency room. I hadn't known much about diabetes but soon learned that I would need medicine the rest of my life. And that I could no longer eat most foods I like — or just two bites of them — or my blood sugar would soar.

That new development was exacerbated by the chemo treatments nearly shutting down my taste buds, so that even foods I have always loved didn't taste good and the mere smell of others — like fish cooking — set my stomach rolling. Queasiness from the chemo made eating tentative at best. And add to this the daily pricking of my fingers, bleeding myself to monitor my blood glucose.

With this double whammy of diabetes and chemotherapy, I quickly lost twenty-five pounds. I had no hair, and my bones were easily visible under my skin.

The doctors had predicted that I would come through it all fine, since I was such a healthy, active person to begin with. But they also warned me about fatigue. I hadn't worried about that too much, though, because of my normal energy and stamina. It was sick people who suffered from fatigue, I figured.

But the doctors were right. Even though my husband had taken over nearly every chore — grocery shopping, cooking dinner, cleaning up, laundry — I was exhausted by dinnertime and in bed by 8:00 P.M. wearing a soft, fleece sleep cap to keep my bald head warm. The diabetes kept me needing something to eat at least five times a day, so I was either hungry or queasy most of the time. Or both.

And depressed. How much I had lost astounded me, even though the surgery had been successful. My active life was gone. I had to leave volunteer activities and a part-time job and still didn't have enough energy to walk around a short block. I felt out of the loop and spent way too much time on the couch. And the doctor appointments! I typically saw the doctor once a year at my annual checkup. Like most healthy people, I suspect, I begrudged that time and hassle because I was always fine. In the eight months following the biopsy, though, I had surgery, a treatment, or a doctor's appointment fifty-five times. This was enough to keep a normally super-healthy person despondent nearly 24/7.

But one pleasure of my previous normal life did not disappear. Every morning, especially in the spring and summer, I like to walk around our yard and see how my flowers and crops are faring. Watching things grow is a tonic and helps reassure me that life goes on, no matter what.

When the daily radiation treatments were nearly finished, what was left of me was still standing, and I hoped that I had survived the worst of it. One Saturday on my morning perambulation, something new caught my eye. It was standing at the front corner of the garage where I couldn't miss it. An iris! One beautiful, blue-and-yellow iris was smiling at me. I had meant to plant irises for years because my mother had blue-and-yellow irises that I loved growing along our driveway when we were kids, but I hadn't gotten around to it.

This wondrous iris—that I had not planted—immediately brought my mom to me at this lowest point in my life, both physically and mentally. I knew she was there, and with tears rolling down my cheeks and a catch in my throat, I said, "Thanks, Mom. I'll be all right."

How to explain this sentimental, unplanted blossom appearing in my garden as if by magic? I like to think it was a message of blooming hope and strength from my mom up in heaven, watching over me with an "attagirl" smile. I could hear her voice saying, "You've survived. Many people don't. Think how lucky you are! No matter how hard things get, always be grateful for your blessings." And I am, especially for the one that's easy to take for granted: good health.

— Becky S. Tompkins —

Dinner with My Dad

Confidence is half the victory.
~Yiddish Proverb

My late father was a complex man who died more than two decades ago. In many ways, I'm still trying to get to know him; the true bonding moments we shared were few and far between. One conversation will always stand out in my mind, as it not only represents who he truly was but who I am to this day.

The third of four siblings raised by hard-working Russian immigrants, Dad grew up in the Bronx during the Depression. As an adult, he survived Japanese air raids on the 58th United States Naval Construction Battalion (Seabees) in the South Pacific during World War II; the tragic capsizing of party fishing boat, *Pelican*, which killed dozens of men, women, and children just off Long Island's Montauk Point on Labor Day of 1951; as well as the numerous challenges of building and sustaining a successful New York City-based fur-manufacturing business that served loyal customers for more than forty years.

Worldly and well-read, his self-acquired knowledge made him very opinionated and, on occasion, a bit of a bully. But Dad easily held his own in discussions on almost any subject despite never having attended college. He lived with an assortment of personal demons — some quite obvious and others, for the most part, left unspoken — but I admired his strength, courage, and ability to press on even through the most difficult circumstances.

Happy to share his positive life outlook with anyone he encountered, my father was always able to cheer me on to complete any task or overcome any obstacle. I was his firstborn, and he expected a lot from me.

Whether I was learning to ride a bike, baking his favorite cookies, or completing a tough homework assignment, I tried to make him proud. No matter what I confronted, "Tomorrow will be a better day" were the words he repeated to me hundreds if not thousands of times.

In my mid-twenties, living in Manhattan and still trying to figure out what I wanted to do with my life, I found myself between jobs due to a difficult economic downturn. Even though I lived in a modest apartment on the Upper West Side, money was tight.

When my father called one morning to invite me out for dinner, I almost declined. But I will always be grateful that I pulled myself together and joined him that evening.

It wasn't the restaurant's great Szechuan menu and bustling ambience. It wasn't the hundred-dollar bill that Dad always managed to slip into my pocket "just to help out" every time he saw me. What changed my life and entire perspective were the words he said to me as we sat in his huge Buick outside my building when he finally drove me home.

"What's really got you down, honey?" he asked.

I looked at him with tears in my eyes and said, "I feel so poor."

Hugging me to his side, he lifted my chin with one finger and told me, "You aren't poor at all. You may be broke, but you aren't poor. Broke means you don't have any money, but poor means you don't have any hope."

I still get choked up every time I share those wise words with others.

There have been more hard times and plenty of other hurdles in my life since that cold winter night, but I've never forgotten the lesson my father taught me. Hope has kept me going through thick, thin, and even thinner. Thanks to that dinner with my dad, I know it always will.

— Jane R. Snyder —

My Mother the Bag Lady

You can never guarantee you'll be the smartest person in the room, but there is no excuse for not being the most prepared.
~Brendan Paddick

I picked up the soft black and white tote bag and touched my face. If only I could kiss the owner one more time. Sorting out my mother's things after her death at age ninety overwhelmed me. Now what would I do with this bag with "Gladys" boldly written in red letters?

My mother loved purses and tote bags. As a child I would ask, "Do you have…?" Mom would dig into her leather purse that held Life Savers, tissues, pencils, paper, and safety pins. A piece of string and rubber bands were essential tools to have on hand. The purse even held a small sewing kit.

Some people might look at the black and white bag and say, "It's just a tote bag," but it was filled with memories for me. I remembered walking down the halls with "Gladys" on my arm. Weekly it went back and forth with me to the assisted living facility with drugstore items, extra snacks, and other things that Mom requested. The large size enabled me to bring clothes and toiletries during her frequent hospital stays. Now the treasured tote made me cry. I put it in a drawer to decide its fate later.

My memories of my mom seemed to revolve around bags. Earlier in my life, a bag held Sunday school teacher's lessons or minutes of the neighborhood garden club meetings. Another one held the Girl Scout leader's handbook and supplies to my childhood weekly scout group.

My mother, an artist, carried a green one that contained a small sketchpad, two artist pencils, and a separate eraser. She might find a cute dog, a small creek, or a beautiful flower to draw along the way. The sketch would later become an oil or watercolor painting.

My parents eventually moved into a senior retirement community in my city. Weekly, a red bag with black monogram initials accompanied her for phone duty at the senior complex. Mom could easily be entertained with a crossword puzzle or book — both of which she kept handy.

She loved to knit and demonstrated it by making gifts for the family. A bag with the logo of the senior complex contained knitting projects. Several seniors knitted blankets for the patients at St. Jude Children's Research Hospital in Memphis, Tennessee. Mom knitted hundreds of hats in multiple designs and colors. When she and the other knitters were featured on a local news program, Mom proudly showed off some of the finished hats.

When Mom started using a walker, she attached a black bag in front. On doctor visits it held a large-print book or a Kindle, which her granddaughter updated regularly. And let's not forget the small box of tissues, breath mints, a tablet of paper, pencil, water bottle, reading glasses, and sunglasses that filled the black bag.

Wherever she went as Gladys, Mom, or Grandma, my mother was ready. I seem to have inherited the trait. One year on a trip with two friends, I took twice as much luggage as they did combined. When I mentioned it, they answered, "We know when we travel with you, we can pack light because you bring everything we need." Or the time I went overseas and took an extra disposable camera — just in case. On the second day one of my fellow traveler's camera broke. And who came to the rescue? My closets contain many totes in colors and sizes that I have used in my own activities and trips. My mother taught me well.

One afternoon, I opened a drawer and saw the black and white bag again, still waiting for me to decide its fate. For several weeks I had been busy with the affairs of Mom's estate and I had forgotten about it. I pulled the bag out and gently ran my fingers down the sides. And then I felt something hard inside, something I hadn't noticed before. I pulled out a small golden pair of clip-on earrings in the shape of angels.

How did they get in there? I vaguely remembered them with all the other clip-on earrings months ago in Mom's jewelry box. Goosebumps ran up my arms. Sensing a heavenly connection, I could almost hear my mother say, "See, I was prepared for my final trip."

A black and white bag with gold earrings will be treasured in remembrance of the best bag lady I ever knew — my mother.

— Sharilynn Hunt —

The Boxes in the Basement

*If the whole world were put into one scale,
and my mother in the other, the whole
world would kick the beam.*
~Henry Bickersteth

We all have heroes, mentors, and people who have influenced us, encouraged us, and motivated us to reach new heights. Some of my personal heroes include political figures like Sir Winston Churchill, Thomas Jefferson, Abraham Lincoln, and Ronald Reagan. Some are sports stars like Peyton Manning, Walter Payton, Michael Jordan, and Pat Tillman. My other heroes and mentors are mostly people you do not know. One of them is named Gwen. She was my mother.

My journey began during an afternoon of spring-cleaning in my basement. It was late April, the week before Mother's Day 2015, when I was surveying the treasure trove of stuff that had collected over the years. As I began sorting through various artifacts and relics I had been hoarding, I encountered two tattered cardboard boxes. I suddenly recalled that I had inherited them from my late father four years before. I had never looked inside them.

My curiosity and anticipation were childlike as I rummaged through each box, realizing at some point that this "stuff" had belonged to my mom. The actual cardboard boxes themselves are not relevant. It was the small miracle that I found in one of them that changed my life. It reconnected me with my mom, who had died twenty years earlier.

There were pieces of costume jewelry, stuffed animals, old photographs, miscellaneous personal belongings, and a red spiral notebook in those boxes. I did not open the little red notebook at first and tossed it to the side as I continued to reflect upon my mom. Each item I found in these cardboard boxes brought back several memories of her. However, it was that little red notebook that kept speaking to me, so I finally opened it.

My mom had always been active and healthy. However, on Mother's Day in 1994 she appeared pale, fatigued, and very fragile. After a few weeks of doctor visits and tests, we got the bad news.

As I thumbed through the yellowing, discolored pages of that little red notebook, I realized I was reading Mom's cancer journal. She was reaching out to me, knowing that someday I would read her journal. She was still giving me advice, encouragement, strength, and motivation through her words.

Mom was an integral part of her patient groups and would often give support and advice to other patients who had little hope or faith in recovery. Mom always said you should not underestimate your power to influence others.

Mom reflected in her journal that the time you have to impact others and influence their lives is limited by the time you have here on earth. Mom was leading and influencing others even during a time when she was fighting for her own life.

Through all of the pain and mental anguish of chemotherapy, Mom wrote in her journal about the importance of keeping the faith and having confidence so that others would not lose hope. My mom found inspiration in the saying, "When you allow your confidence to shine, you unconsciously permit others to do the same."

Although Mom knew what she was up against with her future chemo treatments, she never lost her sense of humor or her positive outlook. She never stopped planning for the future and setting goals for herself, and that was evident in the pages of her journal, even though she got sicker and sicker as the year went on.

Unfortunately, I was on a business trip when my mother lost her battle. I had seen her two days before, at least, but I didn't get to say my official "goodbye" and tell her how much she meant to me on her final day. Her lessons have stuck with me, and I try to be as positive as she was and not let anyone's negativity define me. Mom would always say, "Someone else's perception of you does not have to become your reality."

That was my mom — a real role model.

— Skip Myers —

Surprise! You're Getting Married

*Love isn't something you find.
Love is something that finds you.*
~Loretta Young

My mother kept asking me why I didn't find some nice young man and settle down. At age twenty-two I hardly felt that was a priority. But, because she married at age seventeen, I guess that a twenty-two-year-old daughter who didn't date seemed rather odd to her.

I was happy in my career as an administrative assistant and was considering ways to get a promotion. I wasn't even sure that I wanted to get married. Finally, my mother asked one too many times. I replied rather forcefully, "I don't have to go out and beat the bushes for a husband. When the time is right, he's going to come right up and knock on my door." Mom must have finally gotten my message, because she quit bugging me about it.

Three months later, I had the strangest experience. I woke up one day and found myself saying, "Prepare, for within six months you'll be married." I was mulling this over when I started having thoughts about a specific man, a man I had never met who I seemed to have conjured up, complete with random facts about him. I was so taken aback by this that for several days I could hardly concentrate on my job.

A month after that I called a high school friend, Theresa, whom I kept in touch with, and asked if I could come over and tell her about my premonition or whatever it was. She and I always loved talking about weird things that happened to us, but this time I was sure she would think I was delusional.

I told Theresa everything, starting with the mysterious six-month timetable. "I kept having all these facts bombarding my mind. He has deep blue eyes and a smile that could melt your heart. He loves the outdoors, hunting, fishing, hiking, camping, anything outdoors. He has something to do with Colorado." This didn't sound at all like a man I would marry, because I was definitely not the outdoors type. "He's athletic and loves all kinds of sports." Again, that's not me! I don't have an athletic muscle in my body. "He loves reading and has lots of books. He wants a wife who can cook, sew, keep house, loves kids, and is a strong Christian." That was more like me. I continued, "He's quite a bit older than me, but doesn't look it. And, he drives a little blue sports car." Then, I sat and waited for her to burst out laughing.

I wasn't prepared at all for what Theresa said. "I know that man! He's exactly like that and he goes to my church! He's hunting in Colorado right now. And he just bought a little blue sports car!" She had a shocked look on her face.

"You're kidding!" I exclaimed.

"No, and he desperately wants a Christian wife who wants to raise a family, loves cooking and sewing, and would enjoy his library with him. And," she said, "I think that he said he's in his thirties. He sure doesn't look it."

At this point, I was staring at her, not knowing what to say. "Okay, you're serious, aren't you?"

"You've got to come to church and meet him as soon as he comes back." So, we planned our assault on poor, unsuspecting Lyle.

A few weeks later, I went to church with her and her family. Even though she had not described how he looked, I spotted him in a church of about one hundred people. I just felt like I should be sitting next to that man. When I met him face to face, his smile melted my heart. Of course, Theresa agreed to keep my secret.

A few weeks later, Lyle called and asked me for a date. When he came to our front door and knocked, I told my mother, "That will be my husband." Since I had not told her about my premonition, she just laughed at me.

Although I didn't tell Lyle about my experience until months later, he said that he felt like he had known me all his life. I felt the same. He asked me to marry him. Five months after my strange experience, and five weeks after our first date, we were married. I always wanted wedding bells to ring on my wedding day, but the church didn't have bells. So, I asked God to fill the trees with birds and have them all singing. Lyle thought that was funny and not likely to happen because it was February. But we had a beautiful spring-like day for our wedding and the trees were filled with birds singing joyously, which had everybody talking. God gave us his wedding bells.

On our honeymoon, Lyle told me how his friends had tried to fix him up over the years, but it never worked out. As he told me about a co-worker who tried to get her cousin to go on a date with him six years earlier, I realized that co-worker was my cousin and I was the girl who wouldn't go out with Lyle on a blind date!

Then he told me that he once knew a waitress who had taken in a single woman as a roommate. He invited her to bring her roommate and attend a concert with him. She tried, but her roommate didn't want to go, so she brought another friend. We were dumbfounded when we realized that I was that roommate.

Lyle told me about another set-up that hadn't worked out. He was expected for dinner at a friend's house, when a single woman dropped in on them unexpectedly, just an hour before he was scheduled. They invited her to stay for dinner, but she decided not to, because she didn't want to be considered a blind date. I was that woman!

Three times over the course of six years I nearly met Lyle. I guess I needed a more direct push to finally meet him. We enjoyed thirty-three years of marriage, and had two children and eight grandchildren. My soul mate and best friend died of cancer on Easter Sunday at home, with our daughter and me by his side. I greatly look forward to meeting him again and being by his side forever.

— Rebecca Gurnsey —

A Matter of Hours

Impossible situations can become possible miracles.
~Robert H. Schuller

It was nothing more than a plaster five-and-dime-store nativity, but to me it was as perfect as fine china. During the Christmas season, I loved nothing more than rearranging it over and over, moving animals closer to Baby Jesus or positioning the angels to keep a careful watch over the tiny figurine in swaddling clothes. I remember the glow on my mother's face as she'd turn from the kitchen sink to see me at the piano, strategically placing the sheep in a circle around the shepherd or arranging the three wisemen in a triangle as they carried their precious gifts to the manger.

The small figurines had belonged to my dad's grandparents, and I was touched when the nativity was given to me the January I moved into my first apartment. My mother was boxing up the Christmas decorations when I stopped for a visit. She placed the aged pink shoebox in my hands and told me she wanted me to have the family heirloom I loved so much as a child. I was getting married that September and moving to Massachusetts, and she wanted to ensure I would have the set to display the following Christmas. I lived in the upstairs apartment of a home owned by two very kind senior citizens who lived downstairs, and they generously allowed me space in the attic to store items. That is where the pink shoebox containing my childhood treasure was safely tucked away.

Our first Christmas as husband and wife came, and I couldn't wait to decorate our tiny apartment. We purchased a table-top tree and a few decorations to brighten our home. I began searching the closet where items I'd brought from home were stored, but I couldn't find the pink shoebox that held my treasured nativity. A great sadness poured over me as I realized I must have left it in the attic of my apartment in Pennsylvania. I called my landlord and she agreed to look for the missing box. Only a few minutes passed before she returned to the phone to report she couldn't find it. I felt confident it was there, but pleading my case got me nowhere. I was devastated.

A few years later, we moved back to my hometown in Pennsylvania. As Christmases came and went, I reflected on the memory of my simple nativity. I wondered if my daughters would have loved it as much as I did, and I visualized them arranging and rearranging it as I had.

Thirty-four years had gone by since I left my apartment when I picked up the morning newspaper one day and saw my landlord's husband's name in the obituaries. His wife had passed away long before him, and now they were both gone. Immediately, panic set in. What if my nativity was still tucked away in the corner of the attic? What if the house was put up for sale, and all the contents were cleared out? I would never see my beloved family heirloom again.

My head was spinning when a name popped into my mind. Of course! The name was that of my landlord's grandson's wife. She was close to my age, and I vaguely knew her in high school. Maybe she could tell me what was to become of the house. Perhaps she could solve the mystery of the missing pink shoebox.

I quickly found her on social media and sent a message spilling out the whole story of the lost nativity. In no time at all, I got a response stating her son was moving into the house, and he was in the process of cleaning out the contents. She was more than happy to have him look through the items he had ready to donate to a charitable organization.

The next day, I received another message from her. She believed her son had located the missing box. The anticipation I felt as I drove to the house was almost overwhelming, and my hand was shaking as I reached for the doorbell. A young man came to the door, and I identified myself. He politely asked me to wait while he went to another room to retrieve what he suspected belonged to me. As he returned, he was clutching a familiar pink shoebox. I nearly gasped at the sight of it, and I profusely thanked him. He told me it was a good thing I hadn't waited any longer; the box was just hours away from becoming a charitable donation.

I loaded my precious pink package into the car and joyfully transported it home where I sat down on my living-room floor and gently opened the lid. There it was, each piece wrapped in tissues just the way my mother had given it to me that January day so long ago. Tears streamed down my face as I unwrapped the delicate figurines, smiling at each one the way one would smile when reunited with an old friend. After the tearful reunion, I mindfully placed my precious nativity in a safe place in my own home, never to be abandoned again.

Every Christmas since that day, my beautiful treasure has been placed in a spot that can easily be reached by my young granddaughter. I derive such joy from watching sheep being herded, angels watching over the Baby Jesus, and the wisemen bearing gifts — from whatever position she chooses.

— Tamara Bell —

Chapter 9

Faith in Action

Escape from Hell

*Answer me when I call to you, O my righteous God.
Give me relief from my distress; be merciful
to me and hear my prayer.*
~Psalm 4:1

"Engine 18, respond to 1637 East 16th Avenue. Report of a fire. Time out 1935."

Cap was away. Brad was in charge. He and I were eleven-year vets. Greg was the rookie.

The address was close by. If there was indeed a working fire, we'd have to handle it. Help would be a while arriving.

At the scene, I noticed brown smoke wafting from the rear roof area of an old yellow two-story house. It appeared to be a bedroom fire. The residents assured us everyone was out. As Brad radioed our situation, Greg got ready to fight his first, for real, house fire.

I entered and climbed the stairs, stopping short of the landing. With my face at floor level, I looked down the hall… two doorways on the right and a closed door at the end. Smoke had banked down about a third of the way. I took a mental snapshot.

Back at the front door, Brad was ready to make entry. Greg was still nervously making gear adjustments. I saw myself in him. I knew he'd be telling this story one day. Without Cap, there was no time for the usual training. We needed to knock this fire down and out. I took the line that would guide us back out from Greg. "Get your mask on and let's go."

Smoke darkened all but a foot from the floor now. Visibility grew worse and heat increased as we moved forward. The door at the end of the hallway had no knob—something was lurking—waiting to pounce. I removed a glove and touched the door. It was plenty hot. We could hear fire consuming the house around us.

Brad hollered, "Get ready, I'm gonna kick it in."

On my knees with Greg in tow, I yelled, "Ready; do it!"

One hard kick set the door ajar. Angry flames reached through. One more thrust and the door flew open.

I leaned in and opened the nozzle full blast. The volume of water should have choked the fire, but it raged on, roaring about my head. "Force yourself to hold and fight this beast," I thought. My head was in the mouth of this dragon and it was about to bite down when the life force within possessed me and I bolted back. "I've got to get out. Get out! Get out!" I commanded.

I left the nozzle running in the doorway. Through my ear tabs and hood my ears were burning and the penetrating heat was taking my breath. When I bolted, I sent Greg rolling like a billiard ball into a side pocket.

Out of the flames and perhaps ten feet down the hallway, I was in total darkness. At that point I heard a desperate voice cry out, "No, No, No!" One of my buddies was charging me to come back because the hose was doing the job, or one of them was in trouble. I turned and after a few steps was back in the blinding flames.

Then the building exploded.

For a second everything went bright white, then slammed together again with a fierce shudder. Orange and black spun like a tornado. The explosion ruptured my store of strength and erased my mental image of the interior. I hadn't come in contact with anyone on my return. I instinctively knew I had to use what energy I could muster to get out of the bowels of this monster.

One step and I ran into the wall. The explosion had turned me sideways.

A hurried over-correction caused me to run into the opposite wall.

My helmet was falling off because it was melting and the straps

Faith in Action

had burned off. As I grabbed for it, I collapsed. I knew I had only seconds to live if I couldn't get out immediately. I thought, "Where's the way out?" An answer followed. "You're not getting out. You might as well take your mask off and die in a hurry."

I tried to ward off that enemy, but gave out after crawling just a few feet.

Pressed against the right side wall, all I could see was the raging orange and black storm.

All I could hear was the victory roar of the dragon.

All I could feel was my flesh burning.

Like a View-Master picture wheel, the face of my pretty wife rolled before me. I said, "Find our little boy a father. He'll need a man in his life. I love you." Then my older son to whom I said, "Go to college. It's all prepared for you." Next my sweet little girl; we smiled and exchanged love eye to eye. Lastly my little buddy. "I'll always love you, Buddy."

I knew my face piece would melt any second, but my thought was, "I'm not dead yet." My training reminded me that I had an obligation to fight to survive.

I'd had other training as well. As I pushed myself to hands and knees, I drew a hot labored breath and uttered the name, "Jesus!"

In that instant the roaring ceased. The terror dissipated. The pain dissolved. The fear vanished.

Despite the dragon's blazing rage, I was at total peace.

A soothing voice spoke, "Over here," and I began crawling in that direction. As if someone lifted the corner of a curtain, the fury of orange and black turned into white light. I lunged into the light and found myself sliding down the stairs and rolling out the door.

My crew doused me with water and with my first breath of fresh air I exhaled, "Thank you Jesus!"

Brad and Greg had followed my command and crawled out following the line. Once outside and seeing I wasn't there, the same loyalty that drew me back in for him, drew Brad back in for me. He was trying to scale up the stairs at the same moment I was sliding down them. But he neither heard nor saw me rolling out. Back outside, he was astonished to see me. He approached and said, "Herm, I thought we bought it that time."

We soon learned that the fire was a work of arson that started in the basement. I had only been throwing water through the top of the flames. When the first firefighter of the next company opened the back door and stepped inside, he fell through the floor and hurt his back. As his buddy pulled him out of the flaming hole, the back pain had caused him to cry out, "No, No, No!" The rush of air from that back door being opened fed the fire and caused the explosion.

With my burns and bandages, my wife didn't recognize me, but my escape from hell was just a part of my miracle. My healing was swift. Only skin grafts on my arms reveal I was ever burned. It's the badge of the good Lord's miracle that saved me.

— Herchel E. Newman —

A Miracle in Greece

"Because he loves me," says the Lord, "I will rescue him; I will protect him, for he acknowledges my name."
~Psalm 91:13-15

My friend Steve lived on the East Coast but traveled regularly to Minnesota for business. During one trip, he was dining at his favorite Greek restaurant there when he noticed a waitress staring curiously at him. He engaged her in conversation and learned she was from a small town in northern Greece.

"That's exactly where my twin brother Tom is!" he exclaimed. "He's a Fulbright scholar studying Greek Orthodox icons there."

"I know. I recognized you as Tom's brother as soon as you walked in." She had just returned from an extended visit to her hometown in Greece, where she had met Tom at a local bookstore.

Steve believed things happen for a reason and a few weeks later he learned the reason for his coincidental meeting with the Greek waitress. He was back home on the East Coast when he received word that Tom was severely injured in Greece.

Tom had been walking down a rugged, seldom-used path, near a Byzantine monastery on Mt. Athos. It was the day of the feast of the Ascension of the Virgin Mary in the Greek Orthodox religion. Suddenly, the path, formed by a long-gone waterfall, crumbled and he plunged about a hundred and fifty feet, halfway down a cliff face of the mountain. Tom was knocked unconscious and when he came

Faith in Action

to he saw blood everywhere. Bones stuck out of his left arm. One of his legs was caught in a thorny bush and the other leg hung over the edge of the cliff.

Groggily he tried to determine what was preventing him from falling further. He became aware that he was being cradled on the crimson-colored shoulder of a woman, her arm wrapped around his midsection. He recognized the colors from his study of icons; the Virgin Mary was portrayed wearing crimson. Tom closed his eyes. When he reopened them he was surrounded by a brilliant white light that vanished after a moment.

Severely injured and in mortal danger, he was unable to move. He could see the tops of trees below him and began considering his options. After some time he began to despair. He was tempted to throw himself off the edge of the cliff and put an end to his suffering. No one would ever find him in that remote place.

A booming voice inside his gut responded adamantly to that temptation. "Oh no you don't! Who do you think you are that you can decide your own fate?"

Inspired, an incredible, uncontrollable survival instinct kicked in and he found the strength to crawl back onto the ledge, away from the cliff.

Tom survived the next three days on toothpaste, moss, and a handful of chickpeas and raisins. For water he pressed the damp soil between his fingers, and then licked his hands to quench his severe thirst. The raisins expanded from the morning dew and provided a tiny amount of additional liquid. He conserved his energy by yelling only when he heard a boat arriving at or departing from the coastline far below. During the darkness of night, his mind filled with the faces of everyone he had ever loved. He visualized those people handing him food and drink; he imagined himself thanking them for helping him survive.

Finally, on the third day, Tom's cries for help were heard. In dramatic and dangerous fashion, Greek villagers, monks, and an experienced rescue team arrived and carried him to safety.

The tending physicians diagnosed a broken collarbone and cervical vertebrae, a partially dislocated shoulder, bruised ribs and a severely injured left arm. They said it was a miracle that, despite his arm being shattered in thirty-two places, there was no infection, nerve damage or cut arteries.

When Steve heard of his brother's accident and the severity of his injuries, he was concerned about the limited medical care Tom might receive in that remote part of Greece. He recalled the Greek waitress he had recently met and she referred him to a wonderful local Greek doctor who helped nurse his brother back to health.

Though his recuperation was difficult, Tom knew it was a miracle that Mother Mary had been his first rescuer that day.

But that was not to be the last miracle.

During his recovery, Tom came across a series of twenty-two paintings he had drawn months before the accident. He had titled them "Out of Darkness." The paintings showed in progression a silhouetted person falling off the edge of something, then sprawling on a platform. The person went from a dark to light form as the scenes unfolded. When Tom had painted them, his intention was to portray life as a pre-game warm up, an interim step toward the end result, which is death and then eternal life. In reviewing these paintings after the accident, he was stunned by the striking similarity to his accident. Perhaps God had been trying to get his attention and he had not been listening. At the time of the drawings, Tom was in a spiritual abyss, depressed and feeling alienated from God.

During his recuperation, he experienced an explosion of personal and spiritual growth. Filled with faith, hope and charity, he aligned himself with those who suffer around the world. He knows he is never alone. God is always with him.

Tom does not view his accident as something "bad." He now believes everything happens for a reason. As he says, "We just need to be ready to listen and act on the messages we receive."

— Mary Treacy O'Keefe —

The Check

Courage is being afraid but going on anyhow.
~Dan Rather

At age forty-eight, after twenty-nine years of marriage, I was a widow with four sons at home. Tom died after a long battle with cancer. At the end, I bent down, kissed his forehead and whispered, "It's okay, you can go." It was the permission he needed to leave us and end his suffering.

We believed we had taken care of most of the details associated with his death. I had the necessary account information to handle paperwork for Social Security, life insurance, retirement accounts, and the tedious, time-consuming tasks of becoming a single mom. At least that's what we thought.

In the aftermath of numbness, I began the process of filling out forms, sending for copies of the death certificate, and making appointments to "prove" that my husband was gone and life as we knew it was forever changed.

However, one evening as I looked through the information for a rather large, work-related life insurance policy, I found myself a little alarmed. This policy required my husband's membership in an organization that he had belonged to for ten years. The membership fee was paid annually by Tom's employer.

But what I saw in the folder was an invoice Tom had received for the membership fee. He had copied it and passed on to his employer for payment. I would need to contact them for proof of payment.

The next day I called his company and explained my request. His supervisor indicated she would check on the invoice status and let me know. The invoice was dated several weeks before his death so there had been adequate time for payment. Not one given to deceit, I also called the life insurance company and told them I was waiting on this proof of payment.

However, the next day, Tom's supervisor called. "I just cannot find any record that we have paid this invoice. I cannot imagine how it would have slipped through the cracks, but we apparently failed to update your husband's membership. I am so very sorry."

"Sorry" seemed like the smallest possible word for what I had just been told. Tom's driving commitment after his diagnosis was to be certain we would be financially secure when he left us. The income provided by this policy was one of the provisions to make that possible. And I was being told that the company had overlooked his membership payment! That omission was all this life insurance company would need to deny our claim.

Sick to my stomach, I hung up the phone and raged. "God, I thought You were a father to the fatherless and a husband to the widow. You have taken my husband. How could You allow this to happen as well?"

I finally bowed my head and prayed — but not to God. To my husband! I was not in the habit of speaking to the dead nor did I have beliefs that encouraged it. I believed that our loved ones were content in heaven, healed and whole, and we would just have to wait our turn.

But at this point, I needed to hear from Tom and all I knew to do was demand it. "Tom," I urged. "This is a horrifying situation. And I know that you would have never left us if you had any idea this membership invoice wasn't taken care of. If there is any possible way you are able to speak to me from heaven, you need to do it now and tell me what to do."

I don't know what I expected to happen. Probably nothing. But in the silence that followed, a miracle took place. These words came to me: "Go look at the invoice again." Like a robot, I obeyed this order.

Standing there with the invoice in my hand, I read it over and over. Could I really be missing something?

Then I saw it. At the bottom of the invoice, penciled in, was a four-digit number. Could it possibly be a check number?

I ran to the box that held our canceled checks and record book. Searching through the record book, I found the check number Tom had listed. Yes! It was made out to the organization that carried his life insurance policy—for his membership fee! I sorted through the canceled checks and found the check he had written. It was the proof I needed. The life insurance money would be ours.

Rather than take a chance that his employer would not pay the membership fee in time, Tom had paid it himself and passed on the invoice for them to reimburse him.

As I looked from that invoice with the penciled in number and back to the canceled check I held in my hand, I knew with certainty my husband had clearly led me to the information that I needed. Yes, God is a father to the fatherless and a husband to the widow.

But for one miraculous moment in time, He had allowed my husband to communicate with me from across time and space. This one last message from beyond the grave was an incredible gift that also gave hope and faith to my grieving heart.

— Lettie Kirkpatrick Burress —

Love's Farewell

*No language can express the power and beauty
and heroism of a mother's love.*
~Edwin Chapin

Putting the blood-pressure cuff back in the metal basket on the wall, I looked down at my patient. I brushed some hair back from her forehead and watched her still figure. "Julie, it looks to me like you're leaving us tonight. I'm going to step out of the room and call your family, but I'll be right back."

The fluorescent glare of the hall lights assaulted me as I left her dimly lit hospital room. She was directly across from the nurses' station, a spot we reserved for our sickest patients. I stepped quietly behind the desk and pulled out her chart to locate her emergency contact numbers. As charge nurse of the oncology floor, I had assigned Julie to myself this evening, even though I suspected I was assigning myself a broken heart.

"Hi, David, it's Linda at the hospital."

"How's Julie? Is she okay?"

Listening to the panic in her husband's voice, I tucked away my own emotion for now. "David, she's resting comfortably, but I think you should come. I just checked on her, and I don't think she's going to be with us much longer."

After reassuring David a few more times that Julie was not suffering, and making sure he wasn't driving alone to the hospital, I returned to her room as promised. The months of treatment had made her frail. She looked like a child lying there rather than a woman my age. I thought about my toddler and preschooler at home. They were probably splashing every inch of the bathroom at that moment, soaking our dog and their daddy as he attempted to give them a bath. I missed some precious moments when I was at work, but I had the next couple of days off. I would be with my children tomorrow. Julie was not likely to see her toddler and preschooler tomorrow or ever again.

Pulling a chair up to her bedside, I took a seat and held her hand. "It's Linda. I'm back, and David is on his way."

Julie couldn't open her eyes or speak, but as long as her heart was beating, she could listen. "Your first hospital admission seems like yesterday, but I guess it was six months ago now. When I saw your diagnosis of lung cancer, well, I don't want to say I blamed you, but there was a certain reassurance there. I thought smoking was where we differed. When you told me you had never smoked, I was so angry. I wanted desperately to blame someone or something for what was happening to you. You, though, handled it with grace and peace."

As I teetered on the edge of losing a friend rather than a patient, the door burst open. David was in the lead followed by parents, in-laws, aunts and uncles. When young people die, it is a very different situation than it is for elderly patients. They have not outlived any of the people who love them.

Standing, I steered David toward the chair. "Just talk to her and hold her hand. Let her know you're here," I said softly.

Rounding the foot of the bed, I guided her relatives out of my way until I was standing directly opposite from David. I picked up Julie's other hand, but held it by the wrist. Now that she had her family with her, I resumed my role as nurse. My hand-holding was pulse-checking in disguise.

Soft sobs and murmured voices filled the room, but for the most part, I only heard Julie's breathing. She was having long periods of apnea, meaning she just didn't breathe at times. As one of those periods of apnea lengthened, I could no longer feel her thready pulse in the hand I continued to hold. Instead of whipping out my stethoscope to

Faith in Action | 217

listen for a heartbeat, I stayed still. I glanced at my watch to note a probable time of death, but otherwise remained where I was. I had no desire to rush David or his family into this new reality — life without Julie. Besides, they would notice soon enough.

Her erratic breathing gradually quieted the room. All eyes and hearts were fixated on her, watching this young woman slip away. Finally, her mother asked, "Is she..."

Before the question could be completed, Julie gasped for air. Letting go of her hand briefly, I repositioned my index finger on her wrist, searching for and finding a pulse. This time, though, it was stronger. As her breathing became regular once more, there was a collective sigh in the room. By the end of my shift, her condition was stable, and most of her relatives had returned home.

My two days off passed at the speed of light, and I was soon back at the nurses' station. Just as I arrived, Julie had one of our aides roll her wheelchair over to me. While she normally appeared fragile, her body ravaged equally by the disease and the treatment, she glowed that day. Her smile and her spirit had not been dimmed by her physical struggle.

"Linda, they said you were coming back today, and I was hoping to see you. I've been discharged! David has gone to pull the car around."

"Oh, Julie, I'm so happy you're going home," I said. "And I want to apologize for scaring David and your entire family the other night. It's just that I really thought..."

"No, please don't apologize. That's actually the reason I was hoping to see you before I left. I need to tell you what really happened."

I had crouched down so we were face to face, and I found myself once again holding her hand. On some level, I think I needed reassurance that she was really here.

Taking a deep breath, she looked into my eyes. "The other night," she began, and then she paused. "The other night, when I died, I went to heaven."

"I couldn't feel a pulse," I whispered.

"And you shouldn't feel bad about calling David. How could you possibly have known I'd come back?" she said with an impish grin. "Anyway, when I got there, I asked for just a little more time. That sounds crazy, both that I died and that I asked to come back, but I promise it's the truth. The reason I wanted to come back was because I had one little bit of unfinished business here. I've been given just enough time to take care of it."

"What?"

"My girls are so young. We both know they won't remember me."

I started to object, but I knew she was right.

"That's okay. I understand," she said, patting my hand. "But when they are older, even if David gives them the most wonderful stepmom in the world, they will probably wonder about me. I'm not going to be here for any of their special moments, so I'm going to write letters. Sixteenth birthdays, graduations, weddings, whatever—I need to write down what I would say to them."

Tears streamed down my face as I nodded in reply.

"I won't be with them, but my love will be."

— Linda Kinnamon —

Covered

If you have a mom, there is nowhere you are likely to go where a prayer has not already been.
~Robert Brault

My middle son, Sam, had joined the Marines, something he had wanted since age nine. We knew there was a high probability of him serving a tour of duty in Afghanistan, yet nothing prepares a family for deployment, no matter how much information and communication they get from the Family Readiness Officer (FRO).

His deployment occurred while his father and I were getting a divorce, so emotions were already high. I felt as if I couldn't breathe, moving numbly through work and daily activities. Sam told me not to worry about him, that God is with every Marine at all times.

I believed that, but still, one of the hardest things for military families is the waiting time between each phone call, waiting to hear again the magical words, "I'm okay." All I could do was pray every day, for Sam and for all our service members.

We weren't told the exact day of deployment, but one day we received an e-mail from the FRO letting us know that Sam was already on his way to Afghanistan. We were told that each of our Marines would contact us as soon as he or she was able, but the FRO would keep us updated as possible in consideration of operational security (OPSEC). We all understand OPSEC's importance in keeping our loved ones safe.

As the days passed without word, new reports grimly announced the lost lives. I forced myself to stay focused on what I knew—that each of my children is a precious gift from God and always in His hands. These thoughts, prayers, and the supportive people around me helped me get through the days of not hearing.

Around 10:30 p.m. one night I was awakened with an urgent need to pray for my son. My heart was racing as I got down on my knees and prayed earnestly for Sam. Again and again, I petitioned the Lord to cover him and every Marine with him. Throughout the night, I prayed with fervor, asking God to move these boys into safety, to hide them from the enemies. By 3:00 a.m., I was exhausted and fell into a deep sleep, surrendering to the Lord for whatever was next.

It was several days before Sam called, and I wept in gratitude upon hearing his voice say, "Mom." Then I heard the words, "I'm okay." I asked him what had happened during that night I had felt the strong urge to pray.

Sam asked quietly, "Was it on the news?"

My heart skipped a beat. "Nothing on the news, but I was awakened to pray. Can you tell me what happened?"

He gave a soft laugh. "I knew you were praying, Mom. I felt it. I can't tell you now, but when I get back, I will. But I knew you were praying."

Months later, at work, I was again overcome with an urgent need to pray. I was attending a meeting at the time, but excused myself and went to my office to pray for the safety of Sam and his unit.

The next time Sam called, I asked him about that date and time. He laughed. "I'll tell you when I get back. I knew you were praying, Mom. I felt it."

Months later, Sam returned. I sat in the back seat with him as we drove home, wanting to hold, touch, and look closely at the young warrior who had been returned to us. He was changed—always amazing, he was now an amazing man. At a quiet moment, I asked him about those times when I'd been prompted to pray.

He faced me, inwardly seeing things that were horrible to convey.

"The first time, we were on the helicopter just coming into Kandahar province. There was a sudden firefight, and a helicopter was shot down

Faith in Action

in front of us." He paused, his eyes distant. "Our pilot pulled some pretty fast maneuvers and got us out of there.

"The other time, we were meeting up with another unit. We had a map that our guide, an Afghan, was helping us follow, but the map led us to the wrong place. Somehow, we wound up in a place where there was a dead end surrounded by the Taliban. Every one of us could feel the tension, like we had walked into a trap. But then an old man with a beard, in robes, came out of nowhere and said he could help, that he knew where we needed to be."

Sam shook his head and grinned. "Mom, this man was ancient looking! A little old man! Our guide told us not to listen to him, but the man insisted he was there to help us and could lead us to where we were supposed to be. Against the advice of our guide, we all decided to follow this man. He really insisted he had come to help us, but we didn't know how."

His eyes sparkled. "This little man started leading us out of the city, into the desert in the darkest of night. We were thinking we were really being led into an ambush now, but suddenly there was the unit we were meeting up with! We all turned to thank the old man, but he wasn't there. He just disappeared." He got an incredulous look on his face. "I knew you were praying, Mom. I know God got us out of there. I think that man was an angel."

I wiped away my tears, thankful to God for sending that man, or angel, in answer to this mother's urgent prayer — and for giving me my miracle yet again.

— Patti Wade —

The Christmas Coat

Life is a series of thousands of tiny miracles.
~Mike Greenberg

"I don't think we can afford it right now. Maybe it will go on sale after Christmas," said my mom.

"It's okay, I can make my pea coat last one more winter. We can pray for God to provide one at a reasonable cost, too."

I didn't mean to eavesdrop on my parents' conversation, but we lived in a small house.

I was about seven years old and the third of four children. Christmas was coming and we were getting excited about what might be under the tree for us. Hearing my dad talk about making do with his coat, though, made me a little sad.

Dad had worn the blue wool coat for as long as I could remember. He'd been in the Navy years earlier — before he married Mom. I am ashamed to say I remember being embarrassed when he wore that coat. The wool had been patched in spots and I can't remember how many times my mom sewed on the buttons with the anchors on them. He needed a new coat, but I'd never thought about how much it would cost — or how often my parents made sacrifices like this so we children could have the clothes or shoes we needed or, in this case, some presents under the Christmas tree.

Faith in Action

Earlier that day, my parents had gone shopping and he'd seen a winter jacket that he really liked. It was a heavyweight green and black plaid wool. He felt it was the coat for him, but then he saw the price. It was far more expensive than their budget would allow. He'd recently started his own business, and it was a daily struggle just to pay the bills and feed and clothe four children. As far as he was concerned, unless God had other plans, the coat would have to wait.

It was only a week or so later when Dad came home with a large box and an incredible story.

On the way home from work he'd seen a box fall from the back of a truck that was several car lengths ahead of him. He tried to catch up to the truck to let the driver know something had fallen off his vehicle, but he lost sight of it in the traffic. He decided to backtrack and see if the box was still there.

He was amazed when he saw the large red box still sitting where it had fallen in the middle of the intersection. He pulled over and went to get it — surprised that it hadn't been run over in the twenty or so minutes since he saw it fall. It was a gift box from a local department store. He took it to his car, opened the box, and could not believe his eyes. Inside was the coat he wanted — and it was his size.

It was tempting to keep it, but he thought about the person who obviously bought this coat as a gift — and the person who was supposed to receive it. He drove to the department store and took it to the men's department. The cashier did not recall selling the coat to anyone that day. There was a cash receipt in the box, so there were no credit card records with the name of the purchaser, and no one had called or come in to report it missing, so she told him to just keep it.

He couldn't in good conscience keep it without trying to find the person who bought it, so Dad took out an ad in the Lost and Found section of the local paper naming the intersection, type of truck he saw the box fall from, day and time, but no one ever called to claim the coat. After about a month, he finally felt like it was meant for him.

I remember Dad wearing that coat for years — long after it was threadbare and out of fashion. For him it was something that he could point to and tell the story of how God provided for his need in a very unusual way. More than half a century later, it is still a reminder for me to always have faith that God will provide for my needs.

— Donna Anderson —

A Pink Dress and a Promise

A mom's hug lasts long after she lets go.
~Author Unknown

I was sixteen and more than anything else in the world I wanted my mother to attend my high school graduation the following year. She was suffering from ovarian cancer, and although the expressions on the faces of other family members didn't offer much hope, I firmly believed she would recover and be there.

My mother and I had always enjoyed a special bond, perhaps because I'd been her only child for the first thirteen years of her married life. We shared a passionate love of books and reading. She'd read to me every day until I learned to master the skill myself. Afterwards she continued to share my love of stories by enthusing over my attempts at authorship. An amateur actress, she appeared in numerous local theatre productions. I grew up attending rehearsals and on opening night I was able to mouth every one of her lines.

I especially recall a small party held for the cast and crew one evening after a performance. My mother had bought a new pink dress for the occasion. In my six-year-old eyes, she looked like an angel.

When I was fourteen, my brother was born. Ten months later my mother was diagnosed with cancer. At first I didn't worry. After all, she was my mother. She'd never die and leave me. But as one year stretched to two and she grew thinner and often despondent due to heavy medication, I began to worry.

Two weeks before Christmas the year I was sixteen her condition worsened. I tried to deny the despair I saw in my father's face as we sat by her hospital bed. To strengthen the reality of her recovery I talked to her of the future, a future we'd share.

"And when you come to my graduation, will you wear your pink dress?" I asked her as she lay weak and thin on December 9th.

"Oh, honey, I don't know." She forced a thin smile. "That old thing? Really?"

"Yes, yes, please promise."

"All right, if that's what you really want… I promise." The words were barely above a whisper.

An hour later she passed away.

Somehow I forced myself through the next year and a half of school. My father had drifted away in his own world of grief and my aunt who came to take care of my two-year-old brother had no time for me. When graduation finally rolled around, both declined to attend.

As I sat on the platform with the other graduates, I felt hollow and utterly alone. I'd believed my mother would get well, I'd believed she'd be there for this milestone in my life. No one could possibly feel as bereft of happiness as I did at that moment.

Then the principal was announcing the prize for literature, for outstanding work in creative writing and the student on my right was prodding me. "You won, you won!" she hissed.

Stunned, I remained seated. And then I saw her. Standing at the back right hand corner of the auditorium, my mother was clapping with more vehemence than she'd taught me was ladylike. She was wearing the pink dress.

I stood and made my way to the podium to collect my award, all but staggering under the overwhelming sense of joy. She'd come. She'd promised and she'd come. And she was wearing the pink dress. The moments fluttered wildly in my heart, a beautiful butterfly of joy. In a cloud of happiness so intense I could barely control my movements, I returned to my seat. But when I looked at the back right hand corner of the room she was gone.

Later as I walked home alone in the soft, warm darkness of the spring evening, my award and diploma clasped in my hand, my attitude changed and anger suffused me. Why had she come only for an instant? Why couldn't she have stayed?

I sat down on a park bench by the river and stared at the calm water, and slowly understanding came. She couldn't always be with me, not anymore, but she would be there when I needed her most. She'd kept her promise. She'd come to my graduation and she'd worn the pink dress.

— Gail MacMillan —

74

The Voice

*The most incredible thing about miracles
is that they happen.*
~G. K. Chesterton

Nothing tastes as bad as the Indian Ocean. Not turpentine. Not rotten eggs. Not even cod liver oil or mud. Especially when you are in the middle of it, choking and swallowing large portions, and mercilessly drowning in it.

And that's where I was — although not really in the middle of it, but only a few miles from shore off the coast of Mogadishu, Somalia in 1974. Struggling to breathe and stay afloat, and fighting desperately for my life. And slowly, inexorably drowning in the beautiful, sunlit waves of an inhospitable sea.

My ordeal began when suddenly, and without warning, a surge of stomach cramps hit me. Seconds later the first wave of surf struck and I was sent spiraling to the cold depths below. But I quickly resurfaced and was ready to do battle with this monstrous element. For I was young and in the prime of health and physical condition. And being young and cocky, I felt indestructible and was scared of nothing.

Serving on Marine Security Guard Duty in East Africa, I was one of a group of young marines assigned to protect the U.S. Embassy in the capital of Somalia's tiny, poverty-stricken nation. This was many years before that poor country made headlines and saw other young Americans embattled and struggling for their lives there. It was a time

Faith in Action

when there was still infrastructure, a centralized government, numerous businesses and even occasional tourists. There were even friendly nightspots to wine, dine and dance the humid evenings away, as well as a fair number of Italian farmers and Americans and Europeans of various business interests and occupations with whom to socialize and enjoy the yearlong sunny, sandy Indian Ocean beaches.

But there were no sunny beaches or friendly tourists for me this morning. And no one three miles away on shore — even with a good set of binoculars — would spot me writhing and wrestling with the sea. Nor were there any nearby swimmers or sea vessels to come to my aid. I was totally alone.

Having resurfaced, and with barely time to take a breath, another swell — larger than the first — appeared from nowhere and forced me under again. At the same time, another wave of cramps — this one also worse than earlier — came upon me. As I was sent twisting below the surface, I felt my body grow slack and begin to lose what I always had assumed was a boundless strength and vitality.

A whole minute passed before I resurfaced. Somehow another swell failed to roll in and punish me. So, although I was exhausted, I started for shore. Then, and again without warning, another wave slammed against me with even greater weight and force. I was sent below the glaring surface a third time, coughing and retching on the brine I had already swallowed. But I was also struggling not to gasp for air while submerged, for I had only exhaled a tiny breath before again submerging.

What were only seconds seemed like hours this time. But I had little to contemplate or to reflect upon except the stark realization that I wasn't an atheist and did believe in God. And now would be a good time to pray.

But I had no time to pray. No time left to reflect upon my brief, uneventful life. Let alone time to ask God — whom I seldom prayed to — for divine intervention. I was drowning and about to die. I had swallowed a sea of saltwater and despair, and was physically depleted and spiritually drained.

Then, unexpectedly and not knowing how, I was once more above the surface, coughing up water and gasping for air. But I was barely afloat, and unable to move a single muscle. The end would come soon now, and I had no idea why it already hadn't. Then ultimate despair turned into ultimate terror: out at sea, not more than thirty or forty yards distant, another gigantic wave was heading towards me. And at a hurtling pace! It was at this moment I heard The Voice.

But no, it was more than a voice. Gentle in tone, and powerful and confident in inflection, it was at the same time a soothing whisper and a mighty clarion: both comforting and commanding. It said, "Relax, let go of yourself. And fall back upon the waves and lie still. I will save you!"

I did as I was told and let myself become limp and ceased further exertion. Suddenly, I was on my back, stretched out and calmly floating upon the tossing surface. Then a tide — of a momentous size — loomed above me... but only for a second. The next instant I was riding its crest and being ferried towards shore.

During this not unpleasant ride to shore, I had a sensation of floating on a cushion of air or reclining in a soft bed of flowers. Overhead, all I saw was a perfect-looking noonday sun as well as some scattered, friendly-looking clouds. But in my mind all I heard and kept rehearing was The Voice that spoke to me: its firm, gentle words, and nothing more. And then I was delivered to the shore and crawled out, where I sprawled for an unknown period until my strength and senses returned to me.

This was over thirty years ago, and much has happened in my life since then; some things bad, but many things good. And though I have no physical evidence of the event — no film or tape recording or eyewitness, and sometimes even forget that it actually happened (as I often forget to be a prayerful person) — I know that it did. Especially on lovely sunlit days and whenever I am near the ocean. I also know that it really happened because I am still alive.

Someone or some thing spoke to me in angelic tones one day when I was drowning in the Indian Ocean. It told me that I would be saved. And I was.

— Patrick P. Stafford —

Miraculous Timing

Thank You, Mr. Truck Driver

> *There are only two ways to live your life. One is as though nothing is a miracle. The other is as though everything is a miracle.*
> *~Albert Einstein*

"Hurry up! We have to get going," I said to the kids. It was Tuesday morning, my busy day at work, and we always seemed to be running late.

We rushed out the door. I had a cup of coffee in one hand, a baby in the other arm, and some work papers tucked underneath my chin. I had already asked my ten-year-old daughter to grab my keys and phone. Somehow, with all the things I was carrying, I managed to reach in, lock the door and close it. Only then did I realize my daughter had my phone (which she was playing games on), but my keys were nowhere in sight.

"Where are my keys?" I asked, frustrated because I already knew the answer.

"Oops," she said.

Great, I thought, *now we are going to be really late.*

My daughter managed to find our spare rather quickly so it was only a twenty- or thirty-second delay, but getting locked out is just one of those frustrating things that always leads me to look up and

Miraculous Timing | 233

whine, "Why, God, why? What is the point of this?" As if God has time to worry about me remembering to grab my keys or locking myself out of the house!

About twenty minutes later, we were almost to my parents' ranch, where I was going to drop off the kids so I could head to work. On a little farm-to-market road (the middle of nowhere), we had only seen three other vehicles. One of them was a big 18-wheeler headed in the opposite direction, which was about to pass us. Suddenly, his left front tire blew, and I saw it fly twenty feet into the air as the huge truck came barreling toward us. The truck swerved completely into our lane just a few car lengths in front of us.

In a split second, I had to decide if I should swerve to the left or to the right. Neither way seemed like it would end well at the speed we were going. I thought of my babies snuggled in the back seat.

By some miracle, the truck driver was able to pull that big rig back into his lane before he hit us or I made any drastic swerve, which would have surely rolled our vehicle. We passed him in what felt like slow motion as I realized the tragedy we had just avoided and wondered how that truck driver managed that impossible maneuver.

In my rearview mirror, I saw him pull over on the side of the road to fix his tire. I slowed down but continued on my way to my parents' house in a trance, with so many thoughts rushing through my head. I knew there was nothing I could do to help fix his tire, although I wished I could do something.

I pulled into my parents' driveway and came to a stop. I sat there for a minute, taking some deep breaths. I turned and looked at my babies. My son was snuggled happily in his car seat, and my beautiful daughter was playing with him and talking baby talk. I smiled and thanked God.

"I can't believe what just happened," I said out loud finally.

"What are you talking about?" my daughter replied.

They had been so busy playing that they apparently didn't see the big rig coming. I shook my head and went to turn off my ignition. When I reached for my keys, I cried happy, thankful tears again.

If we had been just a few seconds ahead of where we were on

that road, if we hadn't gotten locked out of the house that morning, I don't think I'd be here to write this story today.

After I dropped off the kids, I stopped on the side of the road where the trucker sat, waiting for a wrecker to pull him to the tire shop. I didn't know what to say. Before I got out of my truck, I saw an unopened bottle of water sitting in my passenger seat. I grabbed it and walked up and handed it to him. It was a hot day and a kind gesture at least.

"I don't know how you pulled that truck back over into your lane so fast," I said.

"I don't either," he replied, shaking his head. "Was that you who was coming toward me?"

"Yes, me and my two babies," I replied.

Tears welled up in both of our eyes. This happened right in the middle of the COVID-19 pandemic, so we didn't shake hands or hug. As I drove off, headed to work once again, I almost turned around because what I had really wanted to say, although I was too choked up to find the words, was "Thank you, Mr. Truck Driver, for saving our lives." And thank you, God, for making me forget my keys!

— Kayleen Kitty Holder —

The Dog Days of Winter

Gratitude is one of the strongest and most transformative states of being. It shifts your perspective from lack to abundance and allows you to focus on the good in your life.
~Jen Sincero

A wail pierced the air, overpowering the sound of ice crunching beneath my snow boots. This chilling sound could only have come from an animal in pain. I stopped to scan the frozen lake I was hiking around, and spotted a furry head frantically bobbing up and down through a hole in the ice about thirty feet from the shoreline. It was a large brown dog. His shoulders churned frantically in the bitter water as his paws splashed his face with icy water.

I yanked off my mittens and tapped out 9-1-1.

"911, state your emergency," a calm voice said.

"A dog has fallen through the ice on a lake. Please, can you send somebody to save him?"

"Do not go on the ice," the dispatcher said. "What is your location?"

"My location?" I hesitated. "I'm on a footpath walking around a lake." I had no idea what address to give her.

A second wail filled the air. That's when I saw a small boy ahead of me on the path.

Miraculous Timing

"Please, Daddy, Buddy!" he bawled as he jerked on a man's sleeve beside him. His father left his side and gingerly stepped onto the edge of the lake, testing the ice beneath his Timberlands as he inched across the frozen surface toward the struggling dog.

"I see a man trying to rescue the dog," I reported to the dispatcher.

"No, do not go on the ice," she repeated. "If you see someone on the ice, tell them to get off the ice!" she firmly ordered.

I hurried over to the child. "Buddy, Daddy, Buddy!" his high-pitched voice continued to plead to his father's back.

"I have 911 on the phone," I yelled out to the man, but I stopped short of telling him to get off the ice. I wanted him to keep going. I wanted him to save Buddy.

I squatted beside the little boy, trying to comfort him and make sure he didn't attempt to follow his father. My shoulders tightened when the ice loudly crackled and white veins shot out from beneath the father's feet. I knew he had to turn around and come back.

But he didn't.

He carefully lowered himself to his knees and began crawling toward the whimpering dog. I pressed my phone tighter to my ear and prepared to tell the 911 operator there was now a man who had fallen through the ice. My other hand gripped tightly onto the boy's shoulder as he anxiously tugged away from me toward his father.

Reaching the watery hole, the father stretched his arm out to grab the dog. A chunk of the ice broke away, plunging his elbow into the numbing water. The dog moaned softly. It was obvious he was exhausted. Only his head quietly bobbled above the waterline now. With one last swipe, the man snatched the dog's red collar and jerked his shaking body out of the water, loudly snapping more ice beneath them.

Everything fell silent except for the anxious sobs and sniffling nose of the little boy squirming under my hand. Wriggling backward, the father dragged the chocolate Labrador by the collar as water seeped through cracks in the ice, soaking his jeans and flannel shirt until he reached the shoreline.

The boy flung himself over the shivering dog and buried his face into his wet fur. His father gave me a grateful nod and then collapsed

Miraculous Timing

over his son, wrapping his arms around him and his dog. I backed away to give them privacy as an unexplained surge of love flowed through me for these strangers as I watched them have a moment alone.

Buddy struggled to stand up on stiff, trembling legs, and the three of them limped down the path for home. I said goodbye to the 911 operator, turned back the way I had come, and headed for home myself.

Hiking back along the lake's edge, I noticed the sun glinting off a fallen tree limb on the water's edge. Half of it was submerged through a wet hole in the ice, while the other half jutted straight up, lodged tightly above the surface and held prisoner in a block of solid ice. How did the ice break under the weight of the dog, but the man didn't fall through it? It seemed against all odds, but they both made it off the thawing lake.

Stepping back into my warm house, I hugged my two boys and our cats. Feeling the same powerful connection to them that I had just felt for complete strangers, my heart danced with fresh joy for my simple life and healthy family. I marveled at my earlier timing, randomly deciding to go for a walk and then stumbling into another family's crisis at just the right moment to help them by safeguarding the little boy so the father could make his brave rescue.

I had left my house eager to take a break from my rambunctious sons. I returned with immense gratitude that I have what is truly important.

— Laura Savino —

The 430 Miracle

*The probability of a certain set of circumstances
coming together in a meaningful (or tragic)
way is so low that it simply cannot be
considered mere coincidence.*
~V.C. King

I had just stepped out of the shower on a cold October afternoon. I dried off, dressed and headed downstairs. On the way down, I kept hearing a voice in my head: "430... 430... 430."

Out loud, I asked myself, "430? Hmmm... what does that mean?" It wasn't as if I was hearing my own voice, just a vivid utterance in my head. While it wasn't making a lot of sense to me (other than maybe it could mean a time of day), it was so powerful that I headed straight to the phone to call my identical twin sister, Shari.

"Hi, Sis. Remember, we're supposed to meet at the nursing home at 5:00 p.m. today to visit Mom. Can we meet there at 4:30 instead?"

She said, "Sure, why?"

Telling her about the "430" voice seemed too weird, so I thought quickly and said, "Well, the traffic will be better before 5:00 p.m."

She responded, "Okay, no problem. See you then."

When I was half a block away from the home my phone rang. It was Shari.

"San, where are you?" She sounded stressed.

"I'm just about there, why?"

"Mom doesn't look so good. Can you please hurry?"

Miraculous Timing | 239

"I'll be there in a minute."

When I signed it at the front desk, I looked at their digital clock — it read 4:27 p.m. I signed in with that exact time and headed straight to our mom's room.

My sister was seated next to our mom's bed holding her hand. Her sad eyes met mine, and I knew. As I stood next to our mom and took her other hand, she smiled back at me. We watched one solitary tear fall from our mom's face as she took her last breath. Still holding Mom's hand, my sister grabbed my hand and shouted, "Unto you, Lord, we commend her spirit!"

A few months later, when we received all the paperwork from the nursing home, I glanced at her death certificate. The exact time of death jumped vividly off the page as I heard that voice echo in my mind again: 430.

Had I not gotten there by 4:30 p.m., I would have missed her last smile and her last breath.

To this day, I'll always be curious about that 430 voice in my head. With no plausible earthly explanation, all I know is that being with my mom at the moment of her passing was one of the greatest gifts I could ever have received.

— Sandy Martin —

The Perfect Wait

The tie which links mother and child is of such pure and immaculate strength as to be never violated.
~Washington Irving

I'd noticed a tiny cyst growing under my right eyelid, so I made an appointment with my doctor. That June day seemed as ordinary as any, other than having an in-office procedure. A little snip, a little stitch, and I was good to go.

"I want you to put antibiotic ointment on it for a few days, which will require a prescription. Where do you want me to call?"

I gave the doctor the phone number of a pharmacy. It was not the one where I usually got my prescriptions filled, but rather the one I'd pass on my way home.

About twenty minutes later, I pulled into the pharmacy's drive-through. The pharmacy worker informed me that my prescription was not ready. "Okay," I replied, "there's no car behind me, so I'll just wait right here at the window." She sort of snarled at me. Maybe people waiting at the window made her uncomfortable.

In a few minutes, a car pulled behind me. I pulled out of line and made a big circle with my car, out of the drive-through and around the building in order to get back in line. Now there were two cars in front of me. I waited.

When I pulled back up to the drive-through window, the woman there snarled at me again and said in a condescending voice, "I told you your prescription is not ready!"

Miraculous Timing | 241

"Sure," I responded as nicely as I could, although heat was rising in my cheeks. "I'll just wait again, but I'll pull around if someone else comes." And that is exactly what happened. Again, I made that large, circular sweep around the building to get back in line.

As if in instant replay, the woman at the pharmacy window snapped at me when I showed up again. "Mrs. Edmonds! It takes at least twenty minutes for us to get a prescription filled!" she exclaimed in an exasperated tone. By now, I was exasperated too — at her!

"This prescription was called in from the doctor's office before I left, and it took me a good twenty minutes to get here in the first place. I have circled around twice and let three other cars go in front of me, so you have had well over twenty minutes to work on it by now!" I retorted. Then, gathering myself, I attempted a calmer tone and added, "I'll tell you what. I will go grab some lunch and then come back. Maybe that will give you enough time."

I drove to a nearby fast-food place and ordered a chicken salad and a medium drink. Then I headed back to pick up my prescription.

As I pulled back into the parking lot, I saw a familiar figure — my son Keith. His apartment happened to be nearby. He wasn't wearing a shirt or shoes, his hair was disheveled, and he was walking along in his sweatpants like he was on a mission.

Keith lives alone in his apartment and holds down a nearly full-time job, but he also struggles with schizoaffective disorder. He has long periods of wellness when he functions fine, interspersed with psychotic episodes that require hospitalization. I pulled the car to a stop in the middle of the parking lot, got out, and approached him.

"Are you okay?" I asked.

"I'm sick," he replied in a monotone voice.

"I can see that," I said. "Come get in my car with me. I'll call Dad, and we'll get you some help."

He walked slowly, robot-like, toward my car and climbed into the passenger seat. I drove the car across the parking lot and pulled into an open space. "I'm calling Dad now," I said.

Keith made no response, but before I could dial the phone, he noticed my salad and drink. "I'm hungry," he said in that monotone voice.

"Sure. Here, honey, have some salad." I opened the salad for him, placed it on his lap, and put the fork in his hand. Then I called my husband.

I never know just how much to say or not say in front of Keith when he is not in his normal state of mind. I wanted to get him help and did not want him bolting from the car. I tried to convey as much information as I could without alarming Keith. My husband asked questions requiring only "yes" and "no" answers and managed to glean enough information to understand that he needed to come right away.

Keith sat in the passenger seat hungrily devouring the salad and drink as we waited for John to arrive. Once his dad arrived, he willingly agreed to go with us to the hospital. I drove while John sat in the back seat with him.

After we had him safely at the psych hospital, I went back to his apartment. Normally, Keith keeps his apartment clean and neat. Seeing it otherwise is always a sign he's sick. This time, his pills from various pill bottles, including Tylenol, were spilled out all over the kitchen cabinet, there were dirty dishes and pots, and one burner on the stove was turned on and red hot.

So many thoughts swirled in my mind. Keith could have been harmed in so many ways. He could have accidentally taken an overdose of meds. He could have set the apartment on fire if anything had been sitting on that red-hot stove. Or he could have walked out into traffic. But none of that happened.

I thought about that slow pharmacy and that unfriendly worker and how miffed I had been at her. Now I wanted to thank her. That long delay had put me in a holding pattern until Keith's path and mine converged. I even had food waiting for him in my car.

Is someone watching over us? Keith and I think so!

— Hannah Edmonds —

Serendipity

Being a mother means that your heart is no longer yours; it wanders wherever your children do.
~Author Unknown

I sat on the rolled out white paper, my bare legs swinging off the edge of the examining table. While I waited, I examined the patterned wallpaper — green embryo-shaped swirls on a cream background.

"Apropos," I mumbled.

An abrupt knock caused me to jump. The door opened quickly as Dr. Graham stepped into the office, his kind smile reassuring.

"Hiya, Jen," he began. "So, we got the results back..." (Was it me or was that smile looking a little more forced?) "I'm afraid you're infertile."

Well. That was blunt. Wham, bam, you're sterile, Ma'am.

His expression remained calm and kind. *How could he be so composed? So unaffected? Where was the back rubbing? And why did he have embryos adorning his examining room walls? That was just cruel.*

And so it began.

The drive home was a blur of blind driving, loud wailing, and a heartbroken apology to the baby I couldn't have. My car was on autopilot as my newfound identity steered me home and into despair so deep that my whole body ached.

As time passed my husband and I began to entertain the possibility of adoption, but it was all too overwhelming. Instead, I pushed through the days, facing each monthly cycle with weepiness, anger, wine… or all of the above.

Then one day I decided I needed a puppy. I'd always loved dogs and had a couple growing up, so this made sense to me. My focus subtly shifted; I desperately needed something to give my love to, to fill the void. Unfortunately, I faced another obstacle. We'd signed a lease that forbade pets.

My husband, however, was on a mission. Unabashedly he pulled the "Infertile Card" and convinced our landlord to make an exception to his own rules: once he did, a fissure appeared in the dark clouds that surrounded me. I had something to look forward to! A puppy would never take the place of a baby, but I needed a home for the stash of love I'd built up for my unborn child.

The first thing I did was call my mother with the news.

She lived nearby and had helplessly shared in my burden of infertility as only a mother could. My news brought her relief and happiness; she was pleased to hear that my husband and I would be starting our search for a puppy the following weekend.

That plan, however, went out the window the next morning. Waiting another four days to begin our search required far too much discipline, so I took a day off from work and set out on my mission, alone. The Connecticut Humane Society was located in a nearby town, which also happened to be the same town where my mother lived. I knew it unlikely that I'd find an available puppy my first time looking, but I had to try. Off I went without a word to my husband, my mother or anyone.

Walking down the aisle alongside the cages was heartbreaking. I tried not to look into the eyes of any of the sad, precious creatures so desperate to be loved. I felt a kinship with them and a terrible betrayal within myself for bypassing them, but I needed a puppy. A baby of another kind…

He was in the third stall. As soon as he saw me he wagged his tail shyly and then sat up on his hind legs, reaching his paws through the bars of the cage and wrapping them around my hand. It was love at first sight. A young girl and her mother were behind me, approaching the cage moments after me. The child was telling her mother that she wanted this same puppy. I ignored them as they lingered, hoping, no doubt, that I would walk away.

I wouldn't move. I waited until one of the attendants came out to check on us and then told her that I'd be taking this dog. A twinge of guilt struck me as I put my needs before the little girl, but this was *my* dog. I was smitten.

They took us into a room where I completed the necessary paperwork. I pulled out my checkbook to pay, the final step before I could bring my sweet puppy home.

"I'm sorry, we don't take checks, Ma'am," the attendant said flatly.

This was the 1980s — we didn't have debit cards and at that point I only had one credit card, which I rarely carried. No problem: I'd run into town and take the money out of the bank.

"I'm sorry, we don't hold the animals for anyone," she added.

I looked through the window and saw the puppy stalkers still wandering around. I couldn't leave — they would get *my* puppy as soon as I left! Trying not to panic I asked if I could use their phone, as this was pre–cell phones. I called my mother, who lived only a few miles away, but there was no answer. I tried my girlfriend. Same result. I began to feel desperate and was fighting back tears when I heard her....

"Jen?"

That voice that I loved and knew so well came from behind me. I turned to see my beautiful mother standing in the doorway, smiling and looking surprised.

"Mom!"

Relief flowed in the form of tears. I couldn't believe that she was there — at the Humane Society of all places — and that she'd arrived just in time. She was on her way to the grocery store, she explained, and for "some reason" wound up taking a turn that brought her completely out of her way... and right past the Humane Society. It was then that she noticed what she thought was my car. Fortunately, she'd decided to come in and check.

My mother paid the attendant in cash and we walked out side-by-side, with my puppy in my arms. I've often thought about that day and how my mother appeared like an angel out of nowhere, a gift of divine intervention. Because of her and my sweet pup, Clancy, I was able to find hope again, which helped me through some difficult days. And Clancy wound up being a wonderful "sibling" to his baby sister, Erin, to whom I gave birth the following year!

—M.J. Shea—

The Call

*Let gratitude be the pillow upon which you kneel to say
your nightly prayer. And let faith be the bridge
you build to overcome evil and welcome good.*
~Maya Angelou

My mother was waiting for me at the bus stop. I was a freshman and she hadn't picked me up in years, so I knew something was wrong. She hugged me tightly, told me to get in the car, and told one of my classmates, who was also my neighbor, to get in as well. My mom drove us the four short blocks home, but those four blocks seemed to last a lifetime. She told us something had happened, and from the way she choked up on the words, I could feel her fright and sorrow.

"The World Trade Center has been hit by a plane," she managed to say. I thought something had suddenly forced all of the air out of the car. I couldn't breathe. She dropped off our neighbor and pulled into the driveway. Inside the house, the TV was still on, and images of the smoke billowing from the North Tower showed on the screen. We were stationed in Germany, where my dad was a soldier in the Army, so it was already mid-afternoon for us. I remember feeling helpless as we watched the second plane approach the Tower on television. I watched it hit, and I felt the strike as if the weight of it would pull me down through the floor.

Being so far away from my homeland when it was hurt was strangely isolating. Suddenly, I was much more aware of the foreign land surrounding us. My mom was on the phone trying to call friends in New York. I'd been born in New York, and my mom had visited the city frequently when she was growing up. When the second plane struck, my mom cried. Not quiet tears; she fell to her knees and cried out loud. She knew seventeen people whom we would later learn had died in the Towers.

The military base was put on lockdown, which meant my dad couldn't come home. I was sitting on the floor, holding our German Shepherd, Hobbes, while my sister toddled around in her walker, blissfully oblivious. Suddenly, I felt an overwhelming need to call my grandfather, Pa, who lived in Virginia. I needed to know he was safe.

Mom told me we would call him later when he got home; the phone lines would be very busy due to the attacks and rescue efforts. But I didn't listen, which was hugely out of character for me. I knew I *had* to call him right that minute. It couldn't wait for him to get home from work.

I went and picked up the phone. To dial out of the house, we had to dial 9, then 0-0 to make an international call. Then we had to dial the country code for the United States — 1 — and then the phone number. I could never remember the number for the house I lived in, much less dialing to the States to Pa's cell phone. We always called him at home. He didn't like the charges on his cell phone from an international call. I knew he'd be annoyed because of the cost, but I didn't care. I had to call him. I had never had such an intense feeling in my life.

Somehow, I dialed the right numbers, including Pa's cell phone. He answered and said I caught him just as he was about to go through security at the Pentagon, which meant turning in his phone because he couldn't take it into his office. If I had called more than a minute later, his phone would have already been turned off.

My voice was shaking when I told him I just needed to know he was safe. He could tell I was upset, so he walked away from the security line toward the parking lot so his signal would be better. He told me he was just fine, perfectly safe, and the guards at the Pentagon were protecting everyone so I didn't need to worry. That is when Flight 77 crashed into the Pentagon, destroying Pa's office.

He told me he would call me back — that he had to go. I didn't know what had happened until it came on the news a moment later. Mom cried again later that day when Pa called back. He was home safe because my earlier phone call had kept him from going into his office. I will be forever grateful for whatever grace allowed me to remember his cell phone number in that moment I needed it.

That urge to call my grandfather was the most miraculous mercy I've experienced in my life. It gave me fourteen more years to share with the most wonderful grandfather anyone could have.

—C. Solomon—

Fleas and Thank You

*I think that someone is watching out for me.
God, my guardian angel, I'm not sure who that is,
but they really work hard.*
~Mattie Stepanek

I owe my life to a flea. If I am honest, I'm sure it was more than one flea. I just like how it sounds to say I owe my life to a flea. It makes me stop and think about how you never know what seemingly insignificant detail could end up being extremely consequential. As it turns out, the existence of those nearly imperceptible fleas played a major role in one of the most consequential events of my life.

Cats get fleas. Having owned several cats over the years growing up in small-town Missouri, this was simply an accepted and acknowledged fact of life. Through those years, we had always been relatively lucky. The few times when fleas were apparent, simple flea treatments from the store had been more than adequate to handle the problem. Thankfully, in 2017, that pattern was broken.

My cat, Boomerjax, was scratching at fleas more than he ever had in the two years since I brought him home from the shelter. It had been about the right amount of time since the last treatment, so despite the increased scratching, I didn't assume anything was different. I ran to the store and bought the same flea treatment I had used on him previously.

A few days after applying the treatment, I noticed he had not improved at all. In fact, he seemed to be even more aggravated. A closer look showed his skin was red and irritated. Not wanting to take any chances, I called the vet's office and made an appointment to get Boomerjax some help.

December 6, 2017 felt like any other day. I ran a couple of errands, watched some TV, read for a while, and then started thinking about getting Boomerjax into his carrier to take him to the vet. As with most cats, it usually took a great deal of time and effort to accomplish this task. To my surprise, on that day, Boomerjax did not put up much resistance. At first, I simply attributed the cooperation to the level of misery caused by the fleas. Looking back, I like to believe it all worked together as part of a bigger plan. I had planned for it to take a while, but now we were running early due to the cat's unusual cooperation. I decided to load the carrier in the car and leave for the vet anyway.

The waiting room offered the standard distractions: TV, magazines, and random strangers with their pets. My distraction of choice was playing a mindless game on my cellphone. When Boomerjax was called to the exam room, I quickly grabbed his carrier and exited my game. What I didn't realize was that I had not simply closed the game app; I had silenced the phone entirely. The vet was very kind with Boomerjax and concluded that he was suffering from an allergic reaction to the saliva in the flea bites. I was given some medicine to put in the cat food, and all seemed right with the world.

Before starting the drive home, I pulled out my phone to send a message to my sister about Boomerjax's diagnosis. To my surprise, the display showed I had four missed calls and two voicemail messages. My surprise turned to shock with the first voicemail. It was the first time in my life I had a message begin with the caller identifying himself as a member of the police department. He asked me to call back as soon as possible. With nervous fingers, I managed to push the button to do just that. After confirming my identity, the officer informed me there was a fire at my house.

As I got closer to home, I found the roads blocked in every direction; I had to be cleared to get through. When I saw my home, I was confused. It looked fine. I was expecting a pile of ashes or at least some visible sign of destruction. One of the firefighters took some information and warned me that the interior did not fare as well as the exterior. When it was finally safe for me to enter, I was walked through the scene. The fire marshal explained exactly what he believed had happened, including the timeline of events.

Due to the materials and design of my century-old house, the fire, which started in old wiring, was contained in the wall until it built up enough pressure to explode through. The full-sized filing cabinet and large freezer that I assumed had been moved by the firemen had, in fact, been blown across the room by the force of the explosion. The fire marshal explained that the build-up of the fire inside the wall would have made enough noise for me to hear from anywhere on the first floor, especially right before exploding through the wall. He felt confident that, had I been home, I would have heard the noise and been investigating — placing me in the immediate path of the explosion. Given the intensity of the force, heat, and flying debris, there would have been little chance of survival.

When the discussion turned to the timing of events, I really understood the important role every small detail can make. The explosion happened shortly after I had left for the vet with Boomerjax. In fact, the first 911 call reporting the fire had come in during the time that I had put aside for wrestling Boomerjax into his carrier. If he hadn't uncharacteristically cooperated, I would have been home and looking for the source of the noise in the wall. And if he hadn't developed an allergy to flea bites for the first time, after our prior successful treatments, we wouldn't have been heading to the vet.

Therefore, I owe my life to a flea, or more accurately to an infestation of fleas.

Amazingly, three years later, Boomerjax has never had fleas again. He's a good boy.

— David L. Bishop —

Finding My Truth

We do not create our destiny; we participate in its unfolding. Synchronicity works as a catalyst toward the working out of that destiny.
~David Richo, The Power of Coincidence

I'd been seeing a gifted healer named Kathy as part of a holistic approach to treating the symptoms of my traumatic brain injury. She gave counsel and did energy healing. I'd been seeing her monthly for about a year and I always felt better after each session. Then one day, as the session ended, she asked me suddenly, "Could you possibly be adopted?"

I laughed and said, "I don't know. I have a birth certificate with the names of both parents who raised me on it. However, I have always felt different from everyone else in the family, so I wouldn't be surprised."

I had said that to make light of the question. Still, later that night, I decided to call my parents. When I questioned my father, he started stammering, and my mother's response was odd, too. I began to search for more information. After several frustrating months with no results, I decided to stop searching and "let go and let God."

Six months later, I was on the phone with Kathy complaining that my mother expected me to go to a three-hour Christmas celebration. I didn't want to attend, but felt obligated. She reminded me I was "grown" and had been considered an adult for more than thirty years. Then she asked, "What do you want to do?"

I responded, "Sit on an island somewhere." She encouraged me to do what would make me happy, and she added that if I decided to go to the islands, she would go with me.

I decided to do it, even though Christmas was only a month away and most places were already fully booked. I told my travel agent that I was flexible as long as the flight wasn't more than three hours, and she said that if I was willing to drive 100 miles to Philadelphia, fly out on Christmas Day and return on New Year's Eve, she could get us to St. Thomas in the U.S. Virgin Islands.

We set off on our adventure on Christmas Eve, but our first day on St. Thomas was disappointing. The beach near our hotel was small and crowded.

We decided to travel to the other side of the island the next day, and we randomly chose a restaurant in another hotel to have breakfast. The restaurant was practically empty, so we were surprised when the waitress sat two women right beside us.

Soon, we were chatting and sharing stories about how we arrived at this isolated location. We were so engrossed in conversation that an hour passed before we exchanged names. When I handed them my business card, which said Sheila Quarles on it, one of the women stared at it. And then she said, "I had a sister who was adopted by a Quarles family in Washington, D.C."

I answered, "I'm from D.C."

She looked at me and said, "I remembered hearing the adults discussing how this family promised to take care of her feet, which needed special attention."

"I had trouble with my feet and had to wear special shoes," I answered.

She then said, "We heard she was modeling. We didn't understand how with her foot problems."

I told her I had been a model for a department store, and my picture had been in the newspaper. Everyone gasped.

I began to cry. I was sitting next to my biological sister.

She had started looking for me six months earlier because our mother had died, and I was the only missing sibling. She further explained that she actually lived in St. Croix and was visiting her friend on St. Thomas when they decided to try this restaurant.

    My sister was returning home that day, and I agreed to go with her to St. Croix. I packed my bags and met her at the small plane that would take us there. She held my hand, and I cried as I looked out the window.

    When I arrived at her home, we actually had some of the same items. We had also sent out the same holiday greeting cards. We had so much in common that I felt as though I was home. She called my aunts, sisters, and brothers and told them I had been found.

    That year, by deciding to do something very different for Christmas, I set off on a miraculous journey and I discovered my truth. And if you're wondering what happened to my friend Kathy, who helped to create this miracle, after I met my sister at the breakfast table, Kathy said, "my job is done." She booked the next flight home. Five years later, I offered to lend my skills to assist Kathy with her business, Inner Journeys, and I've been her business partner for ten years now.

—Sheila Quarles—

One Rainy Morning

> *Coincidence is the language of the stars. For something to happen, so many forces have to be put into action.*
> *~Paulo Coelho*

The beeping of my cell-phone alarm jolted me awake. Summer rain beat against the window of my friend Alice's guestroom, and I wanted nothing more than to pull the covers over my head and grab a few more winks. But home was more than a hundred miles away, and I had a full afternoon of appointments ahead of me. I needed to get on the road. I swung my feet onto the floor and picked up the phone to click on the weather app.

That's when I noticed the low-battery warning. Rats! I'd meant to attach the phone to the charger before I went to sleep. No worries, though. Charging it while I ate breakfast would give it enough juice. I plugged the cord into the outlet near my bed and laid the phone on the bedside table. Then I headed to the kitchen for a cup of coffee and one of Alice's famous blueberry muffins. We lingered longer than I'd intended in her cozy breakfast nook, chatting and watching the rain that was still coming down in buckets.

"My umbrella's where it can't do me a bit of good," I told her.

Alice raised her eyebrows. "Back seat of the car?"

"Right."

We both laughed, and she said she'd walk me out under her gigantic golf umbrella. A few minutes later, that's what we did. I gave

Miraculous Timing | 257

Alice a hug and promised to visit again soon. I knew she was lonely. Her husband had died only a few months earlier, and her only child lived clear across the country.

"I hope you really will come back soon," she said, dabbing at her eyes. "You be careful out there and take it slow around the curves. These mountain roads are slick."

"I'll be careful," I promised, and I meant it. The fifteen miles of back road that led to Alice's cabin were treacherous even in good weather. It would be a white-knuckle trip to the main highway on this rainy day, for sure.

With headlights blazing and windshield wipers slapping, I made my way slowly along. What I needed was some music to help keep me focused. I punched on the radio, but got nothing but static. I reached into my purse, which I'd set beside me on the passenger seat, for my phone, which had hundreds of songs stored on it. But the phone wasn't in the side pocket where I usually kept it. It wasn't in the main pocket with my wallet and sunglasses. It didn't take long for me to figure out exactly where it was. The phone was on the bedside table in Alice's guest room.

If it would've done any good, I'd have laid my head on the steering wheel and cried. This mistake was going to cost me at least an hour. Now, there was no way I could make it to my first appointment on time. No matter. I had to have the phone. I turned the car around and headed back along the same wet, curvy roads I'd just traveled.

I pulled into Alice's driveway and raced through the rain to the front door. She didn't answer when I knocked, so I turned the knob. It wasn't locked. "Helloooo...," I called out. "Crazy me forgot my phone." No answer. "Alice?" I said. "Alice, it's me." Silence was the only response. I made my way toward her bedroom, but pulled up short when I turned the corner into the hall. There was Alice, lying on the floor and staring at the ceiling. I dropped to my knees beside her. Her breathing was shallow, and she had welts on her neck. All the color had drained from her face. I squeezed her hand and put my lips next to her ear. "Can you tell me what happened?"

"Wasp sting," she murmured in a hoarse voice. "EpiPen's in the medicine cabinet."

I rushed to the bathroom and found the pen. "Tell me what to do." "Take it out of the case and pull off the cap. Hold the pen in your fist and plunge in the needle." She pointed to her upper thigh. "Right there. Hold it for ten seconds. Hurry."

Plunge in the needle? I was no nurse. I'd never in my whole life given anyone a shot. It was all I could do to dig a splinter out of a finger. But I slid the EpiPen out of its plastic holder and jammed the needle into her thigh. "Now call 911," she said. I retrieved my phone from the guestroom and, with shaking hands, made the call. Within minutes, an ambulance arrived and took Alice to the hospital. I followed in my own car.

Needless to say, I missed all my appointments that afternoon. In the greater scheme of things, that didn't matter one bit. What did matter was that I hadn't remembered to charge my cell phone the night before. And that I'd left it on the bedside table. And that I'd realized—just in the nick of time—that the phone wasn't in my purse and had turned around. Alice knew she was allergic to stings, but had never, until that day, had a true anaphylactic reaction. But she kept injectable epinephrine around just in case. If I hadn't returned to her house when I did and given her the shot, she likely would have died.

A lucky coincidence? Not to my way of thinking. It was a miracle if I ever saw one.

—Jennie Ivey—

Chapter
11

Answered Prayers

84

Prayers of Thanksgiving

Everything we do should be a result of our gratitude
for what God has done for us.
~Lauryn Hill

"Father in Heaven, please bless my children. Please bless my friends who are struggling. Please do this and do that …" And so my prayers went. They were less about thanksgiving than they were a list of things for the Lord to do.

Who was I to give the Lord instructions?

A moment of reflection following one of my typical prayers brought me up short. Shamed, I realized that my prayers acknowledged little gratitude and praise to the Father at all.

What could I do to change that?

I challenged myself for a week to give prayers that were 100 percent ones of gratitude. Could I do that? Could I suppress my natural tendency to ask for things?

I was determined to find out.

I started small. I thanked the Lord for a sunny day and the flowers outside my window. I thanked Him for the change of seasons. I thanked Him for the gift of prayer itself.

Something happened along the way. Gratitude, it turns out, is contagious. As I became more aware of His hand in my life, I also became more cognizant of the blessings that others brought into my life as well.

A bouquet of flowers from a friend for no occasion.

An unexpected phone call from a distant relative.

A note from a grandchild saying that he loved me.

Another unexpected consequence resulted along the way. The more grateful I became to the Father for His many blessings, the happier I grew.

—Jane McBride—

85

Answered Prayer

*The message of Christmas is that the visible material
world is bound to the invisible spiritual world.*
~Author Unknown

"Lord, what can I do now?" I asked, as I drove home without a Christmas tree for our family.

For weeks our nine-year-old daughter Janelle had been praying for a "real" Christmas tree. She thought the tiny hand-me-down silver tree we usually put up was simply not suitable anymore.

"Mom, our tree is so small — and you've said yourself that someone gave it to you, and some day you hope to buy a real one."

"A real one would be nice," I agreed, "but we don't have money for a real tree or the decorations we would need. What would a big beautiful tree look like without an angel to sit on top?"

I had usually put up the tree in late November. I loved the Christmas season and I felt decorating early was a great way to start the festivities — but not this year. Janelle was so sure that God would answer her prayer for a real tree, so we all had to wait.

The days went by and we were not any closer to getting a real tree. We'd had another poor year on the farm and simply could not afford to "waste" money on a real tree, especially since we did have this old one.

"Please help me to find a solution before this hurts Janelle's fragile faith," became my prayer. But as the weeks went by I began to wonder

Answered Prayers | 263

if maybe we should try to buy one.

About ten days before Christmas, I went into town to pick up our mail and a few groceries. I couldn't help stopping by the lumberyard where a local charity sold real Christmas trees. I just wanted to check out how much they were selling for. I gasped as I came around the corner and saw they only had three trees left. I walked briskly over to them, thinking they must be cheap or damaged to be the only ones left, but I was surprised to see three top-of-the-line trees and they had an out-of-reach price tag to go with them. I walked away knowing we could not afford one of those trees for sure.

That is why I was asking, "What can I do now Lord?"

I prayed as I drove and planned how I would break the news to Janelle. I knew she would be very disappointed and hurt, but we would have to go ahead and put up the little silver tree. Would it be better to have it up when she came home off the bus? Or should I wait, tell her what we needed to do, and let her help me put up the little tree?

Later that afternoon the phone rang. It was our neighbour Ted. We weren't close, so I figured he must be calling to talk farming with my husband Ken.

"No, you're just the lady I'm looking for," he said.

"Oh, really?" I replied.

"First, I'd better ask if you have put up your Christmas tree yet."

"No, as a matter of fact we haven't. I know it's getting late but…"

Ted cut me off with, "Now that my boys are married they wanted a tree for their own places so we went away up north this morning to get ourselves a tree. For some strange reason we ended up with an extra tree and, I wondered… could we give it to you?"

I was speechless. "For some strange reason," he had said. Could the reason have been a little girl's prayer?

I stammered as I tried to answer him. "Yes…Yes… sure… we'd love to have a real tree…." I was sure Ted would hear my heart pounding.

"You don't owe us a thing," he continued. "As I said, I don't know how we ended up with the extra tree, but you are welcome to have it. I'll drop it off in a bit."

I got off the phone shaking my head. How could Ted have possibly known? We hadn't told anyone, and we didn't know him well enough. He'd never been in our home to see our "little" tree. Only a God who truly cares about the little and big things in life could have arranged for Ted to get an extra tree, and then put it in his heart to call and offer it to us.

That day, as the bus pulled into the yard, there was one very excited little girl when she saw a "real tree" in our yard, ready to be pushed, pulled, and eventually cut down to fit into our house. It didn't matter that our decorations weren't the greatest, lights were nonexistent, and there was no angel for the top. After all, a "real Christmas tree" was what she had prayed for, and wasn't having a tree that had truly been delivered by angels better than having one at the top of the tree?

—Annie Riess—

Reflections of Hope in the Snowstorm

It only takes a thought and your angels will be there…
for although you may not see them,
you're always in their care.
~Author Unknown

I was homesick. My husband, Keith, was attending Utah State University in Logan, Utah. We lived eight hundred miles away from my parents and family back home in Northern California. We couldn't afford to go home for Christmas. We would just stay home in Hyrum, and have a simple Christmas with our baby, Ann.

Then a most unexpected gift arrived in a Christmas card: enough money for gas for the eight-hundred-mile drive home. We were so excited. Keith took time off from his part-time job and we packed the car. We had family prayer, asking humbly for safety and good traveling conditions.

We drove all day through Nevada, over the Sierras, to the west coast of California. Everything went well and we finally drove up the familiar driveway, honking the horn to signal our arrival. My family rushed out to greet us, welcoming us with love and Christmas cheer.

We celebrated Christmas in my childhood home, all of us together again for the first time in three years. My family rejoiced when we announced that we were expecting our second child in the spring.

All too soon, the time came for us to return to Utah. My parents gave us some money for gas. With tears and hugs, we started on our way. Hoping to make good time, we drove steadily through the day.

Toward evening, we arrived in Wendover, on the border between Nevada and Utah. Snow flurries swirled around the car. We stopped just long enough to fuel up the car. With no credit card and very little cash, we did not even consider staying overnight in a motel.

If the road and weather conditions were good, we had about two hours of driving to get to Salt Lake City. We thought if we could just make it to Keith's parents' home in nearby Bountiful that night, we could rest. Then we could go on to Hyrum in the morning, and he would make it to work on time.

We drove into the darkening night. Frantic flurries of snow swirled wildly about the car. Keith was having trouble seeing the road, as the headlights seemed dim. He pulled over, and got out to brush the snow away from them.

Then he climbed back into the driver's seat and told me the bad news. "We have only one headlight." A simple statement, but loaded with dread.

With another heartfelt prayer for safety and protection, we felt we had no choice but to head slowly out onto the nearly deserted freeway. Our car bravely slogged through the snowy darkness. We desperately tried to keep our eyes on the white line in the road, but it was vanishing quickly in the accumulating snow. We seemed to be all alone on that dark stretch of freeway. There was no traffic in either direction, and the visibility was near zero.

We knew that our parents were praying us safely through the night. We prayed too, for traction and safety.

Suddenly, out of nowhere, a semi-truck appeared, gaining quickly upon us. It splattered a spray of snow onto our windshield as it passed. Then it pulled into our lane, directly in front of our car. Our meager headlight reflected off the shiny silver doors on the back of the truck.

The driver could have sped ahead. Instead, he stayed right with us, lighting our way. The steady flurry of relentless snowflakes dashed against our windshield. The wipers could barely keep them brushed away. The white line of the road was no longer visible. We cautiously crept along, following the truck.

In those anxiety-filled moments, I felt our unborn baby kick for the first time! The miracle of new life growing within me filled us with wonder. We felt that there were angels protecting us that night, and there was a curious peace in our hearts.

Hours later, we reached the welcome streetlights and plowed roads of Salt Lake City. To signal our gratitude, Keith blinked our one headlight at the semi-truck driver in front of us. This man had stayed with us for more than 120 miles on that drive between Wendover and Salt Lake City. Our one headlight had reflected off the back of his truck as he had lighted our way in the dark night.

It turned out that this storm deposited eighteen inches of snow in twenty-four hours, closing the Salt Lake City airport for twenty hours. But we had traveled safely through the massive storm. We offered a heartfelt prayer of thanksgiving for this miracle.

As I gratefully closed my eyes at last that night, the images of the steadily blowing snow drifted before them. More importantly, though, my mind's eye fixed upon the reflection of the unseen angels and the semi-truck driver who had stayed with us, giving us hope through the darkest hours of that snow-filled night.

—Valaree Terribilini Brough—

87

Miracle on the Hudson

> *In hindsight, I think something remarkable did happen that day.*
> ~Capt. Chesley "Sully" Sullenberger III

It was Thursday morning, January 15, 2009. I was in New York City where I traveled to work on a regular basis. It was about 10:30 a.m. and snow was coming down pretty hard. I had checked the weather forecast because I had a 7 o'clock flight home to Charlotte, North Carolina, and I didn't want to get stuck. The Weather Channel website said the snow was going to quit and it was going to be a nice day.

I went into a meeting with my boss about 11 o'clock and snow was still coming down.

"What are you still doing here?" he asked. "You're going to get stuck up here. You really ought to get home."

So I rebooked for the 2:45 p.m. flight. Seat 16E.

When I boarded the plane, I was on my cell phone, sending texts, talking to people right up until they closed the cabin door. We taxied for about thirty minutes, as is usual at LaGuardia Airport, and we took off.

Sitting back, I felt the steep climb that pressed me against the seat. I opened the newspaper to read the remnants of *The Wall Street Journal* that I hadn't finished that morning.

Answered Prayers | 269

There was a muffled bang that I could literally feel. The whole plane shuddered.

"What could that possibly be?" I wondered.

The plane went into a really steep bank to the left. It was all going so fast. I thought maybe the plane was out of control and it was over. But the pilot, who had identified himself earlier as Captain Chesley Sullenberger, seemed to get control back. He stabilized the plane.

There was no panic. After the initial gasp from everyone, it was very, very quiet.

I was looking around and listening when I heard somebody on the left say, "We must've hit something. I saw shadows."

Then a little later, someone else said, "The left engine is on fire!"

Even at this point, I wasn't terribly worried. I figured we had two engines, and if need be we could fly with just one.

But as time passed I realized how quiet it was on the plane. There was nothing but the whistling of the wind. It dawned on me — we had no power. We were literally gliding and we weren't very high. That's when I sat bolt upright and grabbed my head. I felt a cold fear like nothing I'd ever experienced.

I prayed intensely. I repeated, "Please God, help us. Please God, forgive me," over and over again. Nothing coherent. There were just too many thoughts going through my head.

Yet I still had hope. If they could at least get one engine going... we just needed some power to get back to LaGuardia. We'd only been up for three minutes; certainly we could turn around and make a safe landing.

That hope went out the window when I realized we were getting lower and lower, following the river. When that realization set in — sheer terror — I realized the likelihood of dying on this plane. There was nowhere, no one to turn to but God.

I prayed intensely. I was there with Him. It was the closest I'd ever felt to Him. I didn't bargain: "If you save us, I will..." Instead, I prayed for my family, my children, my wife.

Shortly thereafter, Captain Sully came over the intercom. "This is the captain. Brace for impact."

There was nothing in those words for me but death and pain. A cold hard reality hit me, and there was nothing I could do about it. I was strapped in my seat, completely and utterly powerless.

In the midst of that utter hopelessness, I was looking forward, as crazy as that might sound. What was death going to be like? Was it going to be just complete darkness? Or a bright light? Perfect clarity? Joy? What was it going to be like in the presence of God? I believe God gives us all hope even in dire moments. It was such a blessing to have that sense of hope and that sense of salvation.

I pulled out my BlackBerry. I wanted to get a message to my children… to give them something to carry with them through their lives, some sort of closure. I was trying to do that as I looked out the window, watching the water come faster and faster. I put the BlackBerry down, closed my eyes, and pleaded, "God, please let me see my children again." Then, "God, this is going to hurt so bad."

I was terrified, not necessarily of death and what comes after that, but I was really worried about the pain.

We hit the water. The BlackBerry came up and hit me right on the bridge of my nose, just about knocking me out.

And we came to a stop.

I knew immediately we were okay.

The impact was not terribly traumatic. I knew the plane was intact and not broken up. No one was going to be severely injured.

I got into the aisle, and the emergency doors were open. I saw a beautiful, clear, blue day, twenty degrees, sun light streaming in. It was the most wonderful feeling I have ever felt. Symbolic it seemed, like it was a new day, a new life. A beginning.

I filed out the doorway to step onto the wing, and turned back around to get a lifejacket. No one had announced that we were going to make a water landing and to remember our lifejackets underneath the seat cushion. Of course all the cushions by the exit row had been stripped away and I found none.

I did absolutely nothing right. I did everything wrong, but I still came out of this. If I had gotten out there on the wing, and the wing was sinking, and the ferries were not there, I would have drowned

Answered Prayers

because hypothermia would have overtaken me in ten minutes.

Be that as it may, I stepped out on the wing without a lifejacket. I already saw the ferry coming and it was like a dream for me. So many things went wrong. But so many other things went right. An amazing turn of events.

After that day, I got at least a dozen e-mails of the drawing of the plane with God's hands lowering it down — "What Really Happened on the Hudson River." I truly believe that.

Certainly for me, I came much closer to God that day. It was probably the only time that I've been intimately, truly wholly there and one with Him.

— Warren F. Holland —

Ask and You Shall Receive

Ask of me, and I will make the nations your inheritance, the ends of the earth your possession.
~Psalm 2:8

Several years ago my wife of fifteen years and I found ourselves struggling financially. We had gone through college together, started careers and had two children.

As a veterinarian, I had followed what I thought was God's plan for my life. I'd sold my stock in a very successful multi-man practice to go into full-time teaching. The pay as a teacher is not nearly as good as a practitioner's and the cut was the major contributor to our financial worries. So I had three jobs. I was teaching full-time at a college in Dallas plus teaching night classes part-time for a local junior college. To supplement my teaching salaries I had started seeing patients in a back room of one of the college labs on Friday afternoons from 1:00 until 5:00. It was a modest practice at best, and most of the patients I saw belonged to students so I only charged enough to cover my overhead.

Money was extremely tight and we were not able to pay some of our bills. It was so stressful that my wife decided to take our children and go to her mother's house for a few days to try to decompress, leaving me with the house and my jobs.

I called her Thursday night and asked exactly how much money

Answered Prayers | 273

we needed to pay our bills and not be delinquent or have late charges. She told me we needed $311 to make it until my next paycheck. We agreed to pray that God would help us through this time. We said a short prayer on the phone, and then I did something I had never done before. I got down on my knees and asked God specifically for money. I asked Him if He would bring enough animals to me on the following afternoon so I could pay our bills. I told Him I needed $311.

After I prayed, I went to bed and when I woke up the next morning, I had forgotten about my prayer. I went to school, taught my classes, and went to the lab in the afternoon in case any patients might come to my makeshift clinic. It was an unusually busy day; I saw all of the animals and finished up around five. Since my practice was so small, I only had a student assistant helping me. We did business on a strictly cash basis. If the client had the cash, they paid me and if they did not, I told them they could pay me later. I kept the money I made that day in my shirt pocket. I had always focused on service and caring for the animals, not money, so I didn't even think to count it at the end of the day.

When I got home that night, I was extremely tired and fell asleep on the couch. The phone woke me. It was my wife asking if I had made any money at the practice that afternoon. I pulled the wad of bills out of my shirt pocket and counted it while I spoke to her on the phone. I counted out $310. She gasped and reminded me that was only one dollar short of the money we needed to pay our bills. I looked down and saw a dollar bill on the floor beside the couch. When I had pulled the money out of my shirt pocket, I guess a dollar had fallen to the floor. That dollar added to the rest of the wad equaled the exact amount we had prayed for, $311.

That day marked a big turnaround in our lives. We have never been in that dire financial situation again.

I know this is but a small need, but it was a huge miracle when you realize God provided exactly what we had asked for, to the penny.

— Gene F. Giggleman, DVM —

The Healing Hand of God

The prayer that begins with trustfulness and passes on into waiting will always end in thankfulness, triumph, and praise.
~Alexander Maclaren

My husband and I had agreed to a weekend camping trip with our good friends, Doug and Kathy, fellow youth leaders from our church. Our three young children were just as excited about time at the beach as we adults. We had a great time swimming during the day and at night we decided to gather around a campfire.

We edged our lawn chairs closer to the fire pit as a chill settled over the day. While we were talking and roasting hot dogs and marshmallows on long sticks, I realized that our four-year-old daughter, Elizabeth, had wiggled her chair too close to the fire. I opened my mouth to instruct her to move back when the unthinkable happened. The chair tipped forward, dumping her onto the ground at the edge of the pit. She dropped onto a bed of smouldering coals.

All four adults reached for her. My husband and I grabbed her and ran to the nearby water tap. My first thought was to douse her smoking shorts. I hadn't considered the possibility of burns — until I saw her feet. Blisters swelled like balloons filled with water. Our daughter wailed out her pain. Adrenaline took over as we hustled to

Answered Prayers

our vehicle. We covered Elizabeth's burns with a clean towel and, leaving our older children with Doug and Kathy, headed for the hospital in the nearby town.

"She has second- and third-degree burns on her feet and her hip." I wanted to cry for this innocent child who wept out pain she didn't understand. "You'll want to take her to your family doctor to keep an eye on them."

We headed home where Doug and Kathy waited with our other two girls. Elizabeth sat quietly in the car with me, her feet swaddled in white gauze, the burn medicine giving her temporary relief.

The next day we rented a small wheelchair. Our doctor informed us that Elizabeth would be off her feet for a few months and would likely undergo skin grafting. By Wednesday, an infection set in and Elizabeth's temperature soared. That evening, she hallucinated, experiencing an imaginary card game of Go Fish. We headed to the hospital again.

A child should never have to endure debriding. It is a painful process where the burnt skin is removed. Anaesthetic is useless since the nerves in the burned tissue are damaged. For the next week, our little girl underwent the removal of the decaying tissue while I held her and prayed for God to give us a miracle.

I was supposed to go to a women's retreat two weeks after our camping weekend. I called our group organizer and told her why I had to cancel. "Pray for Elizabeth. She's in so much pain. Pray for healing."

Unknown to us, that request went to the retreat leadership team. While the ladies from our church began their adventure in the Muskoka woods, I made daily trips to the doctor to have the bandages changed and new medication applied. Standing behind Elizabeth's chair, I waited patiently while new gauze and tape covered wicked wounds and I prayed. I prayed that God would heal our daughter and that he would use this moment in time to show his love.

Saturday morning came and I headed out into the countryside to our doctor's home. He'd been very concerned about the infection and insisted that the bandages be changed daily. Sunday morning showed no improvement in Elizabeth's feet. We went to church as a family, her little red wheelchair carrying her down the aisle. She played quietly until the service finished and we headed home. That evening, the phone rang and I made my way to the kitchen to answer it.

"The whole group prayed for Elizabeth." Our group organizer's voice hummed with excitement. "It was something. Over 200 women gathered together praying for a miracle. I can't wait to see what God will do."

Monday morning brought a warm September sun and the girls and I climbed into the van and headed to the doctor's house. He'd warned me the day before that he would not be in the office until Tuesday and to come to his house. We pulled up the long drive and parked. Lifting Elizabeth into her wheelchair, I instructed her sisters to remain in their seatbelts until I called them. I turned toward the porch and spied the doctor coming down the walkway.

"And how's my patient today?"

Elizabeth grinned and waited while he squatted before her and unwrapped her feet. I watched from my place behind the chair, the prayer for healing running through my mind. My heart lurched as his expression sobered. What was wrong? Were her feet worse? Had the infection spread?

"I don't understand." The words came out in a slight stutter.

I locked the chair brakes and moved to the front, leaning over the doctor's shoulder. There in his hand rested one of Elizabeth's feet, the skin beautiful and fresh and pink. Not a mark marred the skin that had been a pucker of scorched flesh the day before. I laughed — a single, shocked chuckle — and he glanced up at me, his eyes frightened.

"I guess that's what happens when 200 women ask God for healing." The words slipped from my mouth and I watched the fear turn to confusion.

"If that's what you want to believe."

I laughed again, this time in amazement. "Do you have a better explanation?"

The doctor shook his head and tried to pull on the mantle of professionalism. "I guess we don't need any more bandaging. Bring her in a week from now and I'll check it over again." I thanked him as he turned and headed for his house.

We sang songs as we drove home and then I spent the morning watching Elizabeth chase her sisters around the yard. Two weeks. She had suffered for two weeks and I pondered all that her suffering had accomplished. Because of it, our family's faith grew, a doctor saw the healing hand of God and 200 strangers learned the importance of prayer.

— Donna Fawcett —

Faith and Warmth

We must remember that the shortest distance between our problems and their solutions is the distance between our knees and the floor.
~Charles Stanley

My three children were at their father's house but would be coming home that evening to a very cold house. Our tiny one-bedroom cottage was heated by a lone fireplace, but I had no money to buy wood. So, I knelt in the tiny front room and began to cry out to God.

Almost immediately, I heard a quiet knock on the door. Drying my tears, I cautiously went to see who was there. I opened the door to a young boy with a very dirty face. "May I help you?" I asked.

Straightening his shoulders, he proudly told me that he had been chopping wood with his father down the street. They didn't have a fireplace so his dad wanted to know if I could use some wood.

Hello? An answer literally minutes after the prayer!

After my incredulous and excited "Yes!" I didn't have to do anything. He ran back to his father and the two of them brought load after load after load of wood. They stacked it neatly against the house, and by my rough calculations there had to have been at least two cords of wood. The father and son had declined my offer of help, so I could only stand there and watch with amazement the tangible answer to my prayer being fulfilled before my very eyes.

With their act of kindness completed, they smiled and left.

Still in a state of astonishment, I gathered up stray pieces for kindling and loaded my arms with the wood. With much joy I built that much-needed fire. Usually, fresh cut wood is hard to get started. But not this time. It ignited right away.

This miracle of grace gave me renewed joy and strength. With a light heart I prepared two loaves of fresh bread, baking one at a time in our miniature oven. My children arrived home to the delicious aroma of fresh bread and the coziness of that incredible crackling fire.

All that I thought was going to be hopelessly wrong, was now abundantly right.

—Brenda M. Lane—

Off the Hook

*Prayer does not change God, but it
changes him who prays.*
~Søren Kierkegaard

"You're my best friend," Marcie told me, lifting the red book in her hands. "I'm worried about you. You have got to quit smoking!" She held the self-help book out to me and said, "This book really helped my husband quit. Maybe it'll work for you too."

I sighed. My husband and children had been nagging me for years and now my dearest friend was stepping up to remind me as well. I had been smoking since I was fifteen. Over the years I had tried numerous times to quit — aversion therapy, hypnosis and many attempts at going cold turkey — but the cravings were so intense and my willpower so weak, I would be miserable and only last a week or two before giving in. Second, I had struggled with chronic depression for many years and each attempt to quit smoking would trigger an episode, exacerbating my feelings of hopelessness and despair.

"Thanks, Marce," I said, taking the book with what I hoped would pass for a grateful smile. "I'm kind of busy lately but I'll get to it as soon as I can." After she left, I took the book and set it dutifully on the coffee table where it sat, radiating guilt vibes at me. "Leave me alone," I muttered. "I'm happy smoking. I don't want to quit."

But I wasn't happy smoking, and I did want to quit. I hated knowing I was addicted to something as stupid as lighting a cylinder

Answered Prayers

of leaves and sucking toxic smoke into my lungs. I knew I was playing Russian roulette with cancer.

I covered the book with a magazine, grabbed my cigarettes and went outside.

Months passed. I shuffled the book from one end of the coffee table to the other, studiously ignoring the bright red cover that said *Hooked But Not Helpless*. Each time Marcie asked if I'd read the book, I'd mutter, "Soon."

One day, in the midst of a devastating bout of depression—sadness and despair so deep that rising from bed in the morning seemed like a mountain too high to climb—I felt strangely compelled to pick it up. In resignation, I started to read. At least I'll be able to give it back to Marcie, I thought, and get it off my coffee table.

Hours later, I finished the book. Its premise for overcoming smoking addiction had been simple but innovative, teaching the reader how to change thinking patterns about smoking, and including good strategies for dealing with feelings of deprivation. Sitting back, I found myself experiencing an unfamiliar feeling... hope.

On the heels of that feeling came an unquestionable knowledge: God wanted me to quit. I put my head in my hands and groaned.

"No way, God!" The very idea made me mad. "I can't do it. You know I can't!"

But the feeling persisted. And it wouldn't leave me alone. Finally, I threw the book down on the table and, I'm embarrassed to say, issued a very irreverent ultimatum: "Apparently you want me to quit smoking, even though you know I'm drowning in depression down here. Well, I think it's completely unfair of you to even suggest it, but here's the deal: I'll try—but I'm telling you this—if I do, You have to do it all. I mean every bit of it. If I have one craving, I'm giving in and smoking."

God, His usual, enigmatic self, didn't say a word.

I got up, put my pack of cigarettes into a drawer and resigned myself to the misery of deprivation.

The rest of the day passed. The family came home and we ate dinner, watched TV and went to bed. Morning came and we all arose and went about our routines. My husband went off to work, the kids left for school and I busied myself with cleaning, laundry and my usual chores. Throughout the day, I kept having the strange feeling that I was forgetting something. I'd stop what I was doing, think, scratch my head, then when nothing came to mind, shrug and go about my work. It took about two days of this before I realized... I wasn't smoking! Not only wasn't I smoking, I had totally forgotten about it! Shocked and wary, I searched my mind for any of the cigarette cravings that had ruled my life for so long. Nothing. I had absolutely no interest in smoking.

That was twenty years ago. I have never had a craving and have never missed smoking. It is as if I had never smoked. Not a day goes by that I'm not awestruck at the magnitude of this miracle, and filled with gratitude — I'm off the hook! Thirty-five years of bondage, broken in a moment by an irreverent, even faithless prayer. And I understand now that our Father listens to and answers His children's supplications no matter what emotional state we are in when we call out.

So the next time you feel like you're all alone in the world and God's too busy or disinterested to listen to little you and your problems, He isn't. Pray anyway. What do you have to lose?

— Tina Wagner Mattern —

A Patchwork of Hope

A quilt will warm your body and comfort your soul.
~Author Unknown

In February 2005, my daughter Julie and son-in-law Mike died in a motorcycle accident. I was stunned and grief-stricken, but the heartache my young grandchildren suffered after losing both parents was unimaginable.

While my husband Walt and I struggled to make sense of it all, family and friends asked, "What's going to happen to the kids?"

In the middle of making funeral arrangements, Walt and I vowed to do whatever it took to raise ten-year-old Cari and six-year-old Michael. After petitioning the courts, we became our grandchildren's legal guardians.

The first few weeks were a blur as we struggled to stitch together the ragged pieces of our lives. A grief counselor advised us to keep Cari and Michael's routines as normal as possible to help them feel loved and secure. Rather than having the children change schools in the middle of the year, I moved into their home. At mealtimes, I prepared dishes their mom used to make; one breakfast favorite was Julie's hot cinnamon rolls.

And each night, I read bedtime stories before we folded our hands and remembered their mom and dad in prayer. Then each morning we recited the Guardian Angel Prayer, just as I had with Julie when she was a child:

Angel of God, my Guardian Dear,
To whom God's love commits me here,
Ever this day, be at my side,
To light, to guard, to rule and guide.

After hugging and kissing Cari and Michael goodnight, I tucked them into their beds underneath one of their mom's quilts.

As a teenager, Julie began collecting quilts after I won an embroidered blue-and-white one for her at a church picnic. Over the next twenty-plus years, I won several for her at local socials, fairs, and festivals. Those hand-stitched quilts had a special place in my daughter's home — and heart.

Months after the accident, we moved Cari and Michael into our home, along with their furniture, clothes, toys, and other belongings. We didn't have space to fit everything, but we made room for Julie's collection of quilts. In each of my grandkids' new rooms, their beds were covered with one of their mom's brightly-colored quilts, which I rotated each season.

When Cari turned twelve, she announced she wanted to paint and redecorate her room. I asked which of her mom's quilts she wanted to use after we were finished and was surprised when she told me she wanted a quilt of her own.

Realizing she was almost a teenager with her own tastes and style, I hugged her and said, "Sweetie, we'll go shopping to find one you like."

"I don't want one you can buy in a store," she said. "I want you to win one for me like you did for Mom."

Choking back tears, I said, "That won't be easy, but I'll try."

I became a woman on a mission, buying chances and raffle tickets, wishing for good luck, with no success.

By late 2009 I'd almost given up hope when I entered the mega-raffle at our parish's fall craft fair, a huge countywide event Julie and I had attended each November. The raffle featured a dozen giveaways, including the top prize everyone coveted — a queen-sized, hand-stitched patchwork quilt.

Answered Prayers

Because the craft fair fell on what would've been my daughter's fortieth birthday, I couldn't bring myself to go. The memory of attending past craft fairs with Julie would be too painful. Instead, I bought my chances in advance.

While admiring the handiwork on display in the parish gymnasium, I printed my name on the tickets. As I dropped my tickets into the huge wire barrel, I whispered a prayer to my guardian angel, "Angel of God, my Guardian Dear...."

The day of the craft fair not only fell on Julie's birthday, it also coincided with opening day of deer season, so Walt and Michael went hunting. Cari was spending the day with a friend.

My sisters Kathleen and Bridget and niece Angie tried to convince me to go the fair with them. Knowing I wouldn't be good company, I declined and moped around the house, missing my daughter more than ever.

Shortly after five o'clock, the phone rang.

"You won a raffle prize," a weary voice said. "We'll be here for about half an hour if you want to pick it up today."

When I arrived at the Parish Center, I spotted a woman sitting behind a long table. Nearby sat the big barrel crammed with thousands of raffle tickets.

When I identified myself, the woman pointed to a large black plastic bag. "Congratulations," she said.

"What did I win?" I asked.

When she answered, "the quilt," I burst into tears of joy.

Staring at the giant container crammed with tickets, I couldn't believe how fortunate I was that mine was the one drawn for the big prize. And I felt especially lucky to have won the quilt for Cari on her mom's birthday.

Then it dawned on me. Winning the quilt for my granddaughter on my daughter's birthday wasn't a coincidence. And it wasn't because of my good luck; I had help from an angel.

Cari's quilt is a homespun beauty, unlike any other in her mom's collection. Scraps of fabric in various colors, shapes, and patterns—once part of something else—had been carefully pieced together and transformed into a loving creation.

    The patchwork quilt is a one-of-a kind work of art that provides comfort, warmth, beauty, and hope — a guardian angel's answer to a grandmother's prayer.

— Donna Volkenannt —

Chapter 12

Dreams and Premonitions

Not My Child!

There is an instinct in a woman to love most her own child — and an instinct to make any child who needs her love, her own.
~Robert Brault, rbrault.blogspot.com

My friend Alice should have been sleeping. In fact, she had been sleeping, but her breathing had quickened until it came in gasps as though she was running. Suddenly she was awake, crying. Her dream had been so real, so vivid she stumbled out of bed and walked to the room beside the one she shared with her husband, Dan, just to check. Yes, all four children were there. It had been a dream.

But what a terrible one! Alice climbed back into bed, wide-awake now, and gripped with a heavy fear. Her mind replayed the dream: Their little family was walking over a footbridge crossing a busy city street. Dan was walking ten feet ahead of Alice with Evan by his side and little Joseph on his shoulders. Alice had the baby in her arm and Ellie by the hand. The baby slipped lower on her hip and, letting go of Ellie's hand for a second, Alice readjusted the baby. In that moment, a strange woman ran beside her, grabbed Ellie, and ran to a black getaway car that sat in a nearby alley. Ellie was gone!

The pain… the horror… the desperation… the futility of running after the car… it gripped Alice all over again until she felt tears raining onto her pillow.

Dreams and Premonitions

"Please, God," she whispered. "Please lift this fear. It was only a dream."

Or was it? The days passed but the heaviness and guardedness Alice felt refused to lift. She told Dan about her dream and the nagging fears and together the two of them prayed over their children. They hadn't known that child trafficking was an issue in this Asian city until the dream alerted them and research confirmed that it was a major problem. "Oh, God," they prayed, "protect our children! Let this dream pass unfulfilled!"

Only when each child was thoroughly bathed in prayer did peace come. In fact, peace came so completely that Alice forgot about her dream until the day their family was restocking supplies in a large city miles away from the little outpost they lived in.

The city was crowded as usual and the footbridge they were crossing was clogged with people. Horns honked below them. Bicycle bells rang. Exhaust choked them. The children's tired feet were dragging, causing a little crowd to collect behind them on the narrow bridge.

"Let's stand to the side and let the people behind us go past," Dan suggested. "We're blocking the walkway."

The children, grateful for a brief rest, plastered themselves against the side of the bridge to let an equally grateful crowd pass them by. And then at the pace of the tired children, the little family made their way toward the bus stop. Dan, with Joseph on his shoulders, walked on ahead with Evan by his side. Alice followed them with the baby on her hip and Ellie holding her hand. Ellie's feet slowed and the distance between Dan and Alice widened.

Suddenly Alice felt uneasy. She glanced over her shoulder to see a lone woman still following them. It was the woman from her dream.

As if on cue, the baby slipped lower on Alice's hip. But Alice remembered the dream and there was no way she was going to readjust the baby now. Clamping her arm tightly across the baby's back in lieu of a readjustment, Alice picked up her pace, hurrying Ellie along. Ellie's small hand was clenched in her mother's iron grip. That woman wasn't going to get this child!

At the end of the footbridge was the alley from the dream. Alice stole a quick glance down the alley. Would it be there? It was. The black getaway car was there idling. Waiting.

Miracle of miracles, a rare taxi chanced past and was flagged by Dan, who had no idea of the drama unfolding behind him. As he opened the door of the taxi to lift the boys into it, Dan was startled as an ashen-faced Alice raced past him, leaped into the car, and pulled Ellie into it behind her.

The taxi doors slammed shut. Bus horns honked, the taxi horn responded in protest, and the little car carrying a family of six pulled away from the curb. The woman from the dream scowled. Her prey gone, she turned and disappeared into the crowd.

— Sara Nolt —

Banking on My Inner Voice

*Our inner wisdom is persistent, but quiet.
It will always whisper, but it will never
stop knocking at your door.*
~Vironika Tugaleva

It was August 1973. I had flown seventeen hours from Los Angeles for my first trip to Sweden. I checked into my hotel and asked how to exchange my U.S. dollars for Swedish krona. The friendly staff pointed out the bank next door. For some reason I changed my mind and decided to go later, after I dropped my things in my room and freshened up.

When I was ready to go to the bank, I again made a decision I did not understand. I chose to walk down all the stairs instead of taking the elevator from my high floor. When I finally entered the hotel lobby I could see something was terribly wrong. It turned out the bank was being robbed. I had almost walked into that bank at the worst possible time, just minutes before.

Because of security demands all the hotel guests were locked inside. Police negotiated throughout the standoff, in which four bank employees were held hostage in a stifling 11x11-foot vault. The employees started to identify with the robbers, and that was how the term "Stockholm Syndrome" was coined.

The ordeal lasted six days. My hotel was surrounded, so delivery trucks could not enter the roped-off zone. We hotel guests bonded with each other. The only food that was plentiful after a while was boiled white potatoes sprinkled with butter and parsley. To this day, that vision or taste takes me back to Sweden.

***

And then it happened again!

It had taken me forever to refinance my house even though interest rates had fallen so much. I dreaded the paperwork. Finally I filled out the forms and went to the mortgage office. When we were finished, I was told to drive to the bank to finalize everything that very afternoon. I threw the thick packet of documents beside me on the front seat of my car and drove to the bank.

As I was pulling into the driveway I thought about people who were superstitious about banking on Fridays. I have never been superstitious yet that thought did cross my mind. I surprised myself by backing out of the driveway and driving to a nearby boutique instead.

I was barely in the door when there was an announcement over the loudspeaker: "Please stay in this store until further notice. The bank down the street is surrounded, with a robbery in progress. We are told hostages have been taken." All of us in the shop could hear the alarm and sirens.

It turned out that the robbers were not apprehended. Some of the hostages were hospitalized and one suffered a major breakdown. That could have been me.

***

They say that things happen in threes. Believe it or not, it happened again!

A few years after the second bank robbery that I avoided, I was at Starbucks, hurrying toward the exit to get to my bank to order foreign currency for an upcoming trip. "Gail!" I heard. It was a former colleague I had not seen in years. I started to say I was in a hurry but then something changed my mind. We found a table and sat down to chat.

We were immersed in conversation when there was an announcement over the loudspeaker: "Stay inside until further notice. The bank in this parking lot has a robbery in progress." We could hear the alarm and sirens.

I have learned to listen to my inner thoughts and to trust my impulses. It has worked for me over the decades, again… and again… and again….

— Gail Small —

Her Final Lesson

If you want to turn your life around, try thankfulness.
It will change your life mightily.
~Gerald Good

On October 19, 2011 I picked up the phone to hear that my best friend since the sixth grade, Pitrice, had died. She was nineteen. She had been in the hospital since August after suffering a brain aneurysm.

On the day of her visitation, I walked up to her open casket with my mom and my friend Kaitlin. We took a long look at Pitrice as I tearfully slid an envelope between her two gloved hands. I had written her a private letter thanking her for the years of friendship and the lessons she taught me. She had always been wise beyond her years, and I asked her to watch over me.

In June 2012, I graduated from an acting program at college and moved back in with my parents. I was a hopeful but nervous graduate as I was thrown into the real world. Not too long after moving home, I desperately began to miss college.

I missed my friends, my student housing, and my roommates. I missed my landlords, my professors, my college fling, and my classes. I missed everything. I discovered that becoming an actress was a lot harder than I anticipated. I wasn't getting anywhere despite my attempts to contact agents and go to auditions.

I was facing a lot of rejection and it started affecting my self-esteem. I avoided seeing my friends because I was embarrassed that they were

Dreams and Premonitions

all doing so well and I was not. My life was going downhill and I had no energy to do anything. Then one night, after spending another day feeling sorry for myself, I went to bed and fell asleep.

I awoke in a room that was completely white. There was no furniture. In the corner of the room, Pitrice stood quietly, staring at me. Her dark skin contrasted with the white walls as she walked toward me. She looked healthy but her eyes were serious.

I immediately began venting to Pitrice about how much my life sucked — my hopeless love life, my nonexistent career, my lack of money, my failing social life, my insecurities, how society had failed me, and so on. I complained about everything. I told Pitrice how much I missed her. I told her that I felt lost and lonely.

Pitrice listened quietly, but then she let out an angry scream. "YOU'RE STILL HERE!" Pitrice shouted. "Move forward."

I froze as I realized that I was bellyaching about my life to a person who longed for the chance to be alive. Pitrice didn't get to graduate from college. She didn't get to pursue any of her dreams. A wave of guilt washed over me as I looked at Pitrice's face. She stared at me as she slowly faded into the white background and disappeared.

I stood there in the white room. "I'm still here."

I gasped as I woke up in my bed from the dream.

"I'm still here. I can still change the things I'm unhappy with."

Since I had that dream, I've been appreciating my life more, realizing it could be taken away at any moment like Pitrice's was. The dream changed me. Simple things like the taste of food and the feeling of the sun on my skin became special as I realized I was still here to appreciate them. I became healthier and looked better. I got in touch with Pitrice's family and to this day we remain close. I found a job, saw my friends and moved on from my heartbreak in college. I found an agent and continued auditioning. I am still taking acting workshops to improve my craft and striving to achieve my dream of becoming an actress.

Now I see the stressful periods in my life as little gifts that help me achieve maturity and growth. Whenever I feel frustrated, I go back to that dream of Pitrice. The dream serves as a constant reminder of the value of being alive and the importance of continually moving forward. Even after death, Pitrice continues to do a wonderful job of guiding me.

— Shannon MacKinnon —

One Last Thing

Dreams are today's answers to tomorrow's questions.
~Edgar Cayce

When I was in high school, I was certain that I had my life figured out. I was going to graduate, go to college, and have a great career. None of my plans included marriage. I thought I would never find someone, mainly because no one had ever been interested in me. At least, that's what it seemed like. I had crushes, and had even asked a boy or two out, but I was always rejected.

This was something that I kept to myself. Nobody knew my deepest fear about my future. Then, one night in December 1997, I had a dream that changed my outlook.

I was walking aboard a Navy ship with my grandpa. He was showing me around and talking to me about my worries of being alone. He said I needed to let go of the idea that I would be alone because he knew I would have love in my life. We stopped in a room where a sailor was standing with his back toward us. All I could see of him was that he was tall and had dark hair.

"Here, sweetheart," my grandpa said. "This is the man you will marry. He will love you more than you know. Please do not worry anymore. You are going to be okay."

I woke up after that to the sound of my sister sobbing downstairs. A chill passed through me, and I knew something terrible had happened. I rushed downstairs, worried that something had happened to my sister's disabled son. I was relieved to see him lying in his crib, just fine, but I turned into the living room to see my family gathered. They all wore sad expressions. The grandfather I had just dreamt about had died.

I didn't want to believe it. I had just seen him a few days earlier. He was healthy and happy. He had just married a few months before, after a long time of being alone after my grandmother had passed away.

My dad told us that it seemed like Grandpa knew his time had come that morning. He had woken up, kissed his new wife, told her he loved her, retrieved his temple clothes from his closet, and laid them out. Then he lay back down and passed soon afterward.

I would also come to learn that I was not the only one who had dreamt of him the night before. I knew then that my dream was him saying goodbye.

Four years later, I was in a much better place. I had more confidence. I no longer worried about being alone, even though I thought marriage was a long way off. I had had a few relationships by then and knew I would find the right man when the time was right. I was preparing to attend school in California. I had also just started to speak regularly to a new guy friend on the phone. He had just re-enlisted in the Navy. Our conversations grew into a long-distance relationship.

In November 2002, I married that friend. Shortly after I did, I was telling him about how I wished he could have met my grandpa. Talking about him reminded me of the dream I had the morning he passed away. I cried, not because I was sad, but because I realized the dream was not just a goodbye. My grandpa had shown me my future husband after all.

— M.D. Krider —

We Dreamed a Little Dream

If two people are meant for each other, it doesn't mean they have to be together right now or as soon as possible, but they will… eventually.
~Nina Ardianti

From the time I was a very little child, my dreams were vivid and real. Most of them were filled with images of playing in sunny meadows or flying over surreal places, so dreams of the more ordinary sort simply passed through my consciousness like the blur outside a train window. But there was one particular dream that felt very special, and I knew it, even though I was only about five years old.

My great-grandparents emigrated from Japan to the Hawaiian Islands at the turn of the 19th century. Four generations later, my family still held onto some Japanese cultural practices. One of them was the *furo* bath where, after washing with soap and water outside the tub, we would enter the hot water to soak. The temperature of the water is notoriously hot. In the old country, it would be heated over burning coals. The entire village would take turns soaking in a large public bath.

Although our modern day *furo* was not heated with coals, but just very hot water from the faucet, I recall being worried that the water would cook me. Boil me alive. I learned to enter very slowly, one toe at a time, as my body acclimated to the searing heat. By the time I emerged, my skin was lobster red. Cooked lobster red. But I loved it. We all loved soaking in the *furo*. It made us feel clean inside and out.

One night, I dreamed that I was sitting in an old-fashioned Japanese furo. My great-grandmother, with her white hair pulled into a tight bun, sat nearby crocheting and looking up occasionally to be sure I was safe. Next to me was a little blond boy. He was a little older than I was, and we didn't speak to each other at all. But we were friends. That much I could tell because of the overwhelming feeling of wellbeing and happiness I felt while with this playmate.

And when I woke up, that was all I could remember: A sweet joy. All I knew was that I wanted to spend time with my friend. But waking life compelled me to focus on growing up, and so I did.

Little did I know that thousands of miles away and across the vast Pacific blue, a little blond boy was growing up, too.

And he, too, had had a dream.

Nearly twenty years later, I was living in California and struggling to end a five-year relationship. One night, I went to bed, sad and uncertain, and prayed to God: "Please, God, help me to know what to do. If it is your will that I marry this man, I will stay with him. If not… if there is someone else for me, please let me know."

That night, I had a dream that I saw a filmy veil that hung like a curtain across the window. I saw the shadow of a figure of a man. And my heart skipped a beat. There was someone else for me.

The next day, I made a clean break. And then, like an ensign that signaled my new beginning, I got a new job, in Newport Beach in advertising. And one week into my new job a blond man walked through the door.

When our eyes locked, something tangible occurred. We both felt it. There was something so familiar about us together. So much so that the company secretary who had been sitting at the front desk came to me later to ask, "What was *that*? Something *happened*. What's going on?"

I didn't know, frankly. All I did know was that there was something remarkable and alluring about this man, and all I wanted to do was be with him. We had our first date of many that night. As time passed, we talked about everything from our families to our career goals, and then finally, our childhoods.

As I explained a bit about Japanese culture, I talked about the practice of *furo-ba*, or hot-tub baths, and how I loved them. He fell silent, and his eyes grew teary. Quietly, he recounted a dream he had had when he was just a little boy living in Texas, in an all white area where no one had ever encountered an Asian family.

He was in a large hot tub with an old Asian woman sitting in the background. Next to him sat a little girl with short black hair. She looked Japanese. And although they did not speak, he felt very happy to be with his playmate.

He said that the sweet dream replayed for three nights, and he was anxious to go to sleep each night. When the dreams stopped, he felt a terrible loss that took him a while to get over. And he was only about eight years old.

What are the odds that two little children separated by thousands of miles had the same dream about each other and then met twenty years later? But we knew it was true because, for some inexplicable reason, we couldn't bear to be apart. And so we weren't — for the next thirty-two years and counting!

Now we have grown children of our own. And sometimes we sit in a large Japanese *furo* together like we once did in a very happy dream, one that continues now even while we are awake!

—Lori Chidori Phillips—

The Climb

*Dad, your guiding hand on my shoulder
will remain with me forever.
~Author Unknown*

I t always takes me a few minutes to realize that it is happening again.

As always, sweat is dripping down my cheek, and my breathing is fast. The weather is perfect. I'm on my bike, pedaling furiously up a steep climb, smiling and laughing despite the effort.

I know he's there, even before I look. As I near the top of the climb, I finally give in to the urge to turn and look behind. Dad is there, two or three bike-lengths behind. If he weren't so exhausted from the effort, I know his smile would be as wide as mine. Just as he's about to catch his breath enough to say something, I jar awake.

I desperately try to hang on to the dream and the feeling for a few moments longer, but it begins to fade. A new day is about to begin — another day without him.

Though it's been over twenty years, I still remember vividly when it wasn't just a dream.

Some fathers take their kids to play baseball, football, or maybe basketball at the park. My dad always took me cycling. For as long as I can remember, it was our perfect getaway — a time to get some exercise and talk about life. In the busy worlds of a social teenager and a working parent, it always gave us the opportunity to solve the problems of the world, or at least to understand them better.

Dad had always been a stronger rider than I was. I still remember the first time he took me up The Climb. He seemed to sail up the hill effortlessly, while I struggled and gasped for air, feeling like my lungs would explode at any moment. Gradually, though, I became a better climber, and eventually I was able to keep up with him.

Then, one day, it happened. As we neared the top of the climb on a perfect sunny day, I surged ahead, and he was unable to match my pace. It was the first time I had ever dropped him on a climb. When he eventually caught up on the downhill, he was smiling and laughing, patting my shoulder as he passed.

"Perfect," he'd say later. "Don't ever let up, not even for me."

Those were days when life made sense, and things were much simpler. It felt like we had all the time in the world, and he'd always be there to support, challenge and encourage me. But fate had different plans, and Dad was about to encounter a climb that he wouldn't be able to conquer. I still remember the first time I heard the word "leukemia." Dad fought hard, but within a year of his diagnosis he was gone.

Cycling, once intended to help me spend time with my dad, now became my escape. I began to ride longer and take more difficult rides. I competed in all the events that we'd planned to do together.

The first time I had the dream was a restless night before my first 100-mile "century ride." It wasn't long after his death. I had been a bundle of nervous energy in the days leading up to the event, but the dream gave me a sense of calm and comfort. From the moment I woke up, I knew it was going to be okay. The ride went well. In a way, I felt like Dad was along for the ride, chasing me up the climbs.

After that, the dream would recur every few months, often before cycling events as I pushed to 150- and 200-mile rides. I would also have the dream after difficult days or when I was contemplating or encountering major changes to my life.

The dream happened the night before my wedding. It happened when each of my sons was born. It happened when my wife was in the hospital—and again a few days later when she came home. It happened the night before I started a new job.

I've spent years trying to understand the dream. Is Dad trying to connect with me, to assure me that he's still watching over the family? Is he reminding me to never let up, to never give in, to never give less than my best? Or is it just my subconscious, conjuring up a treasured memory when life hits unexpected bumps or critical forks in the road?

I have no idea, but I do know this—there are climbs in everyone's life. Some are literal, some figurative. Some are pleasant and mild, while others are cripplingly steep. Climbs seem less severe when we have someone to accompany us on the journey. For whatever reason, the dream always finds me when I need to see my dad. It never disappoints.

Ironically, I still ride my bike up that same climb every few weeks, though not as quickly as I did in my youth. The dream—and Dad—are never far from my mind. Even after all these years, occasionally I'll still look back over my shoulder, half-expecting to see him chasing me up the hill.

Someone once theorized that the dream is just a manifestation of residual grief. They explained that even though many years have passed, I'm still grieving for my dad, and that I'll stop having that dream eventually.

Just between you and me, I hope that day never comes. I don't ever want to stop doing that climb with him.

— Rob L. Berry —

Tested, Not Arrested

It is a good divine that follows his own instructions.
~William Shakespeare

"**M**a'am, I will need you to blow into this, please," said the burly Honolulu police officer matter-of-factly. He had eased out of his patrol car and was holding a small device out to me. I was bright red with embarrassment. Why did he want me to take a Breathalyzer test?

I hadn't been drinking. I had been driving just fine. But it was apparent that my new police officer friend's request was more than that; it was a command.

I put the device to my lips and blew. My attempt was slow and shallow, and it didn't register. The contraption was difficult to blow into. It was tight, like a balloon that had yet to be stretched. I wondered how people, especially those under the influence, were able to produce anything on this handheld machine. The next try, however, proved more fruitful. The police officer seemed pleased with this second performance, and the blowing episode was complete.

The police officer stepped away and leaned into his car. Soon after, he produced a small but thick handheld machine that resembled a calculator. It looked like the ones delivery people use to obtain our signatures.

"You are most definitely lactose intolerant," stated the police officer.

What? It was a lactose test? Why would a police officer test my lactose tolerance, and why test it on that machine? How did he know to test my lactose tolerance anyway?

It was surreal. As I stood there facing the officer, perplexed by the whole ordeal, my dream suddenly ended. Day had broken, and I was awake.

Could that dream hold the solution to my abdominal problems? What if I *was* lactose intolerant?

Slipping downstairs to the computer, I investigated. It didn't take long before the trusty search engine produced answers. The lactose intolerance test seemed to be similar to blowing into a balloon-type instrument. The gases from the participant's breath were contained in this contraption and were then tested. The level of certain gases determined whether the person was lactose intolerant.

I was astounded. This information was all new to me, but it was remarkably similar to the dream, and it deserved my attention. Was God trying to tell me something?

Afterward, it seemed natural to limit my intake of dairy products. The numerous symptoms that I had endured over the years quietly disappeared. I felt good once again.

Who would expect a dream about a Hawaiian police officer to help a person regain health? I certainly didn't, but the results have spoken for themselves. The only test I ever had was the one in that dream, but I thank God for that Hawaiian police officer and for the good health that came as a result of his roadside test.

— Kristi Woods —

The Dream Dress

*Dreams are road signs along the
nighttime highway of sleep.*
~Terri Guillemets

While I spent my final year of high school partying, my best friend Katarina was laid up in a Brooklyn sanatorium, isolated from family and friends. It was just a few miles away from us in Long Island City, Queens, but it might as well have been across the ocean. She spent six months in quarantine after contracting tuberculosis.

The disease had put Kat's life on hold. The treatment and drugs for TB that became available later were nonexistent then. By the time she had recovered I had relocated to another state. She moved back to care for her ailing mother until her mom died.

Kat was not one to whine or complain. Dismissing the unexpected bumps in the road, she picked herself up, worked by day and obtained her high school diploma at night.

After I moved we didn't see each other often, but when we did the friendship was rekindled as if no time had passed. Meanwhile, she was only a phone call away.

One day my phone rang. I had a feeling it was her. "Hi, Kat!"

"How did you know it was me?"

I laughed. "Well, you always did say I was psychic."

It was true. I was intuitive and acted on instinct. She was the logical, sensible one.

"Then tell me why I called," she teased.

I had no idea, but since she sounded so bubbly, I took a guess. "You're getting married!"

"Yes! Can you believe it? You're amazing! A clairvoyant extraordinaire!"

Yes, I certainly could believe it. Katarina had lived through some setbacks, but I knew she would make a wonderful wife and mother. It was about time she got her life on track again.

Four weeks before the wedding, I went to visit her. We sat at the same kitchen table as we had years ago. Katarina was flipping through the family album. Pausing at the photo of her mother as a bride, her eyes filled with wonder and admiration.

"Wasn't she lovely?" she asked. "Mom and I had always dreamed I'd be married in her wedding gown."

I was delighted to see her in such high spirits.

"Where is that gown? I can't wait to see you in it."

"Well, that's the problem. It's here somewhere. But when Mom was dying she became so disoriented that she couldn't remember where she had put it. I didn't want to press her and then it was too late. Maybe you can help me find it."

She went through her mom's closets, opening boxes and trunks that had been shut for eons. We rummaged through the storeroom in the basement that had been shared by various tenants over the years and through boxes in the attic, where all the renters had been allocated some space.

No dress! Finally, we abandoned the search. In a building with many occupants, we surmised someone had walked off with it, intentionally or accidentally.

I wanted to leave her on a hopeful note. "Kat, don't give up. Miracles do happen."

I squinted as if envisioning an apparition. In an eerie voice I proclaimed: "In my mind's eye I see you walking down the aisle in your mom's wedding dress."

She managed a small smile. "If only that were true!"

An idea came to me. "Kat, you have four weeks. Why can't your mom's dress be duplicated?"

A glimmer of hope lit up her face.

"Well, my cousin has just opened a tailor shop on Steinway Street. Maybe if I take these photos to her...."

Three and a half weeks later I returned for the wedding. Disheartened, we sat on Kat's stoop staring at the pavement where years ago we had played hopscotch and skipped rope. The wedding was a few days away and the cousin/seamstress who was supposed to save the day had turned out to be an incompetent novice. It was a totally botched job. The dress was too tight here, too loose there, the zipper appeared to be in backwards, and the bodice had been torn and poorly patched up. Any resemblance to the dress in the wedding photos was only in the wild imagination of the seamstress. I tried to hide my true feelings.

"You'll look beautiful no matter what," I told Katarina, but this so-called dress just didn't cut it. If it weren't such a disaster, it would have been laughable!

"It's not perfect but it will do. It's not like it's life and death. It's just a dress!" Kat sighed bravely.

We parted with a hug and encouraging words neither of us believed. I returned to the house next door where my mom still lived.

I couldn't get Kat out of my mind. I wasn't in the habit of praying every night, but that night I prayed with all my might for her and her future husband to have a rich, fulfilling life. Feeling just a little guilty asking for something so trivial, I prayed, "Dear God, let Katarina walk down the aisle in her mom's treasured wedding dress."

That night I tossed and turned, dreaming about my life and Katarina's — growing up next door, sharing happy memories until her life took a bad turn... first her illness, then losing her mom.

Suddenly, Katarina's mom appeared in my dream. She was standing on a staircase above me, wearing a graceful, willowy white dress — her wedding gown. Her face was as youthful as it had been in that photo album. She was staring straight into my eyes, mesmerizing me. Speaking so softly that I could barely hear, she whispered, "Under the top step."

Under the top step? What could that mean — if anything?

In the morning I woke before the sun came up. It was too early to call Kat, but I did anyway.

"Kat! Under the top step!"

"What?"

"Under the top step, Kat. Look under the top step going to the attic."

"One of your premonitions, Ms. Psychic?" I could envision her smirking.

I almost shouted, "Never mind! Just do it."

Twenty minutes later, as I looked out the kitchen window, I had another vision — Kat walking toward me with a big grin, wearing her mother's treasured wedding dress. Her fingers were gingerly grasping the skirt, raising it off the pavement, while exposing her pink bunny slippers.

There had been a secret compartment under the top step leading to the attic. The dress and the veil had been safely tucked away in there. All it took was for someone to give the step a slight pull.

The dress was taken to the cleaners and restored to its original splendor.

Two days later Katarina floated down the aisle, a vision of loveliness in her mother's wedding dress.

— Eva Carter —

Feelings

All a skeptic is is someone who hasn't had an experience yet.
~Jason Hawes

I was getting that uneasy feeling again, the one I always got when something was about to go wrong. At first, the strange sensation came on intermittently. Some days, I didn't experience it at all. But as time went by, I noticed my anxiety was increasing, especially during my husband Bill's daily commute.

Bill drives over sixty miles in heavy traffic to and from work each day. He's got an excellent driving record and keeps his car in top shape. Still, sometimes I worry. Most days, I keep my thoughts to myself. Yet now I knew I had to tell him about my concern.

"Um, Bill," I started as we sat eating dinner, "is everything all right with your car?"

"What do you mean?"

"I mean, have you noticed any funny noises under the hood or anything else odd while you're driving?"

"Oh, I get it," he scoffed. "You're having one of your 'feelings' again."

After twenty-five years of marriage, my husband was well aware of my quirky intuitions. It baffled me, though, that after seeing how many times my premonitions were correct, he still didn't give them the credence I thought they deserved. I decided to drop the whole thing... for the time being. Yet, in the coming days, during his commute times and whenever I was a passenger in his car, I became more and more certain something was awry with his vehicle.

As I sat in his passenger seat one evening, I decided to broach the subject once again. "When did you have the car inspected?" I asked nonchalantly.

"Relax," he smiled. "There's nothing wrong with this car. It passed inspection with flying colors a few months ago. I had all the fluids changed, and I even had a new set of brakes installed. Enough with your 'feelings.' The car is fine."

Still, I could not be convinced. My instincts were too strong.

Then one night I had a dream.

Bill and I were driving in his car with three friends sitting in the back seat. We were all having a pleasant conversation when Bill decided he was too tired to continue driving and asked me to take over the wheel. He pulled to the side of the road, where we switched seats.

"Be careful with the brakes!" Bill shouted at me as I pulled into traffic. "You have to tap them lightly. You can't hit them hard."

Normally a soft-spoken man, Bill's loud directive took me by surprise, and I experienced a sense of unease. I did continue driving but with added vigilance. We were going along well when suddenly the car in front of me stopped short, and I slammed on the brakes. There was a loud crack, and the car seized right there in the middle of the road.

I wasted no time in waking Bill from his sleep and told him about the dream. He hesitated for a moment and then finally replied. "Okay. I'll make an appointment with the mechanic for Saturday."

Bill knew better than to ignore one of my dreams.

And it was a good thing, too. When the mechanic took a look at the brakes he had installed only a few months earlier, he discovered a defect in the mechanism that was causing them to wear unevenly. At this point, the problem was easy to remedy. Had this defect been discovered during the car's next annual inspection — or later — it would have been a different story.

Does Bill still scoff at my premonitions? Not anymore. Now, after all these years, my husband is finally in touch with my "feelings."

— Monica A. Andermann —

Meet Our Contributors

Mary M. Alward lives in Southern Ontario. She has one grown daughter and two grown grandsons. When Mary isn't writing, she loves spending time with her family, reading, crocheting and spending time with friends.

Monica A. Andermann lives and writes on Long Island where she shares a home with her husband Bill and their little tabby Samson. Her work has been included in such publications as *Guideposts*, *Sasee* and *Woman's World* as well as many titles in the *Chicken Soup for the Soul* series.

Donna Anderson is a wife, mom, and grandmother who lives in Texas with her husband and her dog, Ohbe, a tennis ball–obsessed Golden Retriever. Her hobbies include genealogy, antiquing, writing and trying out new cookie recipes. She can often be found volunteering at the local history museum.

J. Ross Archer is a retired U.S. Army Colonel. Besides bravely and proudly serving, he earned a master's degree in psychology. After military retirement, he was vice president of a college and proprietor of a strategic planning firm. He is a Gideon and Rotarian. John Ross has had twenty-plus short stories and three books published.

Elizabeth Atwater lives in a small Southern town with her husband Joe. She discovered the joy of reading in first grade and that naturally seemed to evolve into a joy of writing. Writing brings Elizabeth so much pleasure that she cannot imagine ever stopping. She sold her first story to a romance magazine when she was seventeen years old.

Carole Harris Barton, author of *Rainbows in Coal Country* and *When God Gets Physical*, is retired after a career in government service. Her stories have appeared in *Chicken Soup for the Soul: Dreams and Premonitions* and *Mysterious Ways* magazine. A widow and mother, she lives in Dunedin, FL.

Hosanna Barton is a wife and homeschooling mom of four living in Southern Colorado. She can often be found in her car, taking her children to ballet, baseball, or heading to the gym. She dreams of having the time to write something truly epic someday, but for now, she's thrilled to make her history come alive by re-telling her memories via short stories.

Lainie Belcastro is an inspirational writer, poet, speaker and storyteller, and is blessed to have many of her true stories published in the *Chicken Soup for the Soul* books. She and her daughter, Nika, co-author children's books through their company, We Plant Dreams, LLC. Enjoy her creative journey at www.lainiebelcastro.com.

Tamara Bell is a regular contributor to the *Chicken Soup for the Soul* series. She recently fulfilled another dream by working in reading intervention, sharing her passion for reading with students at Valley Grove Elementary in Franklin, PA. She and her husband are enjoying semi-retirement, spending more time with their two grandchildren, Clara and Hayden.

Following a career in nuclear medicine, **Melissa Bender** is joyfully exploring her creative side. She recently moved to the Texas coast where she and her husband are renovating a thirty-five-year-old former Parade of Homes fixer-upper. She shares her home renovation and her stories at www.facebook.com/chicvintique.

Born and raised on Cape Cod, **Kristine Benevento** has lived in two countries and three states as a military spouse. Currently living in Vermont, she enjoys family get-togethers and anything her husband and sons are involved in. A former firefighter and EMT, she holds a B.A. degree in Emergency Services Management.

Richard Bennett received both a networking and a programming degree from Wiregrass Technical College in 2009. He lives in South Georgia and enjoys cruising, reading, cooking, devotionals, and listening to sports. He also hosts two podcasts — "620 Life" (Spotify) and "Sighted to Sightless," which is available on YouTube.

Rob L. Berry is a graduate of California State University, Bakersfield. He lives in Bakersfield, CA with his wife and three sons.

Andrea Lebedovych Bilaniuk holds a B.A. from Marymount College, Tarrytown and an MSEd from Fordham University. She is the author of *Blue-Celled Boy* and *Semper Polaris*. Andrea advocates on behalf of pediatric cancer awareness and research. She lives in Northern Virginia and has a son in Heaven and a son at college.

David L Bishop and Boomerjax have returned to Missouri after enjoying six years in Montana. David maintains his passions for reading, sports, and politics, while always enjoying good conversation with friends. Adjusting to the different weather has been a challenge, but there are still no fleas for Boomerjax.

Dan Boyle is a firefighter/EMT from Butte, MT. He is married to Ashley, and has two children, Madison and Ben. He enjoys swimming, basketball, cooking, and reading. He hopes to write more often, on a variety of subjects, in different formats.

Valaree Brough received her Bachelor of Arts degree from Utah State University in 1971. She majored in Elementary Education, with a dual minor in English and French. She has four children, fourteen grandchildren, and four great-grandchildren. She enjoys writing, reading, playing the piano, sewing, and family history.

Lettie Kirkpatrick Burress lives in Tennessee where she writes books and magazine articles. Lettie celebrates life with long hikes, lunch at outdoor cafes, clip-on earrings, and chocolate mint! Her favorite people? An understanding husband, five super sons, three daughters-in-love, and six "grand" children. Learn more at www.writingforhim.com.

Eva Carter is a frequent contributor to the *Chicken Soup for the Soul* series. Her background is in finance, telecommunications, dancing and traveling. She was born in Czechoslovakia, raised in New York and currently lives in Dallas, TX with her husband and two cats.

Amy B. Chesler is an author, podcaster, and award-winning blogger from Los Angeles. Through her work, Amy often highlights the impact of domestic violence and grief on the family system. She's deeply honored to celebrate her eighth appearance in a *Chicken Soup for the*

Soul anthology. Find her @amybchesler on all social media platforms.

Cj Cole is a retired radio diva and advice columnist now living in New Mexico. Getting used to retirement, Cj is now on a quest for new adventures to share with her Chicken Soup for the Soul family

Michele Ivy Davis lives in Southern California where she is a freelance writer and photographer. Her stories and articles have appeared in a variety of magazines, newspapers, and law enforcement publications, and her debut novel, *Evangeline Brown and the Cadillac Motel*, received national and international awards. Learn more at www.MicheleIvyDavis.com.

Kim Garback Diaz has her Master's and SAS in education, and a Bachelor's in marketing. She is the owner of Educational Solutions, a consulting business for parents, families, students, schools, and departments of social services. She lives in the Adirondacks in upstate New York with her husband Ray. They have a beautiful daughter, Jessica.

Dr. MaryAnn Diorio is a widely published, award-winning author of fiction for children and adults. A former university professor, she has written for *The Saturday Evening Post*, *Human Events*, *The Press of Atlantic City*, and Billy Graham's *Decision Magazine*. Learn more at maryanndiorio.com.

Hannah Edmonds is a wife, mother, and grandmother who works part-time in the school system but also enjoys writing.

Karen Ekstrom is a frequent contributor to the *Chicken Soup for the Soul* series. She and her husband David have five children, four grandkids, and a cat. Twenty years living on a Texas cattle ranch gave her lots to write about on her blog, FlunkingFamily.com. Email her at kcekstrom@yahoo.com.

Jackie Eller has been writing since she was a child. Her deep faith in God has always helped her in her life. She attended the University of Kansas and left just three credits short of a degree, but the experience left her a better writer. She is married and lives on a farm with her husband Kenny, three cats, and four chickens.

John Elliott was an officer with the Fairfax County Police in Virginia from 1974 to 1983; Police in Florida from 1989 to 1998; Interpol in Lyon, France from 1999 to 2012. He also trained officers for the Royal

Canadian Mounted Police and for the London Metropolitan Police.

Donna Fawcett is a retired creative writing instructor for Fanshawe College in Ontario, Canada. Donna writes in the freelance magazine market and has two award-winning novels. Her final song on her debut CD won best song lyrics. Learn more at www.donnafawcett.com.

Judy Fleming is a retired home health aide. She has been married for thirty years and has four grandchildren. She enjoys her home in the woods of Northwest Wisconsin with her husband, Dan. While the experience was Judy's, she would like to thank her daughter, Cassandra Kyser, for putting it on paper.

Robyn Gerland is the author of five novels and a book of short stories. She is a regular contributor to the *Chicken Soup for the Soul* series, various magazines and newspapers, and is the past editor of the glossy, *Hysteria*.

Gene Giggleman received his Doctor of Veterinary Medicine degree from Texas A&M University in 1981. He is a full-time college administrator, teaches human anatomy and has a small animal veterinary practice. He enjoys reading, riding motorcycles and bicycles, fishing, gardening, being outdoors, and spending time with his grandchildren.

Sheoli V. Gunaratne is a thirteen-year-old middle school student. Her family originates from the tropical island of Sri Lanka. She enjoys writing stories, poetry, and playing with her puppy Coco. She plans to continue her free-spirited writing.

Rebecca Gurnsey has published *Loving Toby*, a faith-based novel and the sequel, *Saving Vera*. She also published the series *The Taylor Family Adventures: Short Stories You Didn't Expect* and is currently working on another novel. She has retired from a career in business and enjoys spending time with her family and friends.

Bill Hess is a former United States Marine and has been a firefighter and a nationally registered paramedic for over thirty-six years. He is a father and grandfather and enjoys spending time with family, building hot rods and riding side by side with family and friends. Bill plans to write more true-life stories of inspiration and real-life miracles.

Gary R. Hoffman taught school for twenty-five years. He has published or won prizes for over 325 short stories, poems, and essays.

His short story collection, *I Haven't Lost My Marbles: They Just All Rolled to One Side*, will be published this fall by Mockingbird Lane Press. Learn more at www.authorgaryrhoffman.com.

Kayleen Kitty Holder is a journalist and children's book writer. She published a fun kid's book, *Hello from the Great Blue Sea*, with another A-T warrior who illustrated it. All profits will go to the A-T Children's Project. Purchase one to help find the cure for a disease called A-T, which her four-year-old niece is battling.

Julie Rine Holderbaum is a high school English teacher in Minerva, OH. She writes frequently about issues affecting public education for the Ohio Education Association. She enjoys yoga, reading, and spending time with her family. She also writes more personal pieces on her blog, which can be found at thethrillofthehill.blogspot.com.

Warren F. Holland received his Bachelor of Arts from Washington & Lee University in 1990 and his Master of International Business Studies from the University of South Carolina in 1993. He is currently employed by Bank of America Merrill Lynch and lives in Charlotte, NC with his wife and three children.

Sharilynn Hunt, DMin, has written inspirational stories for several anthologies, including the *Chicken Soup for the Soul* series, *Bethany House*, and *Guideposts*. Her books, *Grace Overcomes Today* and *Together WE Pray*, are sold on Amazon. She and her husband love to travel and have almost reached their goal of visiting all fifty U.S. states.

Jennie Ivey lives and writes in Tennessee. She is the author of several works of fiction and nonfiction, including stories in numerous *Chicken Soup for the Soul* books. Learn more at jennieivey.com.

Daniel James works in healthcare. He and his wife watch for lost dogs in the Denver, Colorado area.

BJ Jensen, song signing artist, author, speaker and dramatist, has been the director of Love In Motion Signing Choir since 1990 (www.signingchoir.com). She is married to Dr. Doug Jensen, her favorite cheerleader and encourager. They enjoy living in San Diego, California near their three wonderful granddaughters. Email her at jensen2@san.rr.com.

Susan A. Karas has spent years perfecting her craft, graduating proudly from many writing programs. She won the national Guideposts Writing Contest and has gone on to be published many times in the magazine, as well as in the *Chicken Soup for the Soul* series and various other publications. She is currently working on her first novel.

After decades of working as a registered nurse, **Linda Kinnamon** realized she had too many experiences of heaven to keep them to herself. *Alchemy of the Afterlife* is her award-winning memoir of these heavenly encounters. When she's not writing, Linda loves exploring the mountains of Colorado. Learn more at lindakinnamon.com.

Linda L. Koch is a graduate of the Institute of Children's Literature and has been published in *Good Old Days* and *Willow River Writers Anthology*. Linda has three children and four grandchildren, and enjoys traveling, gardening, and writing. She hopes to publish children's middle-grade novels. Email her at Llkoch@gmail.com.

Catherine Kopp received her B.S. degree from Framingham State College and Master of Education degree from Lesley University. She has been teaching elementary school since 1973. Catherine teaches fifth grade in Denver, CO, where she lives with her husband Jim. During her free time, she enjoys writing, reading, yoga, and gardening.

Melissa Krider is a full-time mom and author living in the Pacific Northwest.

Brenda M. Lane is an American composer and lyricist of Inspirational original music for many renowned individual recording artists and instrumentalists. She continues to write books including award-winning nonfiction and fiction. Branching out with wordsmithing, she is now part of a Product Naming/Tagline team in England. Learn more at www.laneprojects.com.

Geno Lawrenzi, Jr. is a beloved world traveling gadabout journalist who has settled into creative short story writing. He has written over 2,000 articles in his lifetime. Among his passions are poker, the Wild West, famous people, the Caribbean, and justice. He evokes a unique visual mastery, truth, humor, and wisdom.

Suzanne Lindsay lives in Toronto with her two children and works as a freelance producer in the world of commercial photography. Her favourite quote is by Jodi Hills: "She wasn't where she had been. She wasn't where she was going... but she was on her way."

Shannon MacKinnon is an actress who has appeared in various shows such as *How to Die Alone* (Disney Plus) and *Cursed Histories*. She had the joy of writing and performing her play, *Dear Jason*, at the MindPLAY theatre festival. She currently lives in Cambridge, ON with her kitty, Midnight.

A graduate of Queen's University, **Gail MacMillan** has had her work published throughout North American and Western Europe. Recently she has signed the contract for her thirtieth book. Gail lives in New Brunswick, Canada with her husband and two dogs. She is the award-winning author of two books and several short stories.

Mary Beth Magee's faith leads her to explore God's world and write about it in many genres. She is the 2025 Mississippi Poetry Society Poet of the Year, an award-winning author, a storyteller and a speaker on a variety of topics. Magee serves as narrator for The Everyman Puppet Theatre. Learn more at www.LOL4.net.

David Magill lives with his wife Patti in Minnesota. He enjoys writing, reading, and exploring life through a literary lens. David is currently writing many short stories, mostly real life events as relayed to him through his friends and family, or recalled from his own memory. Email him at dpmagill@yahoo.com.

Angela Marchi is a college student and a married mother of a four-year-old daughter. She is planning on receiving her B.S. in Nursing by 2013. Angela enjoys spending time with her family and pets. Email her at windsong81@aol.com.

Joshua J. Mark is Content Director for the online site World History Encyclopedia. His wife, Betsy, passed on from cancer in 2018 and he now lives with his two Beagles, Sammie and Jamie, in rural New York State.

Sandy Martin is an ASCAP Special award-winning songwriter for her original nonprofit theme songs and children's Christian music. She also loves to write poetry, nonfiction short stories, and is a published author in the *Chicken Soup for the Soul* series. Email her at sing2sandy@gmail.com.

Tina Wagner Mattern is a Portland, OR writer blessed all her life with miracles, as her recently published memoir, *Butter Side Up, Thank God* will attest. She is grateful to have shared her stories in ten *Chicken Soup for the Soul* books as well as other internationally known anthologies. Email her at tinamattern@earthlink.net.

Amanda Mattox resides in Southern California with her husband and two rambunctious cats. When she is not working at a nearby university, she enjoys wandering around bookstores and antique shops, practicing yoga, reading, and writing. She holds a bachelor's in English and a minor in communication.

Jane McBride dreamed of writing from the time she was a small child and often made up stories to entertain her friends. These fanciful tales sometimes enchanted, sometimes delighted, and sometimes horrified her audience. Being published in the *Chicken Soup for the Soul* series is a dream come true for Jane. Jane is the mother of five children and the proud grandmother of ten and the even prouder grandmother of two great-grandchildren.

Lisa McCaskill received her Bachelor of Arts from the University of North Carolina at Greensboro in 1987. She is a teacher, writer, and mother of four grown men. Lisa enjoys writing, playing piano, making pottery, and any kind of crafting.

Lynn Maddalena Menna, a retired educator, is a Young Adult author. She lives in Hawthorne, NJ, with her husband, Prospero, and cat, Tiger Lily. Email her at prolynn@aol.com.

Christina Metcalf is a speaker and author of *The Glinda Principle* and four other books. She helps women over forty ditch the excuses, own their brilliance, and finally go after what they want — no wand-waving required. Learn more at www.theglindaprinciple.com.

Skip Myers is a leading security industry expert and speaker specializing in fraud prevention and Internet safety. Skip recently authored a new children's book titled *Say No To Internet Monsters* that addresses the urgent need to protect kids online. He resides in Atlanta, GA with his wife and family.

Carmen Myrtis-Garcia is a retired college teacher and published writer. She founded the Facebook group, Hope for the Widow's Journey, and hosts a podcast interviewing widows. She and her husband lived their dream on a small island in Belize. She has a gypsy soul but resides in Colorado. She is writing a devotional for widows.

Herchel E. Newman is known for his inspiring storytelling gift. He is a founding member of the Word Warriors Writing Group at his church. His life stories have been published in magazines and books, including the *Chicken Soup for the Soul* series. His stories reflect his love of family. Email him at Flashcat555@yahoo.com.

Sara Nolt is the wife of John and the mother of four extraordinary children. Homeschooling, never-ending laundry piles, and written words fill her days while God and his eternal purposes fill her heart.

Carolyn C. O'Brien owned and operated an independent bookstore in Mississippi for sixteen years. She continues her passion for books as a bookseller at Page and Palette bookstore in Fairhope, AL.

Mary Treacy O'Keefe, has an MA in Theology, is a Spiritual Director, speaker and former host of the Hope, Healing and Wellbeing Internet radio show. She was co-founder and President of Well Within, a nonprofit wellness center in Minnesota, which provided free holistic support and therapies to thousands of seriously ill people from 2004-15. She is currently writing her third book. For information about Mary's books and presentations, please visit www.marytreacyokeefe.com or email her at mary.treacy.okeefe@gmail.com.

Nancy Emmick Panko is a frequent contributor to the *Chicken Soup for the Soul* series and the author of award-winning *Guiding Missal*, *Sheltering Angels*, *Chicken Scratchings*, and six children's picture books. A retired pediatric nurse, Nancy enjoys being near the water with her family. Learn more at www.nancypanko.com.

Lori Chidori Phillips resides with her beloved mate of forty years in Southern California where they enjoy spending time with their grown children and learning new things every day. Email her at hope037@hotmail.com.

Kathryn Y. Pollard grew up in Oklahoma spending most of her time locked inside her bedroom writing stories and poems. She resides in Georgia. She is a published author of one novel and several short stories. She loves to teach the Bible and encourage people to enjoy life.

Dr. Barbara Poremba is a Nurse Practitioner and Professor of

Nursing at Salem State University, MA. She earned degrees from Harvard University, Boston University and the University of Massachusetts Amherst and Worcester. Barbara enjoys international humanitarian work, photography, skiing, tap dancing, sea glass collecting and grandchildren. Learn more at www.directory.salemstate.edu/profile/barbara.poremba.

Wendy Portfors is a previous contributor to the *Chicken Soup for the Soul* series. She has several published short stories and a book, *Remembering Love*, which is a personal memoir. Wendy is a member of the Writers' Guild of Alberta. Now remarried, Wendy and Dave enjoy golfing and travelling. They reside in Turner Valley, Alberta. Email Wendy at wportfors@gmail.com.

Sheila Quarles worked in corporate sales until an accident resulted in a traumatic brain injury. Determined not to use Western medicine, she traveled the world for twenty years to study indigenous healing techniques. She became a Reiki Master and partnered with Kathy Morris to establish Inner Journeys, LLC. Email her at innerjourneys@att.net.

Rebecca Radicchi, her husband and crew of kids live outside Atlanta, GA where the summers are hot and the tea is sweet. She's ridden the waves of adoption, breast cancer, and being the mom of a child with complex medical needs. Learn more at rebeccaradicchi.com and on social media to talk about the wild, salty, sweetness of life.

Annie Riess farms with her husband in Saskatchewan. She also teaches piano lessons and does freelance writing. She enjoys spending as much time as possible with family and friends. Email her at annieriess@yahoo.ca.

Patricia Ann Rossi is an avid writer, reader and runner. Patricia volunteers as a facilitator at creative writing workshops for cancer survivors. She is active in her community, and serves on local not-for-profit boards as well as her college alumni board.

Tammy Ruggles is a legally blind writer and artist with Asperger's who makes her home in Kentucky. She enjoys spending her time with family and friends, and using AI to help her with creative projects.

Laura Savino is an airline pilot, motivational speaker, and STEM educator. In her book, *JET BOSS: A Female Pilot on Taking Risks and Flying High*, she takes readers inside the cockpit of United Airlines' widebody jets, offering a powerful blueprint for defying expectations and never selling yourself short. Learn more at laurasavino747.com.

Rachel Schmoyer is the Communications Coordinator of the Bible Fellowship Church Denomination. She lives in the Lehigh Valley of Pennsylvania with her husband and four children.

M.J. Shea writes and paints from her home along the shoreline of Long Island Sound. When she isn't working on illustrations for a children's book she has written she can be found puttering in her yard, thrifting for things she doesn't need or taking her four-legged couch potato, Biscuit, out for a drag. With her daughter off living her best life in California, M.J. and her husband have discovered the joys of living in a small beach town. This is her third appearance in the *Chicken Soup for the Soul* series.

Gail Small is a Fulbright Memorial Scholar. She is the author of seven books and speaks internationally about joyful living and life choices. Travel is her passion, taking her to all seven continents. *Have Bikini Will Cruise* is her latest book. Email this motivational speaker and educational consultant at joyforgail@aol.com.

Candy Allen Smith has written dozens of short stories and has been featured in *Working Mother* magazine and on *MSN Family*. She is working on publishing a compilation of stories about growing up poor in Southern West Virginia, and keeps an active presence on social media. Candy lives on the Delaware shore with her amazing husband, Joe.

Jane R. Snyder is a graduate of Syracuse University (MFA) and Parsons School of Design (BFA). Her writing appears in *Acta Victoriana*, *Paterson Literary Review*, everydayfiction.com, *The Reform Jewish Quarterly*, RESPONSE, jewishfiction.net, *The Jewish Exponent*, *The New York Quarterly*, and elsewhere. Visit: janersnyder.com or to hear her songs — thisjane.com.

C. Solomon grew up overseas while her father served in the United States Army. She has a love of travel and foreign culture, which led her to the study of Anthropology. In her spare time she enjoys crafting and writing.

Patrick P. Stafford lives in Northridge, CA, and works full-time as a journalist, copywriter, editor and poet. He has written for AccessLife.

com, *Wheelin' Sportsmen, Amateur Chef* magazine, *Healthcare Traveler*, and *Northern Virginia* magazine, and has sold poems, articles and editorial pieces both online and in print publications.

Jen Eve Taylor (4/12/1987–17/11/2024) was originally from Sydney. In her twenties she moved to London, the city she loved. She made the most of her short life, writing essays, and her novel *Rebel Rebel*, as well as recording the ups and downs of her life in her www.thecancerchronicles.blog.

Donna Teti has also been published in *Guideposts* magazine, Cecil Murphey's *Christmas Miracles*, and is a winner of the Guideposts Writers Workshop Contest. Through her inspirational writings and speaking engagements, Donna hopes to bring God's comfort to those who are grieving. Email her at is donnateti90@gmail.com.

L. Thorburn is a trainer for the state, creating and delivering soft skills training to state employees and local district staff. Now retired from the Army, she spends her free time gardening, sewing, and having fun with her grandchildren.

Becky S. Tompkins enjoys working with words, both professionally — as a former teacher of English, proofreader/copy editor, and freelance writer — and in her spare time. She also enjoys cooking, gardening, and spending time with her family.

Delores Topliff divides her year between a Minnesota farm and northeastern Mississippi in cooler months. She teaches in a Christian university plus offers writing classes in local libraries. She loves her doctor sons and grandchildren. Travel is her favorite form of education. Learn more about her and her books at delorestopliff.com.

Christine Trollinger is a writer from Kansas City, MO and has had several stories published in the *Chicken Soup for the Soul* series and other publications over the past twelve years. She is a widow with three children, two granddaughters, and three great-grandchildren who are the apple of her eye. Email her at trolleys_2@yahoo.com.

Donna Duly Volkenannt is a wife, mother, grandmother, and breast cancer survivor. She won the 2012 Erma Bombeck Global Humor contest. Donna believes in angels and is pleased to have her story in the *Chicken Soup for the Soul* series. She lives in St. Peters, MO, with her husband, Walt.

Patti Wade's stories have been published in multiple books in the *Chicken Soup for the Soul* series beginning with her story "Real" in *Chicken Soup for the Adopted Soul*. In addition to writing and editing, she is an especially proud mother and grandmother!

Denise Wasko retired in 2016 after spending thirty years in the Early Childhood Education field. She enjoys writing and has written three children's books about the alpacas she has raised on her acreage. Her spare time is spent with her grandchildren and volunteering in her community.

Sheryl K. (James) Winbolt retired from civil service after thirty-five years. She has one daughter, two granddaughters, and three "plus" great-grandchildren (one due in November). She enjoys playing the piano, painting, writing, and spending time with her husband, Don, whom she met in junior high school.

Lisa Wojcik teaches literacy and art to low-income elementary grade children through a Florida public library system. Degreed from the University of New Mexico, Lisa is a science researcher, artist, and writer. Her short stories, poetry, children's literature, and research work can be seen at www.t4studios-bd.blogspot.com. Email her at lisawojcik@hotmail.com.

Kristi Woods writes stories about Jesus and other heroes in contemporary Christian romance and nonfiction, including her gift book, *101 Prayers for Military Wives*. Kristi, her Desert Storm pen pal-turned-husband, and three (now adult) children survived a nomadic, military lifestyle and have set roots in Oklahoma. Connect with her at KristiWoods.net.

Meet Amy Newmark

Amy Newmark is the bestselling author, editor-in-chief, and publisher of the *Chicken Soup for the Soul* book series. Since 2008, she has published more than 200 new books, most of them national bestsellers in the U.S. and Canada, more than doubling the number of *Chicken Soup for the Soul* titles in print today. She is also the author of *Simply Happy*, a crash course in Chicken Soup for the Soul advice and wisdom that is filled with easy-to-implement, practical tips for enjoying a better life.

Amy is credited with revitalizing the Chicken Soup for the Soul brand, which has been a publishing industry phenomenon since the first book came out in 1993. By compiling inspirational and aspirational true stories curated from ordinary people who have had extraordinary experiences, Amy has kept the thirty-two-year-old Chicken Soup for the Soul brand fresh and relevant.

Amy graduated *magna cum laude* from Harvard University where she majored in Portuguese and minored in French. She then embarked on a three-decade career as a Wall Street analyst, a hedge fund manager, and a corporate executive in the technology field.

Her return to literary pursuits was inevitable, as her honors thesis in college involved traveling throughout Brazil's impoverished northeast region, collecting stories from regular people. She is delighted to have come full circle in her writing career — from collecting stories "from the people" in Brazil as a twenty-year-old to, three decades later, collecting stories "from the people" for Chicken Soup for the Soul.

When Amy and her husband Bill, the CEO of Chicken Soup for the Soul, are not working, they are visiting their four grown children and their spouses, and their six grandchildren.

Follow Amy on X and Instagram @amynewmark. Listen to her free podcast — Chicken Soup for the Soul with Amy Newmark — on Apple, Google, or by using your favorite podcast app on your phone. You can also find a selection of her stories on Medium.

Sharing Happiness, Inspiration, and Hope

Real people sharing real stories, every day, all over the world. In 2007, *USA Today* named *Chicken Soup for the Soul* one of the five most memorable books in the last quarter-century. With over 110 million books sold to date in the U.S. and Canada alone, more than 300 titles in print, and translations into nearly fifty languages, "chicken soup for the soul®" is one of the world's best-known phrases.

Today, thirty-two years after we first began sharing happiness, inspiration and hope through our books, we continue to delight our readers with new titles almost every month, but have also evolved beyond the bookshelves with super premium pet food, a podcast, adult coloring books, and licensed products that include word-search puzzle books and books for babies and preschoolers. We are busy "changing your life one story at a time®" and doing it for the whole family. Thanks for reading!

Miracles, Angels & Messages from Heaven

Amy Newmark

Paperback: 978-1-61159-116-3
eBook: 978-1-61159-351-8

More hope, faith and miracles

Chicken Soup for the Soul

Angels and the Miraculous

101 Inspirational Stories of Faith, Miracles and Answered Prayers

Amy Newmark

Paperback: 978-1-61159-104-0
eBook: 978-1-61159-341-9

to brighten your days

If you enjoyed these awe-inspiring stories, you'll LOVE reading *101 Ways to Think Positive* — the book that teaches how a positive attitude can create a happier life. Following are the first two stories from that book.

I Know How This Works

Visualize this thing that you want, see it, feel it, believe in it. Make your mental blueprint and begin to build.
~Robert Collier

We were seated in an outdoor holding area on a bench with the rest of the studio audience, waiting to be ushered inside. The year was 2002, the place was Los Angeles, and the show was *The Other Half*, a male version of the women-centric morning show, *The View*. This incarnation featured hosts Dick Clark, Danny Bonaduce, Dr. Jan Adams and Mario Lopez. The production assistants and show interns were handing out clipboards containing a questionnaire for us to fill out. The questions hinted at the day's topic of discussion: dating disasters. I was sandwiched between my eighteen-year-old niece Jessica and my best friend Lisa, coaching them on how to answer the questions.

"They're trying to find someone who will make good TV," I explained. "Think of the funniest dating disaster you've ever had, one that may have also happened to other women. Something relatable and lighthearted, yet slightly humiliating."

Both Lisa and Jessica laughed, and I said, "See, now you're getting it."

My "dating disaster" had to do with a fellow who pulled up outside my house and beeped his horn rather than come to the door to escort me to his car.

"He completely ruined the moment," I wrote on the questionnaire. My mother was supposed to open the door, usher him inside, and tell him I'd be right down. He had denied me my grand entrance.

I saw the smile on the intern's face as she collected the clipboard, and scanned what I had written.

"Can you tell me a little bit more about this?"

Now that I'm a writer, I understand the concept of the "elevator pitch," but I had no idea what I was doing back then. All I knew was that I was minutes away from seeing Mario Lopez in the flesh (yes, he's better-looking in person, just in case you thought that wasn't possible), with the prospect of talking to him on camera. I turned on the personality like I was there for an audition. In a way, I suppose I was.

Other women were getting interviewed just like me, sharing their dating-disaster stories, hoping Mario, Danny, Dick or Jan would talk about it with them on camera. But I felt something more than hope. I felt like it was actually going to happen. I started to visualize it in my head: Mario approaching me with a microphone, the two of us laughing along with the rest of the studio audience as I discussed my rude date.

As we filed onto the soundstage, I actually began to get flutters in my stomach, sweating even though the studio was freezing. I realized I was experiencing stage fright. As the three of us took our seats, I caught the eye of the production assistant who'd spoken to us, and she smiled at me. I turned to Lisa and said, "They're going to interview us on the show."

"How do you know that?"

"Just a feeling," I said. I'd had it from the moment they handed us the clipboards. Even though the production assistant who'd spoken to me had also taken the time to chat with a few others, I was confident my story was going to make it on the air.

Sure enough, right after the entire audience was seated and the crowd warmer stirred us into the proper level of excitement and anticipation, the assistant approached us and squatted between Lisa and me.

"When Dick talks to you, I want you to tell your story just like you told me."

She turned to Lisa and advised her to do the same. I couldn't believe it. Both Lisa and I had been chosen to speak on national television.

Suddenly, the show was beginning. The four hosts took the stage amid much applause and enthusiastic whooping. They bantered through their opening routine and introduced the topic. Then, Mario Lopez was standing beside me, holding a microphone in front of me as I relayed to Dick Clark and everybody in the entire studio — not to mention the television-viewing audience — my dating-disaster story. It played out almost exactly as I had envisioned it.

It was an incredible moment, exhilarating and somewhat surreal, even if not entirely unexpected thanks to my positive thinking.

—Rachel Remick—

A Dreaded Doctor Visit Ends in Magic

Nobody can be uncheered with a balloon.
~Winne the Pooh

I was seven years old and had just moved with my grandparents to Anaheim, California. I would have to go to a new school, make new friends and, worst of all, get updated vaccinations.

As I sat on the crinkly paper on the doctor's exam table one week before school was to start, with my legs dangling over the end, I dreaded the moment when he would say, "Time for your tetanus shot." The only thing I knew that would make the pain of a shot worthwhile was the balloon I had been promised.

I took that shot like a champ, without so much as a quiet "Ouch." While I waited for the doctor to come back with my balloon, I thought about all the cool things I was going to do with that balloon: I was going to tie it to my doll's arm and pretend she was floating away, only to rescue her at the last minute. I was going to tie it to my dog's tail and pretend she was from outer space and had landed as a scout to report back on whether Earth was a suitable planet on which alien dogs could live. And I definitely planned on rubbing the balloon on my hair to make it stand on end so I could look like a member of KISS, my favorite band at the time.

The doctor returned with a concerned look on his face and delivered the tragic news. "I'm sorry, but we're out of balloons."

All my big plans for that balloon popped faster than that balloon ever would have. I was devastated.

The entire way home, my grandma kept telling me that I should think positively, and everything would be okay. We had a pack of balloons at home that I could blow up. Well, I positively knew that those balloons would never be as good as the balloon from the doctor's office. First of all, we didn't have a helium tank to make the balloons float. And, more importantly, I hadn't had to sacrifice anything for those balloons.

We pulled into our driveway, and I trudged into the house, my day ruined by shots and no balloons. I went straight through the house to the back patio door, ready to go outside and tell my dog all my troubles, when I looked out and saw the most amazing thing my seven-year-old eyes had ever seen. Our entire backyard was filled with floaty balloons! I screamed in delight and ran through them, twirling in circles and stirring them this way and that.

We lived less than a mile from Disneyland. As it turned out, when the wind was just right, the balloons released from the daily parades would land neatly in our backyard.

I will never forget that day of whirling through those balloons and thinking they were all for me because I had to get my shots. And I will never forget my grandmother telling me throughout my life that if you just think positive thoughts, everything has a way of working out in the end.

— Leyla d'Aulaire —